Emotional Business

Emotional
Business

The Meaning and Mastery of Work, Money,

and Success

by David W. Krueger, M.D.

Avant® Books
Slawson Communications, Inc.
San Marcos, California

Library of Congress Cataloging-in-Publication Data
Emotional business : the meaning and mastery of work,
money, and success
Krueger, David W.
1. Work—Psychological aspects. 2. Success—Psychological aspects.
3. Money—Psychological aspects.
I. Title.
BF481.K78 1992 158.7—dc20 91-9319

ISBN 0-932238-64-5

Avant® Books
Slawson Communications, Inc
San Marcos, CA 92069-1436

Printed in the United States

Interior Design by Sandra Mewshaw
Cover Art by John Odam Design Associates

1 2 3 4 5 6 7 8 9 10

Dedication

Our children are our autobiography;
everything else is merely a footnote:
To Ryan and Lauren

Contents

Acknowledgments

The clinical cases and vignettes presented throughout this book are highly disguised to preserve anonymity. Although all were selected to illustrate some aspect of the problems of work, money, and success, these were not necessarily the central issues of psychotherapy or psychoanalysis for the individuals described. I am extremely grateful to the patients with whom I have been privileged to work.

My thanks to Naomi Wise of San Francisco, with whom collaboration was stimulating and invaluable; to Jenifer Pipkin of Houston for her helpful suggestions; to the publisher's manuscript editor, Rebecca Smith; and to Jackie Stanley for her painstaking work on the manuscript. My special thanks to Vicki, who believed and who is always there.

Introduction

The years teach much that the days never know.

—Ralph Waldo Emerson

*To become different from what we are,
we must have some awareness of what we are.*

—Eric Hoffer

Among the greatest joys in life are those that come from finding and following our own direction. This is as true in the arena of work as in our personal life, because for most of us, work occupies the majority of our waking hours.

Almost everyone yearns for self-fulfillment through meaningful work. We want work that makes us feel good about ourselves and proud of our special skills, work that interests, excites, and challenges us to the utmost of our capacities. We long for work that calls for wholehearted commitment, work that is not just a job.

A most basic motivation of all human beings is to be effective, to experience mastery. The pleasure derived from being effective—being a cause—has been demonstrated in earliest infancy and continues in changing form throughout development.

The rewards of work and money are much greater than the material comforts they may bring. We find pleasure in the sense of growth and self-affirmation arising from a lifetime spent mastering a career or a craft. This pleasure is compromised if the impetus for working is purely external (just to make money or win praise from other people), rather than internal. Our work belongs entirely to us and reflects us. The healthy desire to work and succeed comes from within ourselves. Achievement and mastery enhance our self-esteem and self-confidence, just as failure erodes them. Never even trying to achieve, prevents us from gaining much self-esteem at all.

Volumes of sociological and business literature have been devoted to discovering the external conditions that make work more satisfying and workers more productive. Another large body of literature focuses on money and its acquisition, use, and investment. This book focuses on the emotional meanings of work and money, the factors that shape their impact, and the events in human development that make achievement and its enjoyment easier or more difficult.

In the psychoanalysis or psychotherapy I do with an individual, we discover together that person's experiences, feelings, and perceptions, and the underlying assumptions (often unconscious) on which he or she operates. Assumptions that work don't need to be fixed. Those that don't work were usually fashioned to adapt in an earlier time and place and do not fit in the present. Recognizing which assumptions do not work in the present is the beginning of freeing oneself to create new assumptions that are useful here and now.

How to guide a reader through this process, without the usual interchange of therapy or analysis, is a challenge. Psychotherapy and psychoanalysis work through collaborative, empathic exploration of thoughts, feelings, fantasies, and assumptions. Together the individual and I come to understand the past story and create a new one. Meanwhile, the therapeutic focus is on the individual's internal experience and on the process of change and growth, rather than on my own advice, experience, or values.

You and I will attempt to approximate this process by exploring some of the common emotional and developmental themes of work, money, and success, supplementing them with case illustrations and self-quizzes. This is not a fix-it book, ten steps to happiness, or a do-it-this-way program. It is an invitation to reflect on the emotional meanings you attach to work and money, to ask your own questions, and to discover and create your own answers.

In general, the book explores the influence of early experiences on adult assumptions and shows how these experiences can sometimes impose unnecessary restrictions later in life. The first section examines the influence of both conscious and unconscious assumptions on work performance and satisfaction. The second section investigates the emotional aspects of money—the factors that make it easier or more difficult for an individual to acquire, keep, and use it. The third section is devoted to helping you apply these insights to your own life.

By understanding your own behavior and the motives behind it, you can begin to understand your perceptions of yourself and others. The underlying attitudes and beliefs that govern your self-definition will come into focus. As you will discover, your attitudes and assumptions may impede your pursuit and achievement of success or your enjoyment of the rewards of success. You create the future you expect, and these expectations can be examined as diligently as any other aspect of life.

A word of caution: Objectively examining assumptions and internal meanings is an attempt to bring into the clear light of reason, things that may be neither logical nor reasonable. Inoculating feelings with an intellectual label does not immunize you from emotions and their effects.

Psychology deals mainly with metaphors—with symbols. It cannot measure, palpate, seize, or directly map such feelings as pride, fear, motivation, and self-respect, because these are abstract terms used to describe different experiences. Psychologists can't use a surgical probe to repair whatever damage these feelings may have suffered. Yet these abstract concepts are often given a separate existence ("My pride won't let me do it," or "My ego needs it,"); the result is only problems and confusion.

In short, this book is not a volume of labels that will solve problems by naming them. The label is not the thing itself. Instead, this book attempts to introduce you to some new ways of thinking, to give you a broader perspective, as well as help you examine problems surrounding work and money. My goal is to help you discover new options and to provide a framework in which to use them.

DAVID W. KRUEGER, M.D.

Section I

Work and Success

---- **1** ----

What Work Means to Us

The highest reward for man's toil is not what he gets for it,
but what he becomes by it.

—John Ruskin

The more I want to get something done,
the less I call it work.

—Richard Bach

"I just wish I could really excel at something," one of my patients said painfully. "I've been looking all my life for something I can really do well and take pride in."

Work is an expression of the whole human being. It often means more to us than the money or other rewards it brings. "Though I don't need to work financially, I still need to work," a wealthy individual once told me. "Working fulfills me, fulfills my desire to achieve. I say who I am through the work I do. When I'm not working, I feel like an artist without a palette."

For another perspective, consider this statement by a woman who viewed work as a central organizer, a means of self-validation: "My work reassures me. When I feel overwhelmed I turn to the work I know well, and I feel calmed. I became an achiever because it's something I could do that would exist in time and space and become objectively real. It gives me pats on the back." She relied on work to provide continuity and stability in her life. When disruptions occurred, she reestablished internal order by immersing herself in work. Significantly, she could not recall her parents holding or calming her when she was a child. When she became upset, she retreated to her room to take on furiously (what was to her then) work.

How Work Works

Although work is generally defined as purposeful activity, one person's work is another person's play. The difference lies in how each person feels about the work he or she does. These feelings vary not only from one individual to the next, but have also altered over the course of centuries. For most of human history, people have spent their lives raising or hunting food and making tools, clothing, and shelter. Little wonder that our cultural forebears were not enthusiastic about work.

The ancient Hebrews considered work drudgery. The Romans and Greeks regarded it as a burden and sometimes a punishment by the gods for an individual's misdeeds. The ultimate penalty was surely suffered by Sisyphus. In Greek mythology he was sentenced to push a huge rock up a hill only to have it roll back down. He was enslaved to an eternity of meaningless and debasing toil.

According to Christian mythology, work is the punishment for original sin. God sentenced human beings to work "by the sweat of thy brow" to gain basic needs. Many religious denominations consider idleness a sin. In fact, most cultures today consider work an ultimate virtue. The capitalist ethics of our own culture enhance this ideology.

Like early humans, we still live by our work. To a surprising extent, we also live *for* work and consider it rewarding and enjoyable. Through the centuries, as civilization grew more complex, the goals of work expanded beyond the mere satisfaction of immediate physical needs.

Those finding no pleasure or fulfillment in their job remind us how centrally important work is to our emotional life. Those feeling depressed or lost after a long-awaited retirement capture our attention as well. We spend more than half our waking hours at work, whether it takes place in a business office, in a cornfield, or at home caring for children. Work is the stage on which we enact a large portion of the drama of life.

Still, however complete our sense of self and autonomous our self-esteem, work still colors our perceptions of ourselves. To some extent, we define ourselves by the work we do. If self-esteem and self-respect sag, external markers such as work, prestige, and income level become even more meaningful.

The "Monday Morning Cold"

As we all know, working conditions can greatly affect productivity. Personality problems and unrest within a company can make a job unbearable while pleasant environments foster motivation and mutual support. Work and working conditions are changing rapidly in our culture and some people have difficulty adapting. Their work and personal life usually suffer.

Most work and professional difficulties arise from emotional and personality problems, not from technical ineptitude or technological change [Reference 1-1]. Emotional issues are the single greatest cause of absenteeism, especially if the physical symptoms of emotional problems are included. The *Monday morning cold*, *Friday flu*, or day off to recover from a weekend binge are all manifestations of emotional problems that may be related to work.

Why We Work (Besides Money)

Work holds diverse meanings for individuals and they are determined by many factors. Work can build self-esteem, bring gratification, and channel personal ambition and creativity. It can express ethical values and beliefs and meet internal needs. It can be a means of self-assertion and the product of the individual's need for mastery and achievement. No matter how mundane or humble it may be, work can lend dignity to daily life.

Work also can serve as a defense against unwelcome emotions and activities, offer relief from guilt, and offer escape from other life stresses. It may silence internal voices whispering *inferiority*. By working, we may come to feel equal with other people or win acceptance from our family or community. Work can channel aggressive impulses and ward off feelings of insecurity and helplessness. Work earns more than a salary, it earns the right to be master of one's life and fate. No wonder some try to escape into work, or that some suffer an ego-shattering blow when a job is lost.

Historically, men have defined themselves by their vocation or profession and women by their work as mother and homemaker. These traditional roles are changing drastically, but for both sexes work remains crucial. It provides many people with their primary sense of identity, regulates their daily activities, enhances or establishes their self-esteem, and enforces self-discipline.

Work serves the realistic, universal needs for money and something to do all day. In addition, it serves a specific purpose for each individual, varying with the person's history, personality, and internal needs. For example, a self-absorbed, narcissistic person may sustain his self-esteem by working for others' admiration. A chronically competitive, driven person may see her job as an arena for aggressive impulses and a place where she can freely demand love and admiration.

When work engages our attention and challenges our skills, time passes quickly. Boring work, work that makes time drag, fails to hold our attention or stimulate our thoughts and energies.

Meaningful work can define our place in the world. It can also provide us with fellowship and status, with a sense of belonging to a group. When we can visualize our work in a larger context and understand the ultimate purpose of our labors, the act of contributing something useful is our reward. Meaningful work makes us feel contented and productive.

Mastery and Money

All people desire, to one degree or another, recognition, achievement, and mastery. For some, the pleasure of achievement and mastery is sufficient in itself; the reward is intrinsic, and the praise of others is just a nice bonus. Others, however, feel empty or incomplete without recognition for their accomplishments. Pleasing other people is a motivating force for them. But the hollow echo of applause is a poor substitute for a stable sense of self. Psychologically, work cannot create something that is not already present.

Who's That?

Frank came into therapy suffering from feelings of emptiness and depression, stemming primarily from work. He described his despair at discovering, at midlife, that work could not provide his identity: "Even when I do something good, I need feedback," he said. "If I don't get it, I feel empty inside, like a gray room without furniture. I want to make a name for myself one way or the other, even if I lose the company a million dollars. I want recognition, whether it's good or bad. The worst situation I can imagine is to retire and have people in my own company asking, 'Who's that?'"

The Toxic Work-Site

Studies have shown that workers use all their ingenuity to gain control over the way their jobs are done, even when specific tasks are rigidly structured. Human beings have an absolute need to experience the consequences of their actions, stemming from the desire for mastery and pride in accomplishing a difficult task. The experience of mastery *of being effective* may well be the most powerful motivating force in an individual's work. The intrinsic rewards (self-determinism and mastery) are usually more powerfully motivating than such extrinsic rewards as money.

Industrial psychologists have discovered that some of the worst work hazards are neither the machines nor the toxic chemicals but the *toxic psychology* of those operating the machines. The poison in the atmosphere arises from workers' pervasive feelings of boredom and lack of personal power and from the absence of individual recognition for accomplishment. The emotional problems emanating from this *toxic environment* exact a terrible toll on individuals and their work.

The same toxic condition may also arise after retirement, unless the worker retires to some productive activity instead of a deadening idleness. The newfound sense of liberty soon begins to pall, and the supposed joys of freedom fade into a depressing dullness for someone who's lived by a traditional work ethic.

The Middleman

Recognition of our own personality style and emotional needs has to be balanced by a realistic assessment of our strengths and areas of competence. Although Joe was a very successful broker, he gave up his job to become partners with a housing developer. His new job required a change in perspective and approach, but Joe persisted in acting like a salesperson, a middleman between the apartment owners and his own partner. Unable to see himself as half of a team, he alternated sides, telling an apartment owner "I'll get this for you from my partner," and then telling his partner, "We'll have to give him this, and I'll be the go-between." His inability to be part of the team eventually lost Joe the deal.

Joe's earliest childhood experiences as a go-between, mediating between his constantly warring parents, were reenacted in his adult life. He became known as a skilled arbiter for couples having marital difficulties, and his natural inclinations as an intermediary served him well as a broker, where he mediated between his customers and the stock exchange sellers. But these same inclinations interfered markedly with his new position as half of a team.

The Vengeful Conqueror

Some view work as a challenge to be overcome. Once they've conquered the challenge, they lose all interest in the task. Laurel described her dilemma: "I don't do anything unless I can do it well. I master something and then walk away from it. It loses its value after I have conquered it, whether it's buying a new car, starting a relationship, or playing golf. It seems to have an all-or-nothing quality, and after I have it, have conquered it, it's not as meaningful. This attitude is a deterrent in a way, too, because I don't do anything unless I know I can do it well. That keeps me from venturing into new things. Doing well is a kind of revenge."

Laurel described feeling lonely and isolated as a child, looking at the *in* crowd and wishing to be like them. As an adult she exacted a child's revenge for her feelings of rejection, making other people feel as small and frightened as she once felt.

"I can intimidate by my tone of voice," she stated. "I can demean diplomatically; I can control; people become afraid and I like that. When I come across as strong and competent, it scares the hell out of people, and I enjoy that. I feel triumphant, victorious after I give a talk and people are speechless. My talks shut people up. I feel like I'm the best. It's just the opposite of when I was a kid and was never listened to. I was constantly criticized and intimidated by my father. He told me I would never amount to anything, not even to just being a good secretary."

Laurel used her work to avenge earlier intimidations that remained alive inside her adult self. She wanted restitution for her damaged psyche, which still held the residue of her destructive earlier experiences, and everyone around her paid the price.

Achievement in work seems to be the most common and easily recognized path to a sense of self-worth. It is a major standard by which we evaluate ourselves. Most of the impediments to competence at work (including the blocks against acquiring real skill) are psychological. Our assumptions about ourselves and our ability to master our world are the foundations on which our achievements are built. Early experiences can result in inhibitions against achieving or can breed a relentless, unhappy addiction to work. In these situations, the answers clearly reside in the psyche rather than in the work itself.

Fun or Money: Internal Versus External Motivation

Successful work is almost always enjoyable. William Osler, a nineteenth-century physician and teacher, stated, "The very first step toward success in any occupation is to become interested in it. Experience and observation also help us see that success or failure in any endeavor is caused more by mental attitude than by mental capacities for almost all of us."

There's a sharp distinction between satisfaction with the extrinsic rewards of work, such as pay and prestige, and satisfaction with the intrinsic rewards of work, such as the direct enjoyment of doing the work and the resulting feeling of mastery. A study of the enjoyment of work in the United States between 1955 and 1980 indicated satisfaction with the extrinsic rewards had increased, while satisfaction with the intrinsic rewards had declined [Reference 1-2]. Workers had become happier with their paychecks but less happy with their jobs.

The Title Sounded Great

The distinction between extrinsic and intrinsic rewards was a problem for Louise, who was elected to a prestigious position after several months of working toward a goal. Her new post required full-time work in a highly responsible, highly visible position. Three days after her election, a significant thought struck her: "I now realize that I don't really want to do this! I just wanted the recognition and glory of being elected."

The echoes of the applause had barely died when she was seized by the reality of the job in store for her and the realization that she had no interest in the work it involved.

You'd Better Not Have Any Fun

Another patient described himself as a *workaholic*. Jesse recalled how his parents had frowned on having fun. He remembered his father grumbling "If you're going to have fun, it'd better be while you're working." Jesse mentioned a number of hobbies and sports he liked but just couldn't seem to do; these, it turned out, weren't things he'd tried and failed to master but things he'd never even attempted.

Fearing criticism and inadequacy, Jesse wouldn't do a thing if he couldn't do it perfectly, *the first time.* So many enjoyable activities, mastered only with repeated practice, were not available to Jesse because of his attitude.

Travel Tales of the Puritans

People who are driven by the demanding and punitive belief that only relentless work determines their worth may find no escape from this notion, even on vacation. Nor can their friends escape their relentlessly money-oriented travel tales. Such *puritans* come home describing how cheaply they traveled and boasting of the good deals they found—the tailored suit picked up cheap in Hong Kong, the silver jewelry bought for a song in Mexico. Or they're the couple who insist on detailing the number of places they visited, the expensive things they bought, and the exorbitant costs of the trip—and by implication, their ability to afford it.

In either case, these people are emphasizing the external value of their vacation, instead of the good time they had. Their work ethic dictates that value and self-worth can only come from productivity, from saving money, spending money, or producing other tangible results.

The Corporate Image

Another kind of externally-oriented work ethic is embodied in the person who always does what he or she *should* do, constantly focusing on others' evaluation rather than on any internal initiative. Frank relied on work for his identity, saying "I look at my life as a job, I do everything properly. I always do things I'm supposed to do, like the way I dress and the way I present myself. I'm trying to fit myself into the corporate image of my company. The trouble is, I can't behave any differently when I get home. My mind never stops, I'm constantly scanning other people. I always look at myself from the perspective of someone else. I suffer from chronic envy. I have a continuing sense of low importance that keeps me working harder. I always compare myself to other people, but I always find them better than me, or at least I focus on some aspect of them that I see as better or outstanding."

In therapy, Frank began to realize he never compared himself to the whole person, the whole group, or the general population, but always to some specific aspect of somebody else. He wondered why he continually needed to compare himself to others.

Adjusting to Success

Success and failure are often two sides of the same coin. When success is finally attained and the hard times are over, some people feel as though they are on a roll. The spartan turns into a Sybarite, buying a new home, new furniture, new offices, and a vacation cottage. The desire to expand or invest becomes a restless obsession.

Soon enough, the dream of expansion turns into a nightmare of overextension, perhaps into an unknown field of business. What was the epitome of success a few years earlier has been attained and now ceases to satisfy. There's a desire for more, for another victory. The desire for recognition escalates, viewed (or rationalized, if it's useless to the business) as "public relations." Stress increases.

Stress arises not only from the work itself but also from the dramatic changes in lifestyle and social context brought about by success. The change in context is even more difficult to deal with when the individual's external success contradicts an internal self-image.

The School Dummy Makes Good

Jack had started his own computer sales company six years before and achieved remarkable success through dedication, hard work, and intelligent marketing decisions. For the past two years, however, he'd suffered from bouts of anxiety, chest pains, and the certainty on several occasions that he was having a heart attack. After numerous emergency room visits and consultations with specialists, he began to suspect that his problems were probably *in his head*—emotional rather than physical in origin—even though their manifestation was painfully, frighteningly physical.

Jack talked of his work, his success, his changed lifestyle, and finally his childhood. Jack never believed he'd succeed in business, because he was sure he was stupid. During grade and high school, he barely passed, A grade of D appeared most often on his report card. He was held back in the seventh grade. His father would accept only an A on Jack's reports. Jack was sent to his room each day after school until bedtime and forced to study for at least six hours every Saturday and Sunday. He was furiously angry, couldn't concentrate, yearned for freedom, and fell into a stubborn, passive rebellion. "He can keep me in here, but he can't make me study," Jack told himself. He decided that he must really be stupid anyway, or he would make better grades. His father frequently told him he was lazy, dumb, and incompetent, and Jack incorporated the same view into his self-image.

Now, as Jack's success escalated, his anxiety increased just as rapidly. He worried that he really wasn't smart enough to sustain his business. He felt like an impostor. With every business meeting, he grew more anxious and more frightened of further expansion. His physical symptoms seemed to be concrete evidence that something really was wrong.

People Who Succeed— and People Who Don't

George Valliant, a Harvard psychiatrist, has studied a select group of individuals over several decades [Reference 1-3]. He has discovered, contrary to popular mythology, that those who enjoy the best marriages and the most intimate friendship patterns are also most likely to become extremely successful in their professions (company presidents, for example). Many of the successful people in this study were so certain of themselves and their goals that they actually preferred to preside over their own smaller businesses rather than grow wealthy as a vice president of someone else's larger company.

In contrast to these extraordinarily successful individuals, people who are only moderately or slightly successful often have considerably more ambivalent feelings about success or about their career and the commitment necessary for success. While yearning for power, prestige, recognition, and success, they simultaneously feel that the work required to achieve what they want is silly and boring. They may envy more successful people yet refuse to recognize the role hard work has played in the success of those they envy.

The differing attitudes of the successful and less successful are often formed during childhood. The next chapter discusses how some children learn to succeed while others are taught to fail.

Self-Inquiry Quiz

1. What are the labels I attach to myself?

2. Do any of my self-imposed labels limit me or serve as explanations for my behavior (for example, *shy, follower, loser*)?

3. If I would expose my *real self* more, what would be the result? Am I frightened at the thought of exposing myself?

4. How well do I know myself, my self-image, and my body image?

5. As I look at the big picture, do I have a clear overview of the past, the present, and the future, in terms of my goals and standards?

6. What is my internal model of myself? Do I understand my ideals? Am I clear about my internal standards of *good enough*?

7. In my pursuit of a goal or work, is the motivation internal or external? For work, is the goal primarily pay and prestige, or is it satisfaction from the intrinsic rewards of doing the work itself? Or is it all of these combined?

8. Are my goals diverse enough so there is no undue pressure in my life—such as working or being a parent—keeping me from developing other interests or goals? Do I understand that deriving all esteem from one area or directing all my effort into one endeavor creates tremendous pressure and vulnerability?

9. Have I developed my own personal, internally derived definition of success, and formulated my own goals? Do these match my individual needs rather than stereotypic, past, or social ideals?

2

Play and Work

When you like your work, every day is a holiday.

—Frank Tyger

The worst day fishing is better than the best day working.

—Bumper sticker

If you're not certain about play being work, think about the total, hilarious absorption of kittens at play. They ferociously attack pieces of string, rear up on hind legs to bat each others' ears and, with incredible strength and determination, claw their way up curtains. The kittens don't consider themselves cute; they are training for life, not yet aware that they will probably be cared for and protected by humans all their lives. As far as the kittens are concerned, instinct tells them they have, at best, twelve weeks until their mother turns them loose to hunt their own food, fight for a territory, and efficiently escape from larger animals. Little wonder, then, that these tiny furballs are so absolutely (and amusingly) serious about practicing their skills.

Child's Play, Child's Work

Young human beings aren't really too different from kittens. They too learn to explore and assert themselves through play, although a human child has a lot more to learn than any cat. Successful, productive, comfortable, creative adult work is based on the child's effective foundation of a positive sense of self.

Through some very sophisticated research, we now know the motivation for mastery—the desire to feel effective—exists from earliest infancy. Good mothers have known this for centuries; science and developmental psychology are finally catching up. The infant learns that she can influence her environment when she smiles and her mother smiles back. If the parents accurately and consistently respond to the child's needs, she develops confidence in her ability to affect both internal events (feelings) and external events (parental response). This is the pleasure of competence and effectiveness. When a child feels that she has no influence on events, she may conclude that she is incompetent [Reference 2-1].

Another important task of childhood is to develop autonomy; a sense of one's own competent, independent functioning, separate from parents and siblings. The child who says "Let me do it!" is developing autonomy, a self-image, and pride in learning a new task. A four-year-old who succeeds in tying his own shoelaces or an eight-year-old who skates around the block without falling experiences mastery.

Childhood play determines how well an adult will be able to combine work and play. Throughout childhood and into adulthood, the person develops an individual style and an individual play/work ethic. While playing, the child learns to master and manage the external world, how to really do something, be active and effective, exert influence over the immediate environment, and how to be a cause. This childhood mastery is the precursor of work.

Play also allows children to master a painful or frightening event that makes them feel helpless. Such an event is transformed into a game the children may repeat over and over until it loses its painful or scary qualities. After a visit to the doctor or hospital, for instance, children may play act visiting the doctor until their anxiety is lessened, or they may take the role of being the doctor and seize the doctor's power.

At about age eight, when children begin thinking abstractly, they learn to master new events in advance by imagining what will happen and what they'll do. This "anticipatory mastery" may be perfected through playing. The potential entrepreneur can practice making real estate deals in Monopoly, the would-be chef can concoct a witches' brew made of kitchen spices, and the future parent can nurture dolls.

The first atmosphere of play is the home environment, and thus it has a pervasive influence. For example, a child who tries to tie his shoelaces and only manages to knot them may be praised by his parent for making the attempt. Or the parent may scold the child (or worse) for making a mess and then take over the job herself. In the second case, the child will probably not try to tie his or her shoelaces again for a long time. A supportive, dependable, empathic environment gives children a feeling of expansiveness and self-direction, the awareness that they can explore new areas and that they have the power to do things they enjoy. On the other hand, an atmosphere that demands total obedience, unvarying routine, and explicit adherence to parents' rules may interfere with the growth of children's assertiveness and self-reliance.

In a supportive environment, children feel secure and comfortable and engage happily in play. The pleasure of effectiveness, of being in control of something, is the fun of play. A sense of mastery also gives children an increasing core of confidence and self-esteem. They begin to show consistency and endurance in learning new tasks; they feel comfortable enough to try new things and to keep trying right up to the triumphant shout of "I can do it!".

Children then expand the arena of play to include other children, leading them toward cooperation in mutually shared tasks. The child who's learned to tie his shoelaces may teach a friend how to tie hers so the two of them won't have to wait for their parents to do it for them; the child who can roller-skate may teach her friends so they can all skate together. In addition to work competence, play also helps children develop interpersonal skills and facility in social situations.

As children's physical accomplishments and social skills increase, so does their creativity. They begin to internalize, or make part of themselves, a *work ethic*, not the idea that work is a grim duty, but recognition of the pleasure of personal effectiveness. Others' approval and admiration sustain their pleasure in effort and achievement. As children approach adulthood, mastery is increasingly its own reward, although they never lose their need for connection with others and occasional encouragement.

The Successful Failure

Kevin's parents requested he be evaluated by me to see if psychotherapy might help in addressing his school problems. He was sixteen, in the eleventh grade, and his grades had been sliding to *D* and *F* for almost a year. I agreed to see Kevin without his parents present and established with him that whatever we talked about would be absolutely confidential.

Kevin was reluctant to talk to me at first, telling me that he came only because his parents insisted. He mentioned he learned, just that day, that he had missed 118 out of 120 answers on a major test. I commented that he must have known the material extremely well to have come so close to a perfect score. His smile, the acknowledgment of being together in familiar territory, broadened as I asked him what happened on the two he got right.

Our work together went very well, especially after we agreed that it would be his therapy. If therapy was a success, it would be his success, and if a failure, his failure. I demanded nothing of him and only recommended that he say whatever came to mind. With nothing for Kevin to oppose or conform to, we could focus on his internal experiences.

Within his family, Kevin had felt he needed to fail in order to be his own person. His parents demanded perfection, and so mistakes were the only things he felt were truly his own. He felt his parents were intrusive, taking credit for everything he did. He recognized that in the future he would truly have to be on his own, and he was trying, in the only way he could figure out, to establish independence from his parents.

Our Parents, Our Models—Even If They're Not Model Parents

I'm Gonna Be Just Like Mommy

Children's relationships with their parents play an important role in their future attitudes toward work and productivity. From earliest childhood, children identify with their parents, seeing them as models of the people they'd like to be, and as grown-up mirrors of themselves. Children identify with both parents but more strongly with the parent of the same sex. They also identify with their parents' ability, or inability, to achieve.

The family's social attitudes and status may shape—or misshape—the child's progress toward mastery. Some kinds of work may be overvalued and others denigrated, and these values and restrictions are often passed from one generation to another. Children from lower-class families may be taught, from earliest childhood, that they cannot rise above their family's socioeconomic level: "You want to be a doctor? What'sa matter, you think you're too good for us?" Children from higher social classes usually have a wider range of options, because their parents' range of experience has been broader. The parents are thus less likely to limit their children's expectations as to what they can and can't do. On the other hand, such parents may pressure their children to match or exceed their own success: "You don't want to be a doctor? What'sa matter, you want to drive a truck all your life?" Another example is our culture's attitude toward a woman's career outside the home, which many of us (especially those who are middle class) value more highly than people do in other areas of the world.

Although people develop their own ideas and create their own opportunities, the expectations accumulated during childhood play a major role in determining which goals they will pursue later. Parents who are secure about their self-worth, and confident of their femininity or masculinity, encourage children to express themselves uniquely and creatively. They seldom insist that children fit some rigid model. These parents serve as an accurate and complete mirror, reflecting their children's full range of feeling, ambition, and experience.

Children can identify with parents who approach life energetically. Young children have a sense of grandness, of being the center of the world, able to do and be anything. They are right, of course, they are the center of a world of doting parents and grandparents. Children develop both self-esteem and ambition when their parents emphatically reflect this sense of grandness ("What a wonderful drawing!") and simultaneously help contain it within realistic boundaries ("But don't ever, ever draw on the wall again!").

Parents who are visibly proud of a child's expanding accomplishments enhance the child's own pride. Parents who are successful within their work arena and comfortable with themselves as individuals further reinforce the child's sense of mastery. That proud, secure feeling of, *My daddy/mommy can do anything!* translates to, *When I get big, I'll be able to do anything too!*

The parents' relationship with each other is also important. A child's original family offers a model of a woman and a man, a model of loved and loving spouses, and a model of a marriage. These early experiences affect the individual's expectations for both work and love.

All too often, the model is negative. A passive mother often has difficulty dealing directly with aggression and reacts to it with passivity and overindulgent helpfulness. This mother usually will not be able to tolerate assertiveness in her daughter. The daughter will learn to modify her expression of emotion. For example, she'll learn she can cry when she's angry, but she'll learn she mustn't raise her voice or talk back. The father who is uncomfortable with expressing his emotions may demand that his son not cry when hurt, may show no tenderness, and may avoid other such *weaknesses*.

If the mother dominates the father, or devalues his success, or if the father is unreliable, passive, or particularly unsuccessful, a son may have difficulty valuing his own male role. He may also have conflicts about identifying with an *idealized* father who is far from ideal. A daughter who identifies with a passive, dependent mother faces the task of dis-identifying with her model if she hopes to achieve success [Reference 2-2].

Parents Who Compete or Control

Accomplished, successful parents who are also supportive and nurturing will encourage a child to be assertive and independent. If either parent feels threatened by the child's emerging competence and responds in a competitive or constricting way, the child loses not only support and nurturing but also that important early sense of mastery.

A mother who fancied herself artistic enrolled her ten-year-old daughter in a weekly pottery class for children. The mother freely praised the pretty little ashtrays and candy dishes the girl brought home. However, as soon as the daughter turned out a large and exceptionally lovely service plate, her mother promptly joined the class, the sole adult. The mother remained only long enough to produce a matched pair of giant lamp bases before losing interest. The girl was deeply embarrassed by her mother's intrusion, which interfered with the pleasure the girl felt in learning a craft in the company of other children. Clearly, the mother's sudden interest in ceramics lay wholly in her competitive need to surpass her own daughter. The girl, recognizing her mother's envy, felt she was being punished for being *too good* at something. The lesson she learned was that she had better hide her own accomplishments if she wanted to keep enjoying them.

All children have feelings of helplessness. They're very small compared with adults and can't do many important things that are easy for adults (like making lunch, sewing a doll's arm back on, or pumping the right amount of air into a bicycle tire). Play converts children's feelings of helplessness and passivity into activity and mastery. Even if she can't make her own lunch, a child in kindergarten can arrange an elegant tea party for her doll guests.

Parents may restrict their children's play because of their own internal conflicts. *Playing doctor*, for instance, is frequently forbidden since it often involves breaking the sexual taboo against mutual physical exploration. Parents may stereotype sex roles (Chemistry sets are not for little girls) or restrain *play* because of their own unhealthy needs (an over ambitious parent trying to raise a *superchild* may ban board games not specifically labeled educational). Parents who insist on total control over a child, who won't allow the child to disagree with them, may force the child to be passive. A child who must always play the game chosen by his or her parents may decide to stop playing altogether and stare out the window. Such children have difficulty achieving independence because the benefits of their play (and later of their adult work) have been compromised. Their parents prevent them from mastering their environment, from feeling the sense of competence that mastery brings, and from developing the ability to manage stress, which is learned through play.

My Mother Needs Me

"My mother wants me to be a success and be on my own, but I think she'll feel useless when 'her baby' is gone." At age eighteen, Christine had suffered for two years from significant emotional turmoil and had developed anorexia nervosa. In her compulsive desire to be thin, she had starved herself from 125 pounds down to 90.

Her symptoms started when her older brother left home, leaving just Christine with her parents. Christine sensed how much her parents missed her brother, and her disease gave them someone to take care of. Worried about her thinness, Christine's parents focused on every bite she ate and repeatedly attempted to feed her. These events met the emotional needs of both Christine and her parents, although they were quite debilitating for Christine.

By refusing to eat, Christine unconsciously gave up her independence and autonomy so her parents would feel useful and necessary. A closer look revealed that Christine had never achieved complete independence. Her parents had guided her in an over involved, controlling way, making decisions for her and even interpreting her feelings and thoughts. Christine had not been allowed to develop her own sense of self or initiative.

In school, Christine eagerly did exactly what she was told. She felt lost and uncertain, however, if she had to initiate anything herself, and she avoided any activity that seemed new or required her to function independently. She felt secure in what she did, although her underlying boredom and dissatisfaction sometimes surfaced when she realized she was capable of more. As her desire for perfection and effectiveness focused on her body, she began controlling every bite she ate and relentlessly exercised in order to feel *real*.

As graduation neared, Christine realized the time was coming for her to function on her own. She retreated to her parents' waiting arms. Her anorexia guaranteed that her parents would have to take care of her, literally fretting over every bite she ate. With her thin, childlike body and the loss of her menstrual periods, Christine retreated to an earlier time.

During her hospitalization, Christine gradually became aware of her feelings, both emotional and bodily. Only then was she able to do the work she had missed during childhood. She began to develop a sense of herself as a separate and autonomous person. She became aware that a son or daughter might try to be the best child possible by remaining dependent, so the parents could feel worthwhile.

Making a Child Scared of School

Healthy children feel free to explore and develop skills. They can demand privacy, tolerate solitude, and select their own goals. The success of childhood *work* rests on the freedom to develop individuality and separateness from parents—a sense of self. The failure of childhood *work* is shown in academic underachievement, emotionally based learning disabilities, behavioral problems in school, or anxieties that interfere with school performance.

School phobia may also develop when children's growth is stymied. Many children who are starting school feel so anxious about separating from their mother that they develop upset stomachs or other symptoms, that disappear only when they are reunited with their mother.

A child's avoidance of school may be only half the problem. The other half may be the anxious mother who doesn't really want her child to go and subtly, often unconsciously, encourages the child to retreat to an earlier, more dependent stage of childhood.

Enhancing Self-Functioning

Parents who insist on functioning for their children erode coping ability and self-esteem. The most caring approach parents can take is to allow trial-and-error experiences appropriate to the children's age. Naturally, some of the trials will result in errors, frustrating the children and making parents question their decision. Yet this approach allows children to recognize their own effectiveness and come to believe in themselves. Mastering a new skill is gratifying and encourages optimism and an eagerness to experience new situations. Children's capacity to enjoy themselves and their activities is closely connected to a sense of triumph: *I can do it!*

One of the clearest signs of conflict in an adult mind is the still-active assumption (left over from childhood experiences) that some other person, some parental figure, really has all the answers. This magical belief in an all-knowing figure is just the opposite of the healthy self-directedness that comes from having tried and mastered new situations in childhood. An important part of true adulthood is the realization that, although someone may be an expert in some specific area, even experts are only human. Each person has to discover his or her own answers, not absolute answers and not secretly known by someone else.

Children obtain another early sense of the meaning of work from both parents. Even though they may not understand the specific work world of either parent (unless the parent has been working in the home), they can see their parents' attitudes and approaches to work. Children see their parents leave the family each day and they hear how the parents talk about their jobs. Children sense how involved the parents are, note the level of parents' satisfaction with work, listen to parents' stories about successes and failures, see the monetary compensation, and observe parents' zest and eagerness for work. Children also begin to realize how inviting or threatening the outside world is.

A parent who approaches work with positive attitudes is an important model who gives the child something positive to anticipate in his or her own work world, school. With luck, a good teacher will take the child's schoolwork seriously and present it creatively, building the child's self-confidence and sense of mastery. Nothing flattens the child's enthusiasm for school faster than treating schoolwork as a duty, useful only in accumulating facts or winning the teacher's approval.

For several years I have coached basketball at my children's school. I would begin with a team when one of my children turned eight and continue with the same team until they moved to middle school. My son's and my daughter's team started out the same way, none of the children had ever played basketball before. Rather than beginning with the rules and telling them the things they couldn't do, I encouraged them to have fun while being a team. Of all the basics they were learning, I applauded that one thing each child was doing well. Soon enough, all the children learned the other skills. My goal was to give the children a positive experience and build a self-concept of fun and achievement more than to post a good win-lose record. (Fortunately for *my* positive self-concept, we had remarkably good seasons.)

At school (as in later work), learning is most meaningful when it engages the student's curiosity and leads to the feeling of competence. The process of learning is more important than the content, although the content can make the world more understandable. My personal bet is that an increment of self-concept is more useful in the long run than knowing the capital of Greenland.

The confidence-building experience of learning with pleasure, free of internal or external constraint, provides a sound basis for choosing work later in life. Children should learn that they are not bound to the work their parents do. Yet parents can constrict their children's later choices in many ways. They may hold rigid sex-role stereotypes that assume, for instance, that a daughter will become a wife and mother or will choose a *feminine* career. Other parents may impose cultural limitations or rigid family expectations. If grandfather and father have been factory workers, the son may be expected to be a factory worker. In a higher social class, the first offspring may become *a banker, lawyer, or doctor* while the youngest becomes a lifelong source of spicy gossip and forces the parents to continually rescue the *bad seed*. Parents may also insist that a child do only what pleases the parents, or live out the parents' frustrated dreams. The classic example is the stage mother who yearned to be a star herself and now drags her child to every audition.

Adolescence, Identity, and the Work Ethic

As children move into adolescence, their attitudes and personalities begin to crystallize. They consider their abilities and options more realistically and begin to imagine their own future. They can give up their earlier feelings of omnipotence and the unrealistic fantasies of being (all at the same time) a famous attorney, movie star, doctor, and firefighter. Adolescents' growing ability to think abstractly and be future-oriented allows them to choose realistic goals as they begin to plan their career. Adolescents also begin to see their parents somewhat more realistically, and their parents' limitations may naturally be disappointing and disillusioning.

Buffeted by strong and confusing emotions and facing the rational need to reconcile contradictory aims and abilities, adolescents face a difficult task. Nearly all teenagers feel like a dozen different people packed into one; they all need to coordinate these diverse energies and personality tendencies. By learning to adapt to pressing real-life demands, teenagers eventually forge their identity.

Some teenagers have difficulty synthesizing all the different *people* and talents they seem to contain in one skin. They often remain reluctant to commit themselves to any major line of endeavor. They can't bear to close off any alternative. Every talent—even in such unrelated areas as science, sports, literature, and art—is a fragment of a way of life and one's own identity. Choosing just one or two talents, and relegating the others to the status of hobbies, is painful. *Perpetual adolescents* may refuse to accept the limits of making a single career choice and remain as undecided in their thirties as they were in their teens.

One of the major tasks of adolescence is to transform the idealizations of early childhood into internal ideals, permitting more accurate assessment of others and of oneself. Idealizations are those dearly held illusions that people are better, more perfect, more infallible than they really are. Early in life, children's idealizations are personal, they aggrandize their parents or their own abilities. In time idealization spreads to the outer world, taking the form of hero worship of, for instance, a rock star, a movie personality, or a favorite teacher. Later these idealizations also include the general and impersonal, such as religious, political, and educational institutions.

As we mature, we gradually see, confront, question, and disrupt our idealizations; in their place we develop ideals, our own internal standards of being and behavior. We can see our parents as real people with human qualities, including failures and limitations. Our own identity becomes clearer and firmer. We learn to accept reality and its limits and can assess our own capabilities without losing sight of our dreams and goals.

Part of the disillusionment of adolescence is the normal process of emotional separation from our parents and the attainment of autonomy. We come to the inevitable recognition that parents aren't always perfect mirrors, reflecting wholly, completely, and without distortion; they have their own point of view, their own needs and struggles.

When teenagers begin to realize that parents are separate people, they may find that a mentor is helpful. A mentor can encourage a talent or interest that may be a blind spot to parents, or outside their scope of ability.

In therapy, many adult patients finally recognize that they have long been expecting their parents to accurately and completely mirror their own worth and capacity. These patients begin to overcome their problems when they realize they have been looking into an incomplete or distorted *mirror*, because their parents are all too human.

Exalted Ideals and Fear of Criticism

In normal human development, self-esteem and affirmation gradually shift from external sources to an internally regulated source. The guiding question becomes "What is in my best interest?" A set of standards, or ideals, is established. *Good enough* usually lies somewhere between unattainable perfection and flagrant underachievement.

Pseudostupidity

Forced into *pseudostupidity* by family pressures discouraging free inquiry, some adolescents develop inhibitions about knowing and learning. The family may demand ignorance in certain areas, stifling the natural process of inquiry and learning. A puritanical family may require sexual ignorance; a narcissistic family may demand that a child remain ignorant of the difference between the parents' idealized selves and their far-from-ideal real selves; the defensively anti-intellectual family may demand ignorance of the arts, literature, and *all that sissy stuff.*

Whatever form it takes, stifling curiosity may erode the child's ability and eagerness to learn and disrupt the development of a sense of self. The child may come to fear using and expanding his or her talents.

Leave Before They Discover You're Not Perfect

Stan job-hopped. He was certain that if he stayed too long, his co-workers and subordinates would learn everything he knew and he would fall subject to their scrutiny and criticism. Since Stan would begin to feel this way eighteen to twenty-four months into a job, his longest term of employment had been two years.

This brilliant, highly-accomplished professional man was reacting as though he were still a child at the mercy of his powerful, critical, and somewhat humiliating father. Although Stan's extraordinary knowledge of his field and status as a consultant allowed him to reverse this painful parent-child relationship, his past remained alive in the present. Whenever Stan felt that anyone might challenge his authority, he'd flee to a new job. Stan's father had particularly equated worth with achievement and productivity, so Stan felt compelled to perform perfectly but could never enjoy the fruits of his labor.

In love as well as in business, Stan feared involvement and commitment without an escape hatch. His ability to leave was his insurance against criticism and failure. Convinced that he'd be found lacking if he allowed a lover to know him too well, Stan ended his relationships prematurely and moved on to others.

An interesting sidelight was that Stan's father was a professional musician. Stan also loved music but had been tone-deaf since early childhood. Although he tried playing various instruments, his tone deafness had been a real handicap. During therapy, Stan realized that his tone deafness was a generalized way of not hearing his father's constant criticisms; Stan simply *turned a deaf ear* to the barrage of blame. When the underlying issue was resolved in treatment, Stan discovered to his amazement that he wasn't tone-deaf at all, and he began to play the saxophone.

Falling Short of Perfection

Sometimes people fail because their ideals are so high that no amount of talent or trying can ever meet such standards. People with such unrealistic expectations are certain that any effort will fall short and expose them to ridicule, embarrassment, and humiliation. They believe that a perfect score is merely lucky; the exam was not hard enough or the teacher was not smart enough. In this framework success cannot exist, only varying degrees of failure.

The best you can do is to fool the teacher or *luck out* on the test. In this context, any sustained effort toward a goal can only diminish over time, along with pleasure in pursuing and achieving the goal.

People who cannot meet their own impossible ideals gradually try less and less and then not at all, protecting themselves by not even attempting to achieve their aims. They can meet their ideals only in fantasy, or by clinging to the illusion that they could if they really tried, but choose not to [Reference 2-3].

Such perfectionism begins when highly critical parents demand more and better achievements from their children, rather than applauding their attempts and their small successes. Instead of praising children's efforts and the good results, they focus on the one area that needs improvement. With an all-*A*, one-*B* report card, these parents may comment only on the *B*.

If parents consistently notice only what has not been done adequately, their children may begin to see themselves as inadequate. Variations include parents who do not respond at all to their children's achievements and parents who insist on taking credit for themselves ("If I hadn't made you study last night, you never would have gotten that *A*."). Children begin to feel that only phenomenal efforts and results will gain a positive, admiring response. When even perfection doesn't get results, children conclude that they just aren't good enough, and this conclusion becomes part of their self-concept. Such children lose interest in applying effort and suppress their talents for fear of falling short of their own ideals or those they anticipate from others.

I Hear This Critical Voice

Like Stan, Chris suffered from the *"So you got a B"* style of parenting. But Chris, an accountant, exhibited different symptoms. He felt anxious, tense, and inadequate when he sat down to work. "It's like all eyes are turned on me, and I have to perform," he said. His drive to accomplish things would then take on a vindictive tone: "I'm going to do it no matter what." Effort became a personal fight. "I feel like I have to use bulldog tactics to accomplish the objectives," he said. He described how he would delay completing a project, feeling that his work had to be perfect before he could expose it (and hence himself). He would then criticize himself for his "laziness."

As Chris gradually came to realize that perfection was impossible, his depression led him to seek treatment. This is how he summarized his all-or-nothing attitude: "If my work isn't perfect, whatever I do will be criticized. I won't be able to be perfect, so why start work or keep working? I'll just take off."

Chris was haunted by an image of someone constantly looking over his shoulder and judging him. As I learned about his childhood, I said, "I think you still hear the voice of your parents, leaning over your shoulder and pointing out your one mistake or telling you it's not quite good enough. In agreeing with that voice, you feel inadequate, like you'll never be perfect." Chris came to recognize that he could choose to disagree with the voice and could, rather than recreating it, construct his own internal point of reference.

Returning to the Scene of Her Prime

Inaccurate, excessive praise can be just as much a problem as criticism. Inappropriately overvaluing a child's accomplishments can create unrealistic, unattainable ideals.

From her first crayon mark, Robin's every squiggle was treated as a Picasso. Now graduating from architectural school she felt fraudulent, like an impostor. Her parents were proudly urging her to seek a very prominent position, indicating to her and to their friends that they knew she would soon create some spectacular architectural design.

Robin had felt overvalued and pushed her entire life. She had become afraid that whatever she did would never be good enough, would never meet her parents' expectations. In fact, prior to graduation, she had almost failed from a combination of wanting to bail out of impossible expectations and of defying her parents in order to achieve her own autonomy. Robin knew she could never re-create in the real world the adulation she received at home. Understandably, she felt reluctant to proceed.

First Person, Present Tense

Since none of us has perfect parents, a major step toward gaining and feeling comfortable with personal success lies along the road that Chris took, the road of separating your parents' voices from your own, and your parents' aspirations from your own. Adulthood consists, in part, of discovering the freedom to create your own internal model of yourself, with your own standards and ideals.

Having a sense of attainable goals is the opposite of perfectionism.

The only way I know to experience self-esteem is to have internal standards, ideals, and goals and then to live up to them.

Self-Inquiry Quiz

1. Am I vaguely anxious or uncomfortable with feeling good?

2. Do I assume that feeling good will inevitably end in some crisis, some bad luck, or something bad happening?

3. Have I reached long-sought goals only to find I'm no longer interested?

4. After reaching a particular goal, do I ask myself "Is that all there is?"

5. Am I able to relax completely?

6. Am I stopping myself from making important commitments because they seem to close off other alternatives?

7. Are there times I'd rather be well liked than to proceed with what I know to be right for me? Would I rather be well liked than competent?

8. Does it seem selfish to act on my own needs?

9. In discussing controversial issues (business or personal) with one or more people, do I find myself *forgetting* or abandoning my own point of view and adopting theirs?

10. Am I advancing in my work at the pace and level of my true potential?

11. Do I find it difficult to finish things unless there's a deadline?

12. Do I often base my decisions on how other people will perceive me?

13. Am I so concerned with making a mistake that I inhibit my efforts or restrain myself from trying something I really want to do?

14. Are my decisions and progress in my career path consistent with my overall game plan?

15. Do I have a game plan?

16. Do I have a clear perspective of where I am now, in terms of where I've been and where I want to go?

17. Am I afraid to do what I want and need to do because the change would provoke anxiety? Because the change would bring greater exposure? Because I might fail at something I consider really important?

18. Do I feel like a success at home but a failure at work? Or vice versa?

3

Fear of Success: Conscious Assumptions

We have met the enemy—and he is us.

—Pogo (Walt Kelly)

If you think you can, you're right.
If you think you can't, you're right.

—Henry Ford

"I have to fake myself out to win a game," said Marsha, who could swat a ball in a tennis game but dropped the ball on her job.

When we fear success, it's not success itself that frightens us but some anticipated, dreadful result of success. People who suffer from this fear can rarely identify what it is they're worrying about; all they know is that when they come close to succeeding, they feel the generalized sense of dread called anxiety.

Anxiety, the feeling that something bad is going to happen, is a signal that we perceive imminent danger of some kind. *Something bad* has a different meaning for each person, consistent with the individual's experiences and expectations.

Often, people are not consciously aware of what the real danger is for them. Or they displace the danger onto some current fear, such as terror of open spaces; an understandable attempt to control the anxiety by giving it a name and making it specific and real. Displacing the anxiety and naming it lets people feel they can do something about it and don't have to feel helpless. They can stay away from big shopping malls and drive only on neighborhood streets instead of on big, open freeways.

A danger situation is one in which the individual anticipates being helpless. The situation may stem from current reality, such as the danger of being held up at gunpoint. Or it may be associated with a certain set of emotions or with some event that the individual's unconscious links to a childhood event in which he or she felt helpless. This linking, or association, may create a reaction out of proportion to the current, real danger.

A *phobia* is a specific defense against anxiety. In a phobia, avoiding some activity equates with avoiding some perceived danger. The phobia is a stand-in, a representative, for something frightening, something beyond conscious awareness. The danger is symbolically transferred to an external object or situation. This object or situation is avoided in hopes of avoiding the actual, unconscious internal conflict and its anxiety. A phobia is a valiant attempt to master what is otherwise vague and nonsensible.

Some phobias express themselves as inhibitions against achievement. Fear of failure may disguise a conflict that began much earlier in life. Although a moderate and healthy amount of anxiety can drive us toward achievement, a higher level of anxiety can derail our motivation to achieve. The problem is not simply how much anxiety we feel, but the specific cause of the anxiety and what it unconsciously means to us. Our fears can be overcome only when we identify and understand the specific assumptions that block us from realizing our full potential, whether it is a potential for internal comfort, happiness, relatedness with others, a strong sense of self, or successful achievement.

Success phobia is the disturbance of a person's ability to comfortably handle achievement [Reference 3-1]. Fear of success seems contradictory. Why would a person recoil from something that is consciously desired and highly valued? And yet success phobia is a genuine problem for many people.

Forms of Success Phobia

Success can be avoided in many areas of life—academic, vocational, marital, sexual, and parental, to name a few. Surprisingly, fear of success isn't always obvious. It manifests itself in so many ways that it often goes unrecognized. Individuals suffer success phobia for different reasons and reveal it in different ways; there is no simple, single connection between any set of symptoms and any particular set of causes.

An important first step in overcoming a fear of success is to recognize some of the ways it can reveal itself. Three basic areas of phobic avoidance are: (1) avoidance of the final step to success ("I always stop just short of my goals"), (2) erosion of successful accomplishment ("When I win, I lose"), and (3) ambition without goal setting ("I can't set any goal").

Avoidance of the Final Step

I Stop Just Short of My Goals

A graduate student had completed all but the last paragraph of his doctoral dissertation but could not finish it. At that point he decided to switch subjects, he abandoned his initial goal of getting his degree, he became a professional student, and he postponed success. Another graduate student feared she'd be found a *phony* when she took her final doctoral examinations. And yet another student always planned to do more studying than he could possibly manage, forestalling completion of his studies and, in his eyes, success.

People who fear success may avoid taking the final step toward successful accomplishment. Their anxiety peaks just before they finish a task, and it can be allayed only by stopping work before it's done. Some cannot complete a project, they have to keep reworking, redefining, and putting off completion. They may relinquish responsibility for the task or never quite meet the goal.

Graduation from school commonly provokes a great deal of anxiety. One defense against the graduation crisis is to remain a perpetual student, either never managing to get a degree or getting several of them. Yet perpetual students feel inadequate, uncertain, frightened about the future, undeserving of success, and unable to define their goals. A perplexed student thought she wanted to succeed but was actually on her sixth major in as many years.

I Never Finished Because I Didn't Start

A variation on the technique of avoiding the final step is to bar the path to success early, before success can possibly be achieved. We've all heard of students who completely forgot to register, or failed to take the entrance exam, or of job applicants who always arrived late or willfully antagonized the interviewer.

I Choked

The fear of success is whispered in the everyday words, *choke* and *clutch*, describing the sensation of being paralyzed with fear during an examination, a tennis game, or some crisis. Someone who's clearly in the lead may falter when winning is imminent. For example, Marsha described tennis as the only area where she could comfortably express her whole personality, including her feelings of aggression. "But I 'choke' when I'm afraid," she added. "I lose my concentration. I do best when I'm on automatic and don't think about winning. It's like faking myself out." The problem is that some people permit themselves to achieve and be assertive only in a carefully circumscribed arena. In tennis, it's acceptable to be, not just competent, but openly aggressive.

A woman reared in a traditional manner may encounter a problem like this, but still function very ably as a volunteer, as long as she remains free from the taint of competition or money. In therapy, progress in resolving such conflicts can often be assessed by observing the change in someone's game or work.

Don't Let Them Know I'm Good!

Jane, an architecture student who was ready to graduate on completion of a final project, first came for treatment of acute anxiety and depression. She found living with her parents extremely difficult and could tolerate it no longer.

Jane's stress reached unbearable levels when a professor announced that her thesis was the best in the class. Although Jane had consistently made the highest grades in her classes, she didn't want anybody else to know. She was extremely uncomfortable whenever people discovered her *secret*. Sure that the other students were looking at her with envy, she felt acute discomfort. She was convinced that she'd lose all her friends as soon as her competence was recognized and acknowledged.

Jane began interviewing for positions before graduation but felt enthusiastic only about those jobs she couldn't get, the ones that required on-the-job experience, bilingual skills, or other inaccessible prerequisites. Although Jane recognized that she was applying for jobs for which she was unqualified, she continued to re-enact her internal dilemma, insuring that she'd be told over and over that she wasn't qualified. Thus she arranged to be kept from her goals by someone in authority, someone who could keep her in a passive, dependent position.

Meanwhile, she continued to live with her parents, maintaining her fears of independence and her sense of inadequacy. Every time Jane heard that she'd been turned down for a job, she felt relieved. At the same time, she was aware of feeling helpless and unable to change things. Expecting change to come from some external source, Jane placed her fate in the hands of her parents and the potential employers who had been carefully selected to reject her. And yet, once she attained the rejection she had courted, Jane's self-esteem inevitably took a plunge, and she grew depressed.

I'll Never Live Up to Expectations

At significant points, such as being hired for an important job, winning a promotion, graduating, or even getting married, some individuals may sabotage their own plans at the final step. Such people seem to be acting illogically, because often the underlying issues are both emotional and unconscious in origin. But usually these people's emotions can hitchhike on some aspect of reality; usually they can rationalize suddenly abandoning their goal.

Individuals with success phobia may be able to work toward a goal fervently and relatively easily—as long as it is distant and unattainable. They begin to suffer from anxiety when success is in view. One student instantly developed a hysterical paralysis of her writing hand and a feeling of absolute confusion when she entered an examination room. She could not, of course, take the exam.

Some people may interpret their anxiety as a fear of failure or a fear of rejection or humiliation; they may worry that they cannot live up to others' expectations of them, or they may fear criticism. They then abandon their long-cherished goals and substitute others. Women, in particular, often fail to acknowledge their own expertise and will try to avoid situations that might expose their *inadequacy.*

A similar inhibition exists in those who cannot allow themselves to function at their fullest capacity. Fearing criticism or less-than-perfect results, they protect themselves by not trying their hardest. They implicitly reserve the right to use the standard excuse: "If I'd really given it my all, I would have succeeded." People who fear making a mistake may feel constrained from trying.

I Need Constant Feedback

Some individuals require ongoing admiration and have trouble sustaining effort in the absence of constant positive feedback or immediate applause. In contrast, those with success phobia generally feel safest in the background, where no one will notice their supposed weaknesses. The fear of being discovered as an impostor, the feeling of having bluffed one's way to the top, is a common element. "The higher you rise, the harder you fall," is the success phobic's motto. If they are regarded as highly competent, these individuals feel even more fraudulent and inadequate. Lowering their ambitions allows them to retreat from anxiety-provoking situations. As they retreat, however, they may plunge into depression in reaction to their loss of self-esteem.

I Need Structure

Some individuals fret that specific achievements will identify them as separate and distinct from their peers (or their parents) and lead to isolation and disconnectedness. Those who have used structure, boundaries, and externally determined goals to shape their ambitions may fear becoming their own pathfinder and creating their own direction. Failing to achieve a goal or not even trying to achieve it ensures that someone else will continue to gratify their needs and take care of them.

Jane, the architecture student who didn't want her fellow students to know she'd gotten top grades, equated competence and achievement with being abandoned and deprived. Both her parents had subtly discouraged Jane's independence for most of her life. She was the last of four children, and they treated her as the baby of the family, doing more for her than she needed. By focusing all their attention on her when she needed help, her parents encouraged her to act dependent; when she demonstrated assertiveness and initiative, they either ignored or criticized her. Jane concluded, unconsciously, that she'd be abandoned if she demonstrated competence. Finally she seemed to *go on strike* in order to block her own success.

I'll Have to Grow Up

The link between competence and deprivation has a long history for some people. Even in healthy families, it often begins with the birth of the next sibling or with going off to school. Daily occurrences bolster the notion that no one will look after you if you're good, and no one will do for you what you can do for yourself. Even a child who makes substantial and impressive attempts to achieve independence experiences feelings of nostalgia, loneliness, and even bitterness; it's not a total pleasure to be a big boy or a big girl. These ambivalent feelings intensify at every turning point in the years after childhood, in leaving home for college, completing school, starting work, and getting married. Even such celebrated rites of passage as graduation or marriage bring some sense of disappointment, anxiety, and mourning. When these feelings reach an unhealthy level, then any rite of passage can produce a paralyzing urge to stop short of the final step toward achievement.

Erosion of Successful Accomplishment

When I Win, I Lose

Literature describes several famous characters who, surprisingly, fall ill precisely because their most deeply rooted wishes come to fulfillment, as though they cannot stand their own success. Instead of enjoying their victories, Shakespeare's Lady Macbeth and Ibsen's Rebecca West suffer grave illness almost as soon as they know a major wish is about to be fulfilled. In *The Horse's Mount*, Joyce Cary's irascible painter, Gulley Jimson, finds a different route out of success: He paints his most elaborate mural on a wall scheduled for demolition and personally bulldozes the wall as soon as the mural is completed.

Success-fearing people can work diligently toward their goal as long as it remains a safe distance away. But once it is within reach, they become so anxious about success that they adopt some form of self-defeating behavior. They may sabotage their performance, fall ill, or otherwise destroy the product of their efforts immediately after they recognize success. They may consistently make errors, have accidents, be tardy, or procrastinate. Or they may refuse or depreciate the money, prestige, and recognition they've been working for.

The key to assessing self-defeating behavior is to look for patterns throughout a lifetime. Each instance of botched success may look reasonable enough in itself, but a pattern of self-defeating behavior in work, love, and other areas of life is a very effective way to disallow one's full potential.

They'll Discover What I'm Really Like

Consciously striving for success while actively fending it off creates considerable conflict, which is exemplified by this statement: "Whenever I do something really well and someone compliments me for it, I have to point out something that's not good, some criticism or flaw. My response has the effect of undoing whatever I do."

A professional model whose face had appeared nationally in cosmetic ads said, "If I get a compliment about how I look, I think to myself, 'Well, if you saw me without my makeup, you wouldn't think I was so pretty!'" Whenever she started to become intimate with someone, she'd worry that if she truly disclosed herself (that is, revealed herself "without her makeup"), she'd be rejected. When she looked in the mirror, instead of seeing and liking her own face, she focused entirely on her one physical flaw, an almost imperceptible freckle. Despite ample evidence that she had very little to criticize, she could see only her negative side.

Something Bad Is Bound to Happen

A promotion or advancement can bring such depression or anxiety that it disrupts maximum (or even adequate) functioning and prevents fulfillment of a goal. In the corporate world, many respond to significant advancement with major depression. Feeling alone and detached, they may develop a psychosomatic illness or other debilitating symptoms at the moment of success. Even a corporation's new chief executive officer may be depressed by the promotion. Not only are there no more rungs on the ladder, but the support and nurturance provided by colleagues and bosses on the way to the top are also lost. A CEO does not get pats but has to give them to others.

Symptoms of anxiety that arise at times of successful intellectual activity often affect the activity directly. Headaches may occur, concentration may become blurred, ideas may become muddled and confused. Intellectual stamina declines as one approaches the goal.

I Need to Be Challenged, Pushed

Entrepreneurs, on the other hand, may fear that overcoming all challenges or risks will leave them with no sense of usefulness, no motivation, no reason to live. Mike was a brilliant businessperson and a compulsive deal maker, womanizer, gambler, and cocaine abuser. He noted that, on completing a major deal, he would quickly spend his profits or commit them to other projects or investments. Thus he would need to immediately renew his profit-making efforts. He never allowed himself to relax and made sure he was always under pressure from an external source.

Mike didn't realize that the real source of pressure was internal. He was afraid he would feel useless and ineffective without a crisis to handle.

It's Just Luck

Some individuals openly disavow their achievements and the work that went into them, attributing their success to luck, circumstance, accident, or just having been *born to do it*. Others disavow success internally, by feeling like an impostor, by feeling that they've fooled anyone who thinks they're really intelligent.

It Wasn't Me

One woman was convinced that her acceptance into medical school was a mistake. A professional man who was given a prestigious award thought the awards committee had mixed up his name with someone else's.

Yes, but Everything Else Is So Bad

Another way to define success negatively is to declare an accomplishment a failure, camouflaging it so it can go virtually unnoticed. The phobic person can then proceed to the next disguised accomplishment. One who expects to be zapped at the finish line (abandoned, criticized, forced to make it alone) had better not cross the line, at least not while anyone is watching.

Eileen could allow herself to successfully complete her training in a professional specialty and set up a new practice (her lifelong goal) only by referring to her achievements as failures. By orchestrating the breakup of her marriage just a month before completion of training, she could ascribe to the breakup any failure that might occur. As in the past, she managed to attain her goal only by creating some other focus of trouble or anxiety to divert her attention from her accomplishment. Her insistence on perceiving herself as a failure confirmed and deepened her sense of inadequacy.

It's Not Success I Fear, It's Failure

A fear of failure is the opposite side of the same coin as fear of success. It is a fear of success rationalized to seem logical and consciously understandable. Almost all the patients I have treated for success phobia have tried to explain their difficulty (to themselves) as a fear of failure. Indeed, the consequences are the same: avoiding completion of a project, retreating from competition, diverting success, or disowning, depreciating, or eroding the accomplishment once the task has been completed.

Susanna realized in therapy that she always stopped short of achieving her goals because she was afraid she would be disappointed with the results. The self-imposed disappointment of failure seemed more palatable than the disappointment she feared from success. She was at least partially right. Success and money were only symbols for the love and affirmation she wanted at a deeper emotional level. She correctly sensed that external success would not allay her sense of emptiness. As long as success had not quite been attained, she still had the hope of happiness; she maintained this hope by falling short of her goals.

Ambition Without Goal-Setting

I Can't Set a Goal

Failure to set specific goals may ensure that no goal will ever be reached; the feared *perils of success* can thus be avoided completely. People may set vague and undefined goals or avoid setting goals entirely as a defense against feeling too ambitious. Contradictory feelings arise from an internal impediment to success.

Believing in luck and destiny is one way to avoid setting goals and to hide the pursuit of accomplishment. "If I do something well, it's just because of luck, but if I fail at something, it's my fault," one patient stated. Believing in predetermination, fate, or God's will may be the rationalized refusal to accept one's own efforts to achieve success. A person hiding behind a veil of *destiny* does not have to acknowledge accomplishment or fully enjoy mastery.

"I can do things well as long as I don't set goals for myself", said Marsha, the tennis ace. "I work against myself if I set goals, so I don't reach them." In essence, she needed to sneak in the back door to her own successes, to camouflage her goals so she wouldn't sabotage her own efforts.

I've Set So Many Goals, I Can't Possibly Reach Them

An alternate way of handling this problem is to set more goals than one can possibly reach, ensuring that none will be completed successfully. Failure to reach the goals may look like laziness, especially to the person who engages in this pattern.

From this perspective you've actually succeeded in achieving failure, and by your own hand. Ambition may know no bounds and have no realistic limits.

Maybe They'll Just Discover Me

Very intense ambition is often coupled with a passive approach to achieving goals. For example, after obtaining a specialized science degree, one young woman plunged into a fantasy that potential employers would learn of her skills and create a job just for her, though she took no realistic steps toward acquainting potential employers with her expertise. She was disappointed when nothing happened.

This combination of ambition and passivity demonstrates how ambition can remain unfulfilled when one's conscious and unconscious goals are in opposition. Elaborate goals, great expectations, and a sense of being entitled to achievement, reflect the magical thinking of early childhood: The scullery maid becomes a princess, movie stars are discovered at the corner drugstore, and the rookie hits a home run and wins the World Series.

Tomorrow I'm Going to Be Ambitious

It is not uncommon for individuals to suddenly begin feeling the need to work, to have a career, or to develop more well-rounded interests. This pattern often applies to both housebound women and male baby boomers, who are shocked to discover with their first gray hairs that they are already grown up.

Sudden ambition seldom inspires the same intense motivation and careful planning as a dearly held, lifelong goal. For example, a woman who has concentrated since childhood on developing interpersonal relationships, social skills, and domestic interests may find it difficult to suddenly switch goals when she develops other ambitions. Furthermore, she may be comparing herself with people whose successful careers can be traced to interests that blossomed in childhood. Unfortunately, the job market generally shunts untrained or inexperienced newcomers into the humblest, dullest, worst-paid drudgery. It is unlikely to fulfill her modest dream of self-support, much less her dream of glory. The magical promise of fulfillment through work becomes elusive and disappointing, the woman is left with only a renewed assumption of failure.

Fear of Success: What It Isn't

"Burnout" is a state of exhaustion caused by consistent emotional stress. Burnout causes physical and emotional depletion, a sense of futility, general malaise, and the erosion of hope and enthusiasm about work [Reference 3-2].

People suffering from burnout may conclude that they have chosen the wrong profession and withdraw from it. More commonly, however, people describing their symptoms as *burnout* change their line of work without recognizing that their real anxieties lie in the area of achievement and success.

People quit their jobs for a variety of reasons. Boring work is neither challenging or pleasurable and it significantly depletes the employees'motivation. And the vicissitudes of the job market may force highly accomplished, successful individuals from chosen careers. Many people who have the opportunity, intelligence, and imagination to succeed, do not live up to their potential, or suffer when they do. This difficulty reveals an internal, rather than external, impediment to success, *success phobia*.

People who do not understand, or cannot overcome, the psychological factors that prevent them from achieving their full potential—in comfort and contentment, in relationships, or in work—are doomed to repeat their failures, over and over again.

Are You Afraid of Success?

Answer the following questions true or false.

_____ 1. I usually stop short of finishing things.

_____ 2. I'm more concerned about how others see me than about what's best for myself and my work.

_____ 3. I feel like a fraud whenever I succeed at something.

_____ 4. I start too many projects at once and end up not finishing any of them.

_____ 5. I want to do more than what I'm doing, but I can't choose a direction and stick to it.

_____ 6. When I get what I really want, something bad usually happens.

_____ 7. If I can't do something perfectly from the beginning, I don't want to try it at all.

_____ 8. I feel like my husband's/wife's/parent's shadow.

_____ 9. When I start to do something, I remember the voices of my parents, criticizing me.

_____ 10. I've got talent, but I'm still waiting to be *discovered*.

_____ 11. People shouldn't try to rise above their station in life.

_____ 12. I've always been an *underachiever*, I've got the brains but no motivation.

_____ 13. In a crisis, I usually *choke* or *clutch*.

_____ 14. Besides money, I work mainly for praise and recognition. Title and position are more important than how I feel.

_____ 15. Whatever I do and however much I get, I want more!

_____ 16. I'd be nothing without my job.

_____ 17. A successful woman scares men away.

_____18. I feel so let down when I succeed at something that I don't even want to try anymore.

_____19. I hate the person I have become at work.

_____20. If I get too close to someone, or finally get to the top, I'll be exposed as inadequate.

If you marked any answers true, it's likely that you're compromising or having difficulty in the arena of work and success. The key to solving these problems lies in understanding yourself, discovering how these problems started in your earlier experiences, and defining which of your current assumptions about yourself and your world are placing stumbling blocks between you and success.

4

Fear of Success: Unconscious Assumptions

Every difficulty slurred over will be a ghost
to disturb your repose later on.

—Frederic Chopin

What we remember can be changed.
What we forget we are always.

—Richard Shelton

To fear succeeding seems contradictory. But when we understand the conscious and unconscious meanings that success holds for us, our fear becomes easier to understand.

We all have an internal model, a set of conscious and unconscious assumptions about ourselves. Certain assumptions may have been adequate in an earlier context—such as childhood—but are no longer useful. When we understand both conscious and unconscious meanings success holds for us, fears become easier to understand. For example, a woman may succeed in living up to her internal model of being a kind, loving, and giving person. But to succeed at this model may be to fail at her own growth, because having and acting on her own needs may not be part of her ideal.

Unconscious assumptions that are not logical or useful in the current context of someone's life may have been useful at an earlier stage of development. Individuals spend their childhood and adolescent years adapting to their particular family, environment, culture, and biology. If life experiences are extreme—as when one has a chronic or severe illness or lives with an alcoholic, abusive, or excessively critical parent—adaptation must take an extreme form.

Unresolved Issues That Impede Success

When the tasks of childhood—learning how to become an adult—cannot be completed, the unresolved issues continue into adult life. And when some unfinished business from the past intrudes into the present, current experiences may be perceived in their childhood context [Reference 4-1]. Three types of unresolved issues often reveal the unconscious assumptions that impede success: (1) autonomy and mastery, (2) aggression and competitiveness, and (3) narcissism.

Autonomy and Mastery

I Will Follow You

Nina wanted to open a music store but was paralyzed by her fear of the risk. In part her problem was that she had never felt truly grown up. She'd left the house of her overcontrolling mother to follow her high school sweetheart to his choice of college, marrying him just after graduation. Nina's husband, with her subtle support and collaboration, made all the decisions, although Nina felt angry about this arrangement. Nina had never tested her own abilities enough to believe that she could succeed without the guidance of her mother, her husband, or some other all-knowing authority who would tell her what to do, step by step, as though she were still a child.

Between infancy and adulthood are several steps to autonomy and emotional independence. The first steps are increasing psychological separation from parents and from their gratification of our needs. Then comes our growing ability to function autonomously. Finally, we learn to regulate our own self-esteem, motivation, and internal organization without depending on external sources. Triumphant interchange with our environment yields the gratification of positive mastery, which in turn fosters eagerness and motivation to respond to the environment and makes us optimistic about future mastery.

Becoming an individual—emotionally—is a gradual process. Children need to discover novel solutions to problems, and to depart from automatic, stereotyped or ingratiating responses. And parents must allow their children to master new experiences throughout childhood, so they will have a strong sense of self-esteem and confidence in adulthood.

Parents who can't fully accept their child's eventual separation may foster overly intense ties and discourage their child from functioning autonomously. Some parents subtly convey their feelings of abandonment or competition, and in the process teach their child to fear success. Young children can't make distinctions about (or discover the real causes of) their parents' negative reactions; they just feel insecure and rejected when they perceive a parent's struggle for control, particularly if they feel unsure about their attempts at independence. Children who feel insecure and anxious will find less pleasure in the normal growth process, and they may confuse self-assertion and success with aggressive and competitive feelings. If children come to associate abandonment, loss of love, or retaliation with success, they may refuse to succeed too completely or too visibly at anything.

The triumphant "I can do it!" is very different from the passive bliss of being completely taken care of and having all needs met.

You and I, Together, Make a Whole

Some families subtly discourage independence. They may impose their own opinions and decisions on children, quashing creative thought and problem solving. They may insist on doing more for their children than the children can do for themselves, or continue functioning for their children when it is no longer appropriate or necessary. In doing so, these parents rob their children of those important trial-and-error experiences that lead to mastery.

The children of such parents may grow up to exhibit a *fear of success*, which is actually a fear of final separation and autonomy, combined with a feeling of being incapable of independent functioning. In addition, these children may enjoy having things done for them. Spared the stress of ordinary trial-and-error experiences, they develop little tolerance for frustration. In essence, they come to believe that any task has to be done easily and perfectly from the outset, or not be done at all.

I'll Never Do It As Well As You

Parents who demand perfection and rigidly insist there's only one right way for things to be done, rob their children of the chance to answer their own questions. Creativity and expansiveness are difficult when you're expected to adhere rigidly to your parents' party line or to please your parents at the expense of your own inner life.

Stephanie's parents said they were proud when she successfully completed training in accounting. They told her that they were sure she'd be a success but quickly added that she could always come home if she could not make it on her own.

Children who receive inconsistent messages from their parents are likely to feel confused and ambivalent. Their attempts at mastery produce anxiety and insecurity instead of pleasure, especially as they approach success.

Such children may employ a number of psychological strategies to deal with their fear of success and to reduce the anxiety associated with achieving independence and competence. One is to shift attention from important to minor aspects of a task.

Every workplace has at least one person who *can't see the forest for the trees*. He or she completes projects only by working blindly on one detail at a time, never seeing the larger design. Another strategy is to avoid completing the task. A related strategy is to develop a disparaging view of oneself as an *inadequate* performer. These tactics enable many people to avoid becoming too competent and too independent for their own comfort.

Parents of success-fearing children make substantially more critical comments, give more hints and commands, and make more attempts to do their children's tasks than the parents of children who do not fear success [Reference 4-2]. Success-fearing children may also interpret their parents' active participation as more valuable than their own, and may believe that their parents do not want them to act independently. These children may conclude that they're incapable of doing anything alone.

Such children have a devalued view of themselves that is then internalized and subsequently influences their behavior in various destructive ways. They may be sick on days when school competitions or examinations are scheduled. They may remain silent when holding an opposing viewpoint, for fear they won't be able to express themselves well or sound intelligent when they do speak up. They may also use charm and perceptiveness to win the approval of others, trying in vain to build self-esteem by gaining the approval of people they admire. Of course, this tactic doesn't work. You can't feel intelligent and accomplished if the positive responses you elicit aren't based on your intellect or accomplishments. People who try to get by on charm feel there is a huge dichotomy between their true self and their facade.

If You're Scared, There Must Really Be Something to Be Afraid Of

Many adults who suffer from phobias grew up with parents who discouraged their attempts to achieve mastery. In fact, the parents often had phobias themselves, which they transmitted to their children. Their overprotectiveness not only shielded the children from hardships, but also prevented the children from learning perseverance in the face of adversity.

In extreme cases, the parents subjected their children's attempts at mastery to criticism and belittlement, crippling the children's development. The environment itself becomes a source of terror to such children. They learn to fear all sorts of activities, swimming, skating, and bicycling, and later on, driving, flying, and functioning independently at work. The necessary compromises and detours take much of the joy out of living.

I'll Be Taking Something Away from Others

As success-fearing children grow into adulthood, each new sign of independent functioning may be greeted with redoubled fear, an unconscious fear of losing their parents' love, or of hurting their parents with their successes. Any achievement or significant attempt at achievement is a step into unknown and frightening territory. The only safe course is to inhibit advancement. Since any achievement represents a severance of the bond with their parents, such individuals abandon their efforts before success can be achieved.

Although a certain amount of anxiety motivates people to achieve, phobics are so anxious that their ambitions are derailed. Their anxiety is channeled instead into somatic or physical symptoms, such as palpitations, dizziness, shortness of breath, and faintness. The phobic attempts to contain these symptoms magically by finding a medical cure. However, the problem is not simply the level of anxiety but its specific causes, the unconscious assumptions.

I'll Take Something Vital Away from You

The normal development of independence from parents involves increasing amounts of self-functioning and self-regulation. Separation and independence are a process, not a single event.

In addition, separation occurs within the context of family relationships, not outside of them. Families that stymy the maturation process with too much or too little parental functioning cannot produce fully independent children. For example, a woman who had difficulty separating from her mother may still feel incomplete and desperately want someone else to make her feel whole.

When such a woman has a child, she may become intensely attached in a *twinship* that is emotionally life-supporting for both mother and child, rather than just for the child. Separation then becomes hazardous to both, as it would be for Siamese twins sharing vital organs. The child's unconscious fantasy is that independence would take vital and powerful things away from the mother. The child thus remains emotionally bound to the mother, robbed of autonomy and independence. The growing child feels increasing anxiety about separation, which remains active into adulthood.

Unless I Please You Completely, You'll Abandon Me

Rachel came for treatment at age thirty-two, frustrated by her inability to make significant changes in a life she found disappointing. She was a realtor, but she'd been unable to have the kind of career she wanted and felt capable of achieving. She experienced extreme discomfort in fully expressing herself and being assertive on the job, especially with superiors. She agonized when she had to close a sale aggressively. She felt guilty and anxious whenever she had negative feelings about other people. She agreed too readily with the comments and opinions of others and searched for ways to mirror others' views, even when she could make a better deal by relying on her own expertise. Her efforts seemed governed by an overriding desire to ingratiate herself with others.

Rachel was intelligent and had done well in school, but her special interest since childhood had been to please people. When her parents expressed doubts about her ability to *behave herself* without their supervision, Rachel declined a scholarship to a distant prestigious college to attend junior college in her hometown.

Instead of earning a bachelor's degree, she married Jack, her childhood sweetheart and the son of her parents' best friends. Rachel supported Jack through college and graduate school while she studied, after work, for her real estate license. In her relationship with Jack, she explicitly agreed with his ideas and decisions. Terrified of being alone, she fiercely clung to Jack even though they fought much of the time they were together. She placed all her hopes in her husband's achievements, which she considered more important than her own goals. In short, she gave herself over entirely to Jack and relinquished her separate hopes and desires.

Rachel's long avoidance of self-sufficiency started to depress her when she turned thirty. Her efforts to establish her own identity were confusing and self-defeating, she couldn't take advantage of new opportunities. Offered the chance of a partnership in the real estate office where she worked (with the attendant legal, financial, and task responsibilities that partnership entails), she put off the decision for months. She was terrified by the risk and felt helpless rage over her despair, her immobilization, and her inability to overcome feelings of inadequacy. She turned to feminism, not in the hope of changing the future for all women, but in a desire for reparation of what she felt men had done to her. Her fear of autonomy, adult responsibility, and a full, separate selfhood overwhelmed her at times.

In therapy, Rachel recalled that neither of her parents would respond at all if she expressed any feelings contrary to their own. If she engaged in behavior that didn't meet their ideals, they would simply return to what they were doing before she *interrupted* them. She recalled her mother's withdrawal when she expressed anger or even excitement or joy. "I became very controlled," Rachel remembered. "I still am terribly controlled inside with my husband and at my work. All my passions are in total control. I am just now realizing how angry I am at my mother for withdrawing from me. She said it was 'weak' of me to be angry or to have other strong feelings."

Rachel's reserve and inhibition were the result of innumerable rejections by her mother, who seemed to have discouraged autonomy and encouraged dependent behavior. Rachel described being the best daughter possible, feeling that she couldn't even think any thoughts or feel any feelings contrary to those of her parents. She still looked to her mother for approval and confirmation.

Since Rachel's parents wouldn't acknowledge any behavior on her part that didn't express their own feelings, a part of Rachel was consistently ignored as though it simply didn't exist. Rachel experienced a sense of unreality when she had feelings or ideas her parents wouldn't approve of. It was as if she saw only a third of herself when she looked in a mirror; she had come to believe that a partial reflection was all there was to her. Her parents had managed to create a daughter who was wholly an extension of themselves, an extremely *good* daughter who tried harder and harder to please them, a goal that was forever elusive.

As a girl, Rachel felt any achievement led her parents to withdraw. Lonely, Rachel would then approach her mother, who would start to care for her again. Rachel feared that this fragile contact with her mother might be destroyed if she demonstrated any anger.

As an adult, Rachel described herself as having a horrible sense of direction, an obvious handicap in the real estate business. She would become lost on the way to the houses she was trying to sell, turn up late when clients were waiting, or exasperate those traveling with her. In Rachel's personal life, her husband either drove or navigated for her. Getting lost was all the more distressing for Rachel because she was certain there would be severe consequences for making even a single mistake.

Rachel's poor sense of direction didn't represent some innate deficit. She was able to discover this in therapy, as she explored the need for dependency that was keeping her from finding and creating her own direction. The lost parts of herself and of her memories became evident as she examined her unconscious assumptions. Rachel remembered, reconstructed, and worked through her early experiences until she was able to relinquish her past, including her crippling perception of herself as only a portion of a complete person.

Aggression and Competitiveness

I'll Pay for My Success in Other Ways

Edmund came for treatment at a time of major success. He had just earned over a million and a half dollars in commodities trading, and he felt (curiously to me, familiarly to him) miserable about it.

At age fifty-three, Edmund was beginning to think of retiring in eight or ten years. Although he had earned several million dollars over the past twenty years, his net worth was remarkably small. He was an astute businessperson who had somehow managed to sink his profits into incredibly bad investments. Edmund recognized that he'd consistently chosen the worst investments for himself with the same skill with which he could pick, for his clients and his company, the one commodity position that would fly. He was puzzled about this, since he never willingly sabotaged himself. But the evidence was insurmountable; some force inside him countered every positive move he made.

The same force seemed to operate in Edmund's personal relationships. In three marriages, he'd chosen women who were not genuinely interested in him, with whom warmth and intimacy were impossible.

Edmund was the second child of highly solicitous, achievement-oriented parents. His older brother, Paul, gained his father's favor by being the athlete of the family. Edmund fell under his mother's nearly exclusive and overwhelming care. Edmund and his mother became so enmeshed that their very thoughts and feelings seemed to be unified. Edmund often didn't even have to speak his thoughts aloud; his mother *just knew* everything he was thinking.

This attachment alienated and probably infuriated his father, and a chasm grew in the relationship with his second child. The few times his father would play with him, he'd prod Edmund to "run faster, try harder." He would make Edmund run out for passes, each time throwing the football a little farther than his son could run, and would explode if he felt Edmund wasn't trying hard enough. These *games* would last two hours, leaving the boy exhausted both physically and emotionally.

As an adult, Edmund thought daily of his father, an omnipresent critic forever finding fault. This fantasy of an ever-present, ever-critical father (sometimes generalized to any stronger authority) maintained the presence of a powerful loved and hated parent. Edmund tried to escape from this presence by forming his own firm so he wouldn't have a boss, but the emotional issues persisted. His father's presence, watching and judging, continued to possess his emotions.

With women too, Edmund kept trying to resolve his childhood conflicts. Intimacy with a woman meant risking the loss of his identity, as it had with his mother. He struggled to maintain his separateness by keeping an emotional distance from his various wives and lovers. Feeling close to a woman made him feel "smothered, crowded, like she's going to try to take over and tell me what to do. Then I have to move on." When he felt crowded during his current marriage, he would spend an evening with one of the many other women in his "stable," letting sexual conquest and domination appease his anxiety for a while. But intimacy with a woman would again raise the specter of his father, criticizing and punishing his success, angry over Edmund's special closeness to his mother. Edmund both desired and feared such a relationship with a woman.

At work, Edmund continued to hear his father criticizing him for not trying hard enough, together with the sympathetic voice of his mother telling him, "You're working too hard, darling, you're not resting properly." These parental ghosts kept Edmund in a childhood emotional state, as though he'd never left home. He wanted to rebel, to do something drastic to escape these oppressive fantasies.

Edmund's "killing" on the commodities market made him especially restless and anxious. On the one hand, he was afraid of separating emotionally from his mother and finding his own autonomy; on the other, he feared his angry father's punishment for success. For Edmund, all successes were tainted by the pleasure and gratification he felt in displacing his father in his mother's affection. He unconsciously equated a highly successful com-modities deal with his father's discovery and resentment of his "successfully" exclusive relationship with his mother. With this unconscious emotional equation, every success awoke his fears. He abandoned the taboo successes by squandering money on bad investments. This equaled a retreat to early childhood, before little boys have sexual feelings about their mothers or competitive feel-ings about their fathers. Getting rid of the money served as the punishment that destroyed the evidence of success. By punishing himself, Edmund was imitating, allying himself with his father. Losing his profits flung him back into dependence on his wife— who, of course, was equated with his mother—whose income supported them while Edmund's money was tied up in playing the market.

Inside this middle-aged man was a little boy, torn between his desire for independence and his fear of growing up. Edmund couldn't give up his wish for the gratifications of early childhood. He consciously desired success but also perceived it to be forbid-den.

I'll Lose Everything I've Gained

A seed is planted in childhood that eventually grows into a person's view of competition and cooperation. This seed is what Freud called "the Oedipal situation." In ancient Greece, Oedipus was banished at birth from his parents' kingdom. When he grew up, he returned to his homeland, unknowingly killed his own father, and married his mother. Freud believed that modern families also harbor a largely unconscious Oedipal scenario. For a girl, the Oedipal fantasy is to win the exclusive love and attention of her father; the opposite side of the coin is fear of angry abandonment by the mother should the girl succeed. For a boy, success would lie in winning the exclusive love of his mother, but it would provoke retaliation by his father. For both sexes, incomplete resolution of this normal developmental stage may allow the unconscious equation of success with competitive success over a parent. Success can thus become a dangerous achievement.

In a healthy family, this phase of growth resolves itself naturally as the child develops a firm sense of sexual identity and internal boundaries. The boy begins to identify with his father and to sublimate, or rechannel, his desire for his mother's special, exclusive love. He realizes that, although he's small and limited now, there's a promise of future mastery; someday he'll be like his father and will be able to choose his own relationships, find his own wife. The girl, too, learns to identify with her mother. She realizes that she will be like her mother some day and will love another man, free from boundaries and constraints.

In some families however, the Oedipal situation evolves into a pathological issue and emerges in work inhibition. One scenario is when parents are actively competitive with their children and are threatened by their children's capability, attractiveness, or expressiveness. In other families, a parent may respond to the child in a somewhat seductive manner, so that the child's wish to be attractive and desired comes dangerously close to actually being granted.

When a parent is seductive, "success" violates a mighty taboo, so that the child has to retreat from success and accept a protective, self-imposed defeat.

When parents are alienated from each other and the child can win the opposite-sex parent's exclusive affection by taking sides, the Oedipal dilemma is intensified. This situation may arise when at least one parent is excessively self-centered, or emotionally needy, or when a parent is psychologically or physically absent (through death, divorce, or prolonged separation).

Physical intimidation or abuse from a parent, or even a sibling, may reinforce the unconscious idea that assertiveness brings retaliation or abandonment. In an atmosphere of violence or of hostile competition, the child anticipates not only physical attacks but also swift retaliation for fighting back. Parental physical violence makes the Oedipal fantasy seem like reality since there is actual retaliation by the parent. A child who learns to inhibit or withhold assertiveness grows into an adult who cannot be fully assertive at work. Competition is also inhibited, because it is identified unconsciously with the original rivalry and the resulting punishment. Such constraints undermine self-confidence, self-esteem, and effectiveness and may result in a chronic sense of inadequacy.

A child who has learned to inhibit aggression and to regard success as taboo reacts with passivity, abandoning or distorting goals or substituting other, less desired ones. As in Edmund's case, being and acting as a full-fledged adult produces conflict because success is attached (as it is for all children at a certain stage) to exclusivity and erotic feelings. For such adults, failure before the final step to success seems to guarantee safety from retaliation.

I'll Be Judged Critically
and Retaliated Against

Norman, a young physician, was presenting his first lecture at his alma mater, in the same classroom where he'd sat as a medical student. As he took the microphone, he suddenly remembered the many professors who had stood behind that same microphone and was so overcome by anxiety that he couldn't utter a word for fully a minute. He was seized by a fantasy that someone in the audience would accuse him of masquerading as a teacher, shouting that he should still be in the class, not standing in front of it. He imagined his audience glaring angrily at him, ready to pounce on him for his youth and ineptitude. Later that week Norman received a letter with the return address of a law firm; he was convinced before he opened it that he was being sued for impersonating a doctor.

Norman's fantasies repeated a common theme of his childhood. His father, who had not finished college, was openly supportive of Norman's educational pursuits yet apparently felt threatened at the same time. The father was frequently away on business trips, and Norman and his mother developed an intense closeness during his absences, a closeness that persisted even when the father returned home. Norman constantly feared his father's criticism and retaliation. When he took the microphone in the lecture hall, every man in the audience turned, for him, into a demonic version of his father, and Norman became an impostor, the object of criticism and harsh judgment.

When Oedipal conflicts are not resolved, the final step to the successful completion of any task brings terrible anxiety. The more visible the success—a promotion, graduation, marriage, an award—the greater the anxiety. The fear of retaliation (primarily in men) or abandonment (primarily in women) inhibits effort. In some cases, people are able to achieve only in the areas their same-sex parent did not achieve. Or they may reach a position just short of parity with that parent before they stop.

I Can Never Surpass My Mother, or I'll Be Abandoned

Betty Ann began to have difficulty concentrating and studying for her examinations during the final months of nursing school. She became so anxious that she even considered dropping out and abandoning her career plans. Her mother, it turned out, had also studied nursing but had dropped out of nursing school when she became pregnant a few months before graduation. To Betty Ann, completing nursing school was, unconsciously, a direct affront to her mother; she was eclipsing her mother on common turf. To graduate, Betty Ann had to break the mold of her model.

Those who can never allow themselves to match or exceed their parents' level of achievement may be perpetuating an Oedipal battle in which they must continually lose and which requires them to relinquish success or its enjoyment. Sometimes the thrill of victory is spoiled by the image of someone else being defeated, a real or imaginary opponent who suffers from the loss.

Cybel, an attorney, stated, "Childhood seemed like a series of win-or-lose situations. It always seemed that, whenever I won, someone else lost or suffered for it. It wasn't necessarily physical warfare, but a series of win-or-lose arguments, using bitter sarcasm to reduce myself or others to tears. I realize that when I win in a legal situation in court now, I feel bad and pity the opponent." Thus, the thrill of success is tainted by an opponent's imagined agony of defeat.

Maybe a Thousand Victories Now Will Make Up for the Past Defeat

Sally, on the other hand, derived much of her pleasure in life from the defeat of others. She was a competition addict. As an upper-level executive in a city hospital, she supervised a vast empire of managers, supervisors, and line staff.

Sally delegated much of her own work and power to the most favored of her direct subordinates. But when these subordinates began to gain too much power of their own, or failed to show their gratitude by agreeing with her, *thus returning Sally's power to Sally*, she would abruptly withdraw her favor and the power that accompanied it. She would suddenly transfer her former favorites' best staff members, publicly ignore or belittle them at meetings, and withdraw the more enjoyable and empowering of their delegated tasks. Throughout the hospital, it was considered dangerous to become *Sally's pet*, and a constant stream of transfer requests emanated from her fallen favorites.

This pattern was self-defeating for Sally. On many occasions during her career, she found herself left with only passive, alcoholic, or burned out subordinates. Her more capable staff members were either transformed into trembling yes-men or fled from her supervision.

During childhood, Sally had actively competed with her mother and brothers for the rare and valuable attention of her father. He was a handsome, prominent, powerful elected official who spent most of his time in Washington, D.C., and came home only for holidays. Although she felt that her father preferred the boys, Sally, the middle child, managed to make herself the center of attention at home and at school. Tall and quite obese, she was bossy and controlling with her mother, younger brothers, and schoolmates; she was intensely flirtatious with her father, older brothers, and teachers (of either sex). Denied something she wanted, Sally would unleash her anger with such fury that her mother and brothers would not dare set any limits for her. Her mother, who was preoccupied with presenting the public image of a perfect wife to her famous but continually absent husband, seemed to young Sally weak and ineffectual. Sally greatly preferred her father and identified with his role in life. Nonetheless, neither her flirting nor her temper tantrums could keep him at home with her.

Before the age of forty, Sally had attained her hospital management position, using her competitive skills not only to pass the promotional examinations but to obtain a far broader scope of power than was held by others in her particular job category. She remained unmarried and flung herself into her work, extracting much of her personal identity from her title and the power it conferred.

She drew her friends largely from among the hospital's middle-class patients, especially those with permanent physical handicaps and those graduating from the alcohol detoxification ward. She also courted the personal friendship of the most flamboyantly gay men among her line staff, although she privately viewed homosexuality as a psychological illness. She was estranged from her brothers and had virtually no contact with anyone in her original family except a female cousin of her own age, whom she'd occasionally visit on vacations.

Many of Sally's subordinates, peers, and bosses were critical of her habitual lateness, her lengthy "liquid lunches," her misuse of office hours and staff for completing her personal chores, and the union grievances that chronically arose over her arbitrary decisions. Sally's critics were mollified by her considerable intelligence, charm, and managerial acumen and were quite possibly intimidated by the fierce fury she displayed in confrontations. Nearly six feet tall, weighing over 220 pounds, with long, clawlike, scarlet-painted fingernails, she was a formidable opponent.

Despite her growing dependence on alcohol and the constant troubles in her division, Sally maintained her position and gradually increased her power for over a decade.

When Sally was fifty, the hospital director decided to retire. He was a silver-haired, courtly, and rather remote gentleman, much like Sally's father. His replacement was a man fifteen years younger than Sally, six inches shorter, and some hundred pounds lighter. Sally had enjoyed a daughterly relationship with the retired director, but she fell into a confrontational one with the new director, especially after he responded with obvious repugnance to her flirtatious approach. After the second monthly meeting of the top-management cabinet, he was heard to whisper of Sally, "What a frightening witch!"

During the next five years, Sally expanded her empire, adopting and then abandoning a favorite subordinate each year, without the new director's interference. Then Sally took a promotional examination for the next-higher job category. She placed too low in the rankings to ever expect a job opening, leading her to suspect that the hospital director had influenced the rankings.

All the *opponents* she had created by that time had been vanquished or had fled, so she unleashed her aggression on the director himself. She openly challenged his authority and publicly embarrassed him in an executive meeting with a long, sarcastic attack on his personality and his decision-making capacity. A tenured civil servant, Sally didn't have to worry about being fired. But a week later she received a memo ordering her to report to a new position, a *paper job* on the sidelines where she would have virtually no power and no employees to supervise directly. Sally had effectively been demoted and removed from competition.

Within a year, largely as a result of her increased alcohol intake, Sally's weight had increased to nearly 320 pounds; she was barely able to walk. When her old friends asked how she was doing, she replied that life had lost all meaning. Several of them ventured to suggest psychotherapy; the suggestion infuriated her. "Nothing's wrong with me!" she insisted.

Aggression Must Be Covered Over at All Costs

Sally was an unusual woman. Open and aggressive competition to be the best and favorite child, its ambivalent results, and her parents' apparent inability to help her discover her own limits, led to an addiction to competition in adulthood. She needed to continually reaffirm her own self-esteem by crushing the self-esteem of others. She eventually carried this pattern to self-defeating lengths, possibly in the unconscious hope that someone (the hospital director in lieu of a parent) would seize control and set some boundaries for her and her uncontrolled aggression.

More commonly, however, when ghosts from the past persist in adult life—when competition to be the favorite child produces internal conflict about rivalry, initiative, and assertion—the result is inhibition of aggression. And the anxiety and guilt caused by self-assertion may manifest itself in one's work. Current success can seem frightening because of its unconscious connection with leftover childhood taboos on sexuality and aggression. Personal performance must either be sabotaged directly or, if an accomplishment is completed, depreciated by being labeled inconsequential.

The problem is not innate inability but inhibition. When aggression is wrapped in conflict, identifying oneself as inadequate can resolve the problem. People who use this defense then have to enact their inadequacy in their lives and careers. They can't openly express any strong feelings, especially if self-expression seems too assertive to them. They often direct their feelings of aggression back on themselves, transforming the aggression into guilt and depression, which then erode any feelings of competence that might be sneaking in.

Such ambivalence about achievement and success are captured in the words of a man who had just completed a particularly noteworthy accomplishment: "I'm amazed. I just felt like I didn't have it. Sometimes I wish I didn't."

Narcissism

Problems with narcissism, or one's sense of self—including self-esteem, confidence, and initiative—are the most common problems I encounter. They are to our present time what neuroses were for many decades. Therefore, Chapter 7 is devoted entirely to this subject.

Can You Make and Enjoy Money?

Answer the following questions true or false.

_____ 1. Talking about money, even with my family, feels embarrassing and seems taboo.

_____ 2. I go on spending sprees I can't afford.

_____ 3. I seem to consistently lose money on investments.

_____ 4. I feel afraid and paralyzed about investing my money.

_____ 5. I don't seem to be taking the initiative to learn more about managing money or investing, and I still rely on other people to make decisions for me, even though they're not experts.

_____ 6. You've got to step on other people to really make money.

_____ 7. I need to have money in the bank to feel "real."

_____ 8. No matter how much money I've got, I always want more.

_____ 9. I use money to gain love and admiration, to compete with others, to show off my prosperity, or to gain revenge.

_____ 10. I grew up poor, and although I'm doing all right now, I still feel poor and insecure.

_____ 11. I have difficulty admitting my mistakes and cutting my losses.

_____ 12. I'm pretending to be content with my financial status only because I'm afraid to make any changes.

If you answered true to any of these questions, you're probably having some difficulty gaining, managing, or enjoying money. Whether your job pays you *enough*, these problems will continue because the questions are about your feelings and assumptions. Feelings are at least as real as dollar bills.

5

Work and Success: For Women Only

I must refuse the compliment that I think like a man.
Thought has no sex. One either thinks or one does not.

—Clare Boothe Luce

I thought how unpleasant it is to be locked out;
and I thought how it is worse, perhaps, to be locked in.

—Virginia Woolf

The developmental process is lifelong. Although early relationships lay the foundation for later relationships, we can find many new ways, as adults, to realize our full potential. History cannot be changed, but we can free ourselves from its grip.

Women now participate in many activities once reserved for men; sex-role stereotypes are gradually fading. But their residue remains. For many generations, the traditional woman had to restrict her ambitions and interests to the accepted *feminine* role, which entailed marriage, children, and domestic activities. Only after the children had left home (if then) could she expand her interests and work outside of the home.

Through the centuries, only especially clever women or those in unusual circumstances have been able to circumvent the presumed order of male dominance and female domesticity. The family system has traditionally focused on containing, rather than expanding, expectations for females. That pattern persists to some extent today.

For instance, in a group of closely studied prize-winning children's picture books, the female characters were usually neat, passive, and somewhat dull [Reference 5-1]. Their status was determined primarily by their relationship with males: the helper of a worker, the wife of a king, the admirer of an explorer. No mothers with outside careers were depicted, and women were absent from the worlds of politics, science, and sports.

Until recently, girls have not been encouraged to compete in sports and other contests, precluding them from learning to win and lose gracefully. Membership in a serious, cohesive, intense team is an important experience for participating in later team efforts, such as working in a corporation.

There remains a good deal of difference in the degree of organization of children's sports and in how much fuss is made: Girls play on informal teams in a few sports for a few spectators. Boys play on highly organized teams for various sports and compete before cheering, crazed parents.

The highest-status sports for girls are nonteam activities in which competition is intense but relatively subtle, such as ice skating, horseback riding, golf, archery, and tennis. The difference becomes most apparent in middle school and high school, when boys' team sports are accompanied by cheerleaders and bands. Meanwhile, girls' sports merit little attention, and girl athletes may begin to seem *unfeminine* to some.

Girls are still frequently conditioned to assert their rights as individuals and defend themselves with such passive techniques as crying. Studies of normal families found that girls are allowed to *run to mommy* much longer than boys, and to call on masculine help for defense. They are encouraged to be less physically active and aggressive, less impulsive than boys, and are forbidden to be sexually curious (or at least as open about it).

The inhibition of girls' natural aggression begins early. There is, instead, an early emphasis on learning to get along with people. In an elegant work, *Toward a New Psychology of Women*, Jean Baker Miller describes the affiliative model of relatedness and cooperation held up to girls, as opposed to the competitive model that guides boys, men, and business [Reference 5-2].

Differing sex-role expectations are obvious, whether you look at the names of the executives on a corporate ladder or at the rosters of children's soccer and baseball teams. A girl's right to establish or achieve her own personal goals is still deemphasized, and her role of helping others is emphasized. However, things are changing, a third of today's managerial slots are occupied by women, compared to 14 percent a decade ago.

Like Mother, (Sort of) Like Daughter

Any child will attempt to conform with the image that achieves love and respect. A girl's mother is her most important source of these rewards. If a girl sees her mother as passive, deferential, helpless, and vulnerable, she is likely to believe that behaving assertively will contradict her mother's worth and risk the loss of maternal support. For her part, the mother may not feel comfortable enough about her daughter's assertive tendencies to support them.

The girl may then mistake the desire for mastery and independence as an aggressive, competitive urge and end up feeling guilty and anxious. If specific circumstances (such as severe spankings, intense rivalry with a sibling, or an abusive, alcoholic, or dysfunctional family) make her aggressive feelings, and the need to contain them, more pronounced, she may learn to equate aggression with punishment or retaliation. Expecting punishment, she may feel inhibited about asserting herself.

The mother who has difficulty dealing with aggression can tolerate only as much aggression in her daughter as she herself feels comfortable with. For example, she may teach her daughter by words and example to express anger only with tears. The mother molds the daughter, the daughter identifies with the mother, and a pattern is established. It becomes extremely difficult for the daughter to adopt a different style of relating to others.

One of the first successes any child achieves is a positive relationship and identification with both parents, especially the same-sex parent. The girl identifies with her mother as an ideal and a model, she regards success as living up to an ideal of herself based on the model of her mother. If her mother is unassertive, then being "successful" may mean learning to be passive and submissive, to have a poor self-image, or to be a hypochondriac. Winning then becomes losing. For a girl to successfully live up to an ideal like this, the idea that a woman neither has nor acts on her own needs, she must fail at her own growth. Alternatively, growing and expanding require the girl to fail at living up to this ideal of herself. A girl who *succeeds* at being like her mother may prevent herself from attaining other success in different contexts.

Where Was the Bionic Woman When We Needed Her?

Along with the child-parent relationship, a whole gamut of environmental forces affect the child. The child's primary models include not only mother and father but to a lesser extent siblings, surrogate parents, teachers, and mass media figures (for example, television characters and media stars). Emotional disruption or some other major problem in the family unit gives these other models increased importance. For example, when one parent is lost through divorce, or death or is unavailable emotionally, surrogate parent figures gain greater value for the child.

Only very recently have girls had any major female heroes, while boys have always had superheroes. Before Wonder Woman and the Bionic Woman, there were no socially accepted, omnipotent female fantasy figures. Most of the powerful women, such as the Greek goddesses, had to weave at least some of their power into traditional feminine allure. Nonetheless, girls, like boys, fashion private fantasies of omnipotent figures and of themselves as omnipotent.

The importance of the mother in modeling ambition, career, and values, is underscored by a recent finding. It was found that both sons and daughters of women in high-status positions achieve high positions themselves, much more often than children from families in which only the men held high-status positions [Reference 5-3].

Only in recent times have girls and women had the opportunity to identify with women who are accomplished professionally. My female classmates in medical school noted that they had no women professors in medicine to identify with or use as models. The medical students, psychoanalytic candidates, and psychiatric residents I currently teach and supervise (about 50 percent of them women) say the same thing.

Daddy's Girl:
The Role of the Father

The father is also vitally important to his daughter. For a girl's healthy development, her father must be comfortable with both her femininity and her potential to become a powerful person. The father is the first man a girl loves (just as the mother is the first woman a boy loves) and the first person she competes with and for. Furthermore, her parents' relationship becomes a girl's prototype for the way relationships are negotiated between two people and among a group, the family.

The bulk of evidence now suggests that girls who have difficulty establishing self-esteem and comfort within themselves have something in common: the absence of empathic, encouraging responsiveness from their fathers, together with a failure on their mother's part to serve as an attractive model. Hints of this issue appear when, for example, a father seems to prefer playing or working with his son rather than his daughter. Because a young child does not have conscious, adult logic, the girl may conclude that she is less valuable as a person than her brother.

The father plays an important role in establishing the groundwork for his daughter's future success and comfort. He needs to encourage her competence, physical activity, and intellectual accomplishment. He should be able to enjoy her curiosity and zest. Later, if he becomes afraid of the strength of her adolescent passions and cuts off the companionship that nourished her, she may perceive his discomfort as a preference for a more demure, passive type of woman and conclude that something is wrong with her, particularly her emerging womanhood. She may feel abandoned or spurned or assume that she's sexually unattractive. Just the opposite may be true. She may actually be too attractive, too competent, too bright, or too tempestuous—and thus too threatening for her father's comfort. Often, for just this reason, a father severs his relationship with his creative, energetic, blossoming daughter at the beginning of her adolescence.

The Families of Successful Women

A group of extremely successful female executives were asked about their family histories [Reference 5-4]. Of all the possible variables, the most consistent finding was that these very successful women had a father who recognized his daughter's ability and value with no stereotypic limitations. Consistently, these fathers supported the girl's freedom of exploration and expression. They regularly participated in their daughter's activities, extolled their daughter's ability to choose her own activities regardless of sex-role designation, and engaged in aggressive, competitive activities with her. In the successful woman's family, both parents encouraged their daughter to establish her own standards for measuring herself and her achievements, rather than letting her boundaries be set by gender stereotypes.

Successful individuals who are comfortable with their success grew up in families that not only praised them for their achievements but also tended to view all their children as individuals. The parents had equally important functions in the family and supported each other's roles and abilities. Each parent related to the child as a separate person, not as an extension of himself or herself (which would, of course, imply imposition of the parent's own wishes, ideas, and feelings). These parents emphasized in their words and their interactions that both girls and boys have equal rights to the options available to both sexes.

When children can express themselves without constraint, they're free to explore the world and their own talents without feeling limited by gender. Parents provide this climate of self-expression through their interactions with each other and with their children. The specific content of the interactions is less important than the quality of the process, because children are more deeply impressed by what is done than by what is said.

The Rebel with a Cause

Career choice can be very difficult for the girl whose family has been inflexibly *traditional*. In choosing a career, she must deal with her past identifications, her expectations, and her conflicting feelings about sex roles. She may want full autonomy and competence and yet feel that she doesn't deserve them. The emerging young woman may also receive conflicting messages from those who want her to do well, but not too well. Her family and society may confuse her with contradictory values and expectations.

When parents or society try to limit an adolescent girl's achievement and independence, she may become rebellious. Internal conflict about dependency may cause rebellion to persist into adulthood. A grown woman who has not resolved the issue may adopt a provocative manner on the job, irritating and annoying the people who have to work with her. Demotions or firings may result.

A rebellious posture may prevent a woman from holding a job for very long, and struggles with authority figures may become a recurrent theme in her life. For her, work becomes a duty, a structure, a demand imposed on her by authority figures—a symbolic struggle of dominance versus submission, obedience versus control.

A Collector of Injustices

Roberta was failing in business school. She had done poorly for the first two years of her graduate training and was having serious problems in the last six months, and was facing a suspension from school. As she presented several scenarios of victimhood, it became evident that she was a collector of injustices. Although her descriptions of unfair treatment revealed that she had in fact set herself up to fail, she continued to engineer these situations both in school and in interpersonal relationships.

Roberta had become involved with a man she felt was emotionally unavailable and married to his work. When she became pregnant, he abandoned her, which further validated her operating hypothesis of victimhood.

She had exceedingly high expectations of herself and had risen to a level of success beyond anyone in her family, none of whom had completed an undergraduate degree and certainly had never imagined obtaining the kind of education Roberta was getting. Her progress and success had been difficult for her to accept, and she unconsciously sought to nullify, or at least counterbalance, her achievements.

Roberta was, without being aware of it, ambivalent about her success and what it would entail, especially in terms of responsibility. She created face-saving excuses and tales of unjust treatment to avoid the criticism she feared most: that she went beyond (what she believed to be) her own abilities. She was concerned about the negative effect of success once she graduated;

she actively fantasized about being on her own, taking care of herself, making decisions herself, not having the nurturing support of others, and even having to support those who were in her charge.

Roberta wanted to do everything she attempted perfectly from the beginning. On a vacation at the beginning of her therapy, she declined an opportunity to windsurf in Acapulco because others would see her, and she might not be able to do it flawlessly the first time. She rarely enjoyed anything, because she felt she needed to be an expert from the beginning in order to avoid embarrassing failure.

Roberta's inner needs for continuing affirmation and nurturance were at odds with her definition of success and responsibility. The status and power she coveted were in direct opposition to affection and tender relationships. Her behavior was not intended to be self-sabotaging, although the result certainly was. Roberta's intent was to live up to an internal model of herself as loving, compassionate, and noncompetitive.

Caution: Women at Work

In the work world, women are increasingly gaining positions of power, especially at the lower-middle and middle executive levels. Until the 1970s, these positions were largely closed to them. Many female executives, however, find themselves to be *strangers in a strange land*. They've been somewhat grudgingly admitted but not exactly welcomed. Even their potential mentors and models, women who have achieved higher positions, have often been inaccessible. Since many companies have promoted women only in response to *quotas*, women who already have a position in the corporate world may feel that the newcomers are their potential competitors for a limited number of jobs and may abruptly suspend all help.

Serious problems also arise from the clash between corporate values and *feminine* values, although the latter may include some of the worthiest characteristics of humanity. The existing corporate structure requires that those in power adhere to a highly *masculine* set of behavior. The executive is expected to be openly and aggressively competitive, genial and mildly cooperative with peers, while somewhat ruthless toward them (in intention) and toward subordinates. Demanding (rather than forbearing) toward lower-level employees. Furthermore, the mid-level executive is expected to relay the orders of higher executives who are even more remote from the mass of employees, without imagining (and hence, at times, protesting) the practical impact of the orders.

One national company, for instance, was taken over by a corporation known for its traditional orientation. Headquartered in the sunbelt, the new management promptly issued dress regulations requiring all female employees to wear skirts, hose, and heels, whether or not their jobs required public contact. The order may have seemed reasonable enough to the male chief executive officer, basking in the southern sun, but to the lower-level women executives in the company's northeastern offices, it seemed cruel and unenforceable considering the frigid northern winters.

Above all, the corporate structure demands that those holding power compartmentalize their feelings to the point of *doubling*. Two nearly separate personalities are formed, with the ruthless executive coming to work and the decent human being existing only on weekends and after five. Boys have traditionally been taught to partition off or disregard their feelings much more consistently than girls. A boy who is urged not to cry when he's hurt, is often mocked for taking care of a sick animal, Boys who are encouraged to distinguish between the girls he dates *just for sex* and those who might be marriage partners, is learning to separate his sensitivities into well-defined pigeonholes. Girls, on the other hand, are taught to react to others with their whole being, with all their sensitivity intact and active.

Many women who hold corporate power complain that, to get ahead, they have to be more masculine than the men. They're not only expected to do their jobs better than men in the same position, but worse yet, they're expected to act nurturant on the outside while being tougher than the men on the inside. A female executive's corporate uniform, a severe suit feminized with a softly tailored blouse, is a visible symbol of the flattened, *masculinized*, emotional state many women maintain with difficulty.

Corporate success remains a highly stressful achievement for women, and many cope with the anxiety of independence and assertion by developing an inhibition or fear. For example, one woman couldn't drive on an expressway or open road. By choosing routes through neighborhoods (all of which reminded her of home), she created the illusion that she had never left home and thus didn't have to face the anxieties of feeling independent and separate.

One person's success may be disregarded or depreciated by someone else. The ability to recognize and tolerate differences and to perceive a wide range of viewpoints and ideals is important in determining what constitutes success. Compare, for example, the woman whose idea of success is the achievement of an officer's position in the military with the woman whose ambition is to be a warm, engaging mother who rears her children successfully and creatively.

Women and Money

Some women emerge from a traditional cocoon of learned helplessness, including not being involved in money management. The traditional view of women's money-management skills—which tends to deprive them of information about and direct control over money—disallows mastery and enhancement of self-esteem.

Men and women regard money differently. Men view it as representing power and identity; women more frequently view money as security and autonomy [Reference 5-5]. A recent survey by *Money* magazine expanded on these differences [Reference 5-6].

Men generally viewed effective money management in terms of long-range strategies, such as planning for taxes and retirement and choosing investments. Women, in contrast, viewed good money management in terms of short-range goals, such as finding bargains, balancing the checkbook, and eliminating debts.

Today women of all economic classes seem to be more aware of money management as an important component of their work, whatever its nature. But adopting an active role in money management takes time and effort. Small steps may include reading the business section of the paper and watching the financial segment on the television news. Each partner furthers empathic understanding by recognizing and respecting (though not necessarily agreeing with) the other's point of view.

Women Who Fear Success

"I know I have a lot of potential and talent," said Margaret, a doctor's wife, "but I've never really allowed myself to use it."

Many women fear success so much that they sabotage their own best accomplishments or avoid accomplishing anything at all. As with any other problem, the reasons for female success phobias vary from individual to individual. However, several types of success phobia are especially likely to afflict women: (1) cultural and role conflict, (2) fear of failure, (3) fear of deviance, and (4) ambition without goal setting [Reference 5-7].

Cultural and Role Conflict

The summer before starting college, Janet, age eighteen, proudly told her parents that she had been offered a terrific summer job. Her parents responded by questioning her ability to do the job and pointing out how inconvenient it would be to drive her to and from work. Angry, frustrated, and defeated, Janet retreated to her room, not venturing out for hours. Her parents, imposing their own needs, had refused to recognize or respond to Janet's needs. They did not take seriously her ambition and her excitement about spending the summer working in her own field of interest.

Only in recent years have women been able to disregard constricting sexual stereotypes in order to realize their full potential. Steps toward fulfillment are not easy in the face of protests by family members and others, by society as a whole, or by one's own heart.

Traditional ideals may actively interfere with the pursuit of contemporary relationships and roles. A woman may feel overwhelmed by the double or triple responsibility of working a full day and then coming home to be a homemaker and perhaps a primary parent. Recently, after speaking on this subject at a gathering for women, I was asked, "Can you tell me how to handle the stress of working a full day, then hearing my husband is bringing home a business associate so that I suddenly have to prepare an elaborate meal?". My response was to question the unstated assumption: that it was her duty to comply with her husband's demand and, at the same time, deal with her feelings and the additional work without protest or negotiation.

Being consciously aware of women's issues is not enough for women who have internal conflicts about achievement or who feel less significant, less powerful, and less important than others whom she must please. Success and competence do not fit easily into the self-image of women who believe that kindly, loving feelings are inconsistent with feelings of expansiveness and assertiveness. Valuing femininity without letting it become a constraint is important in the development of mature and successful women.

Parents may say they want their daughter to be independent and successful, but they often unwittingly give signals to the contrary. They may emphasize from an early age the importance of marrying, of pleasing a husband, of being a good wife. Parents may react to their daughter's potency and vitality as if these were destructive forces; they may reinforce the idea that a girl should respond rather than initiate.

The more "traditional" her family, the more difficult it may be for the adult woman to resolve such issues. She may have received dual messages from those who want her to do well, but not too well. The problems and contradictions of her own internal voice may be intensified by the contradictory values and expectations of her parents and society.

I'm Too Competitive

Some women do not have the same general sense of personal entitlement to growth as men . As soon as a young man indicates an interest in a profession, everyone encourages him. The women in his life—first his mother, often his sisters, later his girlfriend, then his wife and his secretary—all serve his desire for advancement. On the other hand, the traditional woman excels in her support of others, but may overlook her own growth and development. Some women feel guilty and ashamed of their competitive feelings, men generally do not. Competitive striving for achievement is considered *de rigueur* for men; women often feel they have to justify their ambition to strive and succeed in the public arena. A woman's *forbidden* competitive feelings, especially toward men, may stimulate an inhibition about competing at all. Men may unconsciously fear competition that matches too closely their personal history of competition (for instance, the inevitable competition with their father), but successful competition is part of the male ideal. A man is not likely to say "I'm too competitive." He's more likely to say "I'm having trouble being competitive enough."

A woman's *feminine upbringing* and her sensitivity to others' feelings may sometimes be detrimental. For example, once when Valerie was shutting out her opponent in a racquetball game, she suddenly imagined how frustrated and low her opponent must feel and eventually lost the game by two points.

Since childhood, Valerie had an acute sensitivity to her mother's feelings; when her mother felt hurt, Valerie blamed herself. Likewise, Valerie assumed responsibility for her opponent's feelings and identified with her hurt and frustration; she helped her opponent feel better by performing badly herself and eventually losing the game.

Many people have trouble conceding that the fields of medicine, business, and law are not intrinsically masculine, just as a woman's ambition, accomplishment, and success do not require a departure from femininity. Until recently, a successful, independent woman was often considered a failure *as a woman*. Not too long ago, an essayist stated, "Nobody objects to a woman's being a good writer or sculptor or geneticist if, at the same time, she manages to be a good wife, a good mother, good-looking, good-tempered, well-dressed, well-groomed, and unaggressive." [Reference 5-8].

Many still believe, as did eighteenth-century philosopher Jean-Jacques Rousseau, that "a woman's dignity consists of being unknown to the world; her glory is in the esteem of her husband, her pleasures in the happiness of her family."

A compliant desire to do things *right*, as family and social pressures dictate, indicates a supportive, nurturing role rather than the autonomous, creative, responsible role of a mature adult. A woman's ability to satisfy her own need for self-expression, however she defines it, depends on her perception of the restraints and restrictions of the traditional female role. One woman may see them as insurmountable; another may see them as a challenge to be overcome. Regardless, a woman must overcome these internal obstacles if she is to achieve personal or professional success.

Along with their own anxieties about succeeding, women may suffer the disapproval, overt or covert, of society, family, and perhaps her husband. In many corporations, she may also have to face the resentment of male supervisory personnel, who are often less than overjoyed by the presence of women in their ranks. These traditional men may resent requirements that women be hired and promoted into positions of greater rank, responsibility, and reimbursement, than the humdrum clerical and secretarial work they were confined to for so many years.

The women's movement has brought a new set of arbitrary social expectations. A professor at a major women's college recently indicated that the women who sought supportive advice a generation ago were those who wanted to enter a profession. She said—as college counselors have confirmed—the women most apt to feel "peculiar and vaguely unjustified" are those who want to marry and start a family without having a career. The stereotyped view of a woman as wife, mother, and nurturer is no more tyrannical than the view that personal fulfillment can be found only in the active pursuit of a career. With new pathways available for feminine fulfillment, new conflicts and problems have also arisen.

We must develop the ability to recognize and tolerate differences and to perceive a wide range of viewpoints and ideals about what constitutes success. For example, one woman's idea of success may be an officer's position in the military; another woman's idea of success may be rearing children successfully and creatively. Both ideals are valid.

Fear of Failure

The Reluctant Violinist

Nina, introduced in Chapter 4, made elaborate, well-researched, and well-funded preparations for starting her own business, a music store. In her own business, Nina expected to be able to use her talents more fully than in the routine office job she'd taken to support herself. Although intelligent and competent, she still couldn't believe in her own abilities. "It's frightening to go into business on my own," she told me. "It's easier for my husband because his father was in business, and he's sure somehow that he can make a go of it. I feel as though any undertaking or change like this is threatening, and I fear the worst—like starving." After all her careful planning, Nina gave up the project at the last minute, so fearful of failure that she couldn't even try to succeed.

Nearly everyone who fears success seems to explain it as a fear of failure, which seems more understandable and logical than a fear of success. Falling ill emotionally or physically or sabotaging one's efforts just when the goal is in sight does not make sense to the conscious, logical mind.

The attribution of success anxiety to fear of failure is more pronounced in women who have particularly low self-esteem and who associate shame with failure. It occurs most frequently among women who have never enjoyed consistent, acknowledged experiences of mastery and success. Low self-esteem may result when the child identifies with a mother who seems unsuccessful, incapable, or inadequate. It can be intensified by a parent who consistently responds to the child critically; rather than applauding things the child does right, the parent focuses on the one flaw ("for your own good" or "to help you do better"). The girl increasingly defines herself negatively and critically, assuming that since her parents are all-wise and all-powerful, they must be mirroring her accurately.

My Mother, Myself

Fear of failure also arises in women who were overly attached to their mother during childhood and perhaps still are. Such a daughter avoided autonomy and independence, preferring to maintain a tight bond with her mother. The mother, feeling dependent and incomplete herself, needed a dependent child to feel more whole (and perhaps fend off emptiness or depression). The mother discouraged her daughter's independence and full self-expression by functioning for her, rather than allowing her to become more self-sufficient. As a result, the daughter came to feel less than complete herself, because her mother could always do things better and faster. She felt that she needed her mother in order to function. Mother and daughter became emotionally enmeshed.

Nina, who didn't dare open a music store, had this sort of relationship with her mother. "My mother tried to control my emotional reactions so I would be automated and predictable," she remembered. "She couldn't handle a free spirit. She's a dead person inside. It was like Mother wasn't there psychologically. She was always withdrawing from me. Anger was not acceptable to her. In some way, I was afraid of being harmful to my mother if I asserted myself. I was careful not to feel too much of anything. I tried to get love from doing a job well and feel good about myself outside of my work, but it never worked out. I'm afraid to take risks—to make a serious commitment."

Nina transferred her dependency to her husband. Later, seeking therapy to counter her despair, she mentioned that she wanted to be in treatment forever. She would have liked to substitute the therapist for her mother. But as she learned to understand herself and the source of her depression, she quickly realized that this wish echoed her earlier avoidance of autonomy. When Nina's treatment ended, she was happy with herself and her marriage, and was no longer depressed; she owned a music store and played violin in an orchestra.

I Can Control One Thing in the World

I have seen many patients with anorexia nervosa, the self-starving disease, who had an overly dependent relationship with their mother. A major increase in autonomy and responsibility—the onset of adolescence, graduation, marriage, or child-birth—frightens these women and forces them to confront their lack of a fully separate selfhood. In retreat, they center their lives on something over which they have complete control, their body.

Controlling food intake is, for them, a positive, exciting experience of mastery. One anorexic woman stated, "I can walk into a roomful of people and know there's one thing in the world that I can do better than any of them, and that is being thinner." This experience was so important to her that she was still counting calories when she weighed eighty-two pounds.

I'll Stop Just Before the Finish Line

Fear of failure generates more fear of failure. From early childhood, people who never try (or stop short) because they fear failure do not allow themselves the confidence-building experience of increasing mastery that fuels later, greater endeavors. Confidence, self-esteem, and skill all stem from trial-and-error experiences accompanied by accurate and encouraging parental feedback. Thus a fear of failure, by precluding new attempts at mastery, can be self-perpetuating. The impediments to working and succeeding that result may look like laziness to someone else or may be attributed by the person suffering from this difficulty to a lack of motivation or interest in work.

Individuals sustain this fear by refusing to recognize their accomplishments as successful or by focusing on a negative aspect. Thus they have scant opportunity to build self-confidence. They may feel like an impostor or a fraud, expressing the notion that they haven't progressed through skill and hard work but through good luck, a good connection, or someone else's help and guidance. Their hope for future success is that their luck or connections will continue. They never acknowledge that *good luck* comes to *good players*.

Such individuals minimize their success and disassociate themselves from it as though threatened in some way by achievement. Most often, however, fear of failure precludes achievement, because those who suffer from it are unable to attempt anything that might result in success. Like Nina, who suddenly decided not to start her own business, those who fear failure usually abandon their efforts before any outright success can allay their fears.

Fear of Deviance

Fear of deviance, a special type of fear of success, is based on the anticipation of negative consequences if one deviates from a set of expected behaviors. The fear of deviance was illustrated nearly two decades ago in a classic study by psychologist Mathilde S. Horner [Reference 5-9]. She asked male and female undergraduates to complete a four-minute story about either John or Anne. The two stories began with the same sentence: "At the end of the first term finals, John/Anne finds himself/herself at the top of his/her medical school class."

Story completions indicating a fear of success emerged in 62 percent of the female sample but in only 9 percent of the male sample. Three basic fear-of-success themes were present when the story was about Anne: (1) social isolation and rejection (Anne feared she'd lose all her friends if she succeeded), (2) Anne's discomfort and fears about not feeling feminine if she succeeded, (3) disavowal by the female respondents that a woman could actually achieve what Anne did (Anne is a code name for a group of male medical students).

Horner found a positive correlation between fear-of-success imagery and later inhibition of performance. The performance of women who revealed fear-of-success themes in their stories decreased whenever they had to compete against men.

This study illustrates a particular kind of fear of success, namely, a fear of being viewed as deviant from the feminine norm and a fear of being rejected because of this deviation. An important aspect of this fear is its relationship to external reality, to a set of norms that are social as well as internal. The fear is directly related to sex-role conflict in the real world.

A fear of deviance is a particular problem for women with high ambitions, given the social context in which they must achieve their ambitions. Contemporary women grew up in an earlier, more traditional world and internalized its traditional values to some degree. For women raised in an era when female success consisted mainly of being desirable to men (with a good marriage and motherhood the very pinnacle of success), the shadows of these ideals may still be present. The more heavily these goals were emphasized by a woman's family and the fewer the individual or creative alternatives allowed during her childhood or adolescence, the heavier the threat of social ostracism for defining success in a different way. Having a career would mean stepping outside the bounds of conventional behavior. Worse, this nonconformity would have to take the form of a personal rebellion, because it would require the woman to disidentify with her family, her mother, her own past, and her own ideal. For some, the pleasures of mastery and self-fulfillment may be sufficient to overcome these barriers, but others may find them insurmountable.

If a Woman Were Just More Like a Man

The woman who regards career activities as masculine may fear loss of femininity and attractiveness if she strives for a career. She may shrink from any attempt to expand and may limit her horizons to the traditional, domestic ones. Anthropologist Margaret Meade, one of the most successful and unconventional women of her generation, has noted that a woman's success calls into question her femininity.

Maria, a capable and successful businesswoman, struggled to avoid knowing that she was more active, energetic, and competent than her husband. Fearing that her competence would damage his pride, she inhibited her expansiveness and limited her ambitions. She had grown up as the favorite child of an unsuccessful father and had been nagged and criticized by her mother, who was apparently jealous of her daughter's abilities. Maria resolved not to repeat her mother's pattern. She married a man who seemed the very opposite of her father, only to discover, as is so often the case, that he was essentially the same.

A woman may impede her personal success in an effort to maintain the balance in a marriage or a family. Remaining dependent on her husband may preserve the relationship. Sometimes a woman may maintain the marital equilibrium in tiny ways; for instance, she may ask her husband's guidance about something that she understands perfectly well and can decide for herself. The asking creates (or maintains) her dependent role.

Lillian Rubin did a study in which she interviewed 160 successful women [Reference 5-10]. One of the women Rubin interviewed, a highly successful executive, described herself initially only as a good cook. This disclaimer of power and disavowal of success reveals the difficulty many women have in integrating the various aspects of themselves. Some women even label themselves "successful impostors" when they are effective in the world.

Women who are changing their world and their horizons are not always able to change their basic image of themselves. To be competent and to feel competent may be wholly different. They may avoid acknowledging their competence to themselves and others, or they may fear stepping out of traditional feminine bounds. When a woman is caught in a bind between her old patterns and new ones, she may vacillate between her traditional ideals and her newly found competence. She may fear being strident, aggressive, and unfeminine, worrying that power will corrupt her humane, nuturant instincts.

Many women allow themselves to be competent only in volunteer positions, where their competence can be channeled into the traditional cultural expectation of helping others. They satisfy their ideal of *a good woman* by striving for a form of success free from personal gain, occupational competition, or independent financial reward. Their energy and competence are applauded but are free from financial compensation, one of the benchmarks of success. Volunteerism may also be a way to avoid direct competition in the world or with men. Although volunteers often compete energetically for public praise and organizational power, volunteerism may represent a compromise with the prohibition against entering the *official* world of competition and power, the work world.

The woman who was raised to be compliant rather than assertive, to be giving to the point of martyrdom, to be dependent, perhaps timid, and centered on her family, may be tormented by guilt when she wishes to pursue work outside the home. She may feel that *proper mother love* does not permit her attention to stray from her children. She may even suffer echoes of the separation anxiety she felt as a child and hesitate to leave her children lest something harmful befall them.

Ambition Without Goal Setting

Many women learn to fit into someone else's mold instead of establishing their own goals and standards. Choosing vague and undefined goals, too many goals, or failing to set goals at all, may serve as a defense against feeling too ambitious. Belief in luck or destiny may disguise the fact that a goal is being actively pursued. In contrast, a woman who can develop an internal point of reference—her own direction, drawn from her own desires and standards—can develop an autonomous sense of self.

Casting Her Own Shadow

Margaret, age thirty-three, entered treatment in a state of depression and despair. She felt that she was not a person in her own right but just the shadow of her husband, a prominent physician. She was angry and frustrated but afraid to change this secure position; she was aware of the gratification her current role gave her, as well as her fear of failing should she attempt greater independence. She wanted freedom and independence but had no idea of how she meant to achieve them. For all her ambition, she had not made any specific plans for attaining some reasonable goal.

"I really can't feel free, can't release myself," she said. "I can't seem to use my potential and talent. My whole life actually centers around my husband, being the perfect doctor's wife, and having everything I do in that role being approved of. It's as if I can't do anything without his approval. I enjoy the praise I get for such wifely things as preparing perfect meals and being a gracious and beautiful hostess. My husband is security for me. He knows what he wants out of life."

Margaret was constantly depressed and persistently felt that something vital was missing from her life. Yet she avoided taking on any major responsibilities outside the home. When asked to give talks in public, she refused, and she wouldn't assume a leadership role in her community.

Margaret identified strongly with her mother. This continuing bond included sharing her mother's interests and pursuits. She noted that she could do well only in areas in which her mother had done well—but could never do quite as well as Mom. She was careful not to compete with her mother. Margaret's mother had acquired a college degree, but Margaret dropped out of college during her final semester. Whether preparing meals or dressing for a major social event, Margaret always left something out; the effect was never quite complete: "I never could complete anything, I always leave just one thing undone. I never really do anything quite as well as I can. I guess it's an insecure feeling. If I look nice and sound bright, I laugh at myself or make some stupid remark to put myself down. If I feel really attractive, I might dress in some cruddy way."

When Margaret received a compliment, she felt guilty, as though such praise was undeserved. She always found some way to sabotage her efforts. Saying something stupid, appearing slightly

askew, or leaving something undone were her methods for disavowing completeness and success.

As a little girl, Margaret saw her mother behave deferentially
toward her father, who was also a physician. He seemed to favor
Margaret's brother. While Margaret did household chores, her
father took her brother with him on his hospital rounds. Even in
such small matters as the amount of play time he shared with each
child, her father gave priority to his son.

During psychoanalysis, Margaret acknowledged her anger
and frustration with a father who played favorites and a mother
who seemed to regard herself and her daughter as unimportant.
Margaret had been cloaking her anger in the same shroud of
ingratiation that her mother used and had continued to ask herself
a despairing question: "Why can't I be free and independent like
other girls?" The answer lay buried beneath the blanket of her
unconscious.

Early in adolescence, realizing that she would never receive the
love and respect from her father that she wanted, Margaret became
promiscuous in an effort to repair her self-image and simultaneously avenge herself for her father's unresponsiveness. Her father had
not affirmed her as being attractive and womanly, so she turned to
other men who might represent him. Although her sexual adventures were open and active otherwise, she was careful to conceal
them from her parents. She found every man who pursued her
exciting but simultaneously found the procession monotonous:
"They all just wanted sex." Like her father, her sexual partners were
afraid of closeness, intimacy, and emotional depth. Her assumptions about men were validated by the men she chose.

Something had always interfered with Margaret's achieving
any goals. In essence, she had never established her own set of
goals; after marriage, she simply mirrored those of her husband.
She recognized that she sabotaged her own endeavors because she
was unconsciously afraid of surpassing her mother. She assumed
that, if she surpassed her mother, she would be exposed as small,

insignificant, and incapable and would feel all alone. She restricted her aggressiveness as though it were the exclusive domain of the male (as demonstrated countless times by her father and brother) and allowed herself to do only such *womanly* things as household tasks and studying for a teaching degree. Even having an orgasm was difficult for her, because the frightening prospect of letting go with a man would mean unleashing her aggression and sexuality.

During psychoanalysis, Margaret finally emerged from her husband's shadow. She completed college and went on to study for a doctorate. In a letter she wrote after her treatment ended, she indicated that she had completed her Ph.D. and felt happy, secure, and whole—she was now casting her own shadow.

Mid-Life Issues

Many women invest themselves deeply in mothering, believing that the career of motherhood is the noblest of all endeavors and that producing healthy children far surpasses producing income. Other women may feel guilty about the conflict between motherhood and another career and will only permit themselves to direct their attention outside the home after the children have grown up.

Sometimes, in mid-life, a woman will finally allow herself to consider her own development and fulfillment. It's as though she feels she's paid her dues, has put in the requisite amount of time fulfilling other people's expectations, and can now proceed to blow the dust off her shelved ambitions and desires.

This stage can be difficult for women who continue, in some subtle way, to be a prisoner of sex-role stereotypes. They remain vulnerable to their husband's demands for attention and even to the demands of their grown children. The husband may resist any change in his wife and his home, perhaps resenting the disruption in the well-established marital routine or the loss of his wife's constant services and attention.

The more a woman's sense of herself has been grounded in her identity as a wife and mother, the more difficult will be her readjustment when she enters the work world. She may feel that being female, attractive, and lovable is incompatible with being assertive and successful, and she may also feel more dependent and less competent than men.

Women looking for outside work in mid-life also face the hard fact of devaluation in the occupational marketplace, stemming from years of "not working."

The woman between thirty and fifty, especially, has a multiplicity of choices for her domestic, personal, and career roles. She may find it difficult to work out a stable lifestyle that allows the growth of her own interests while satisfying her desire to be a good mother and a loving wife. Since there is no universal or traditional precedent, she needs more than average self-esteem and strength to settle on a manageable pattern; it is difficult to find validation and approval for any particular choice. Young children are bound to want their mother around as much as possible, and children and husband are both likely to blame the working mother when things go wrong. Other women may envy her or disapprove of her arrangements, so she often finds herself facing her dilemma alone.

The husband who originally encouraged the mid-life woman to work outside the home may later become unexpectedly demanding, resenting the fact that her attention is focused elsewhere. For instance, he may complain vociferously when he discovers that dinner won't be waiting for him if his wife comes home from work at the same time he does. Several motives may play a role in his reaction: The husband may be ambivalent about his wife's working or perhaps more dependent on her than he knows. He may feel threatened by her competence. He may want her to outshine other women but not to outshine him. He may need her to be dependent on him so he can feel masculine and paternal.

The woman who puts all her energies into being a dedicated mother and who derives all her pride from managing her household often finds that this career is a transient one, lasting only until the last child is grown. Thus the woman who makes a career of mothering is without a job at mid-life. But even the woman whose primary career is outside the home may have to face confusing internal and external pressures when she reaches this stage of her life.

Self-Inquiry Quiz: For Women Only

1.   What is your own personal definition of success?

"The tragedy of life doesn't lie in not reaching your goal. The tragedy lies in having no goal to reach."—Benjamin F. Mays

2.   What does money represent to you? What does money management entail for you?

If you have been regarding money and money management stereotypically, perhaps seeing money as autonomy and security, and if you have been focusing on short-term money management, perhaps finding bargains and balancing the checkbook, consider the other viewpoints in the Money section of this chapter.

3.   How much do you rely on others for direction, affirmation, and self-esteem?

Self-esteem is developed originally through feedback from others, but its base is within the self. All the compliments and reassuring feedback in the world won't enhance self-esteem if you feel undeserving of such comments. If you feel undeserving, the praise will be disavowed, disregarded, or attributed to a lack of information. Self-esteem cannot be implanted or transplanted.

4.   Do you read the business section of the newspaper and watch or listen to the financial portion of the broadcast news to balance your awareness of events?

These small behavioral changes can expand awareness and promote different ways of thinking.

5.   Do you believe that, if you're competent and work hard, your boss will offer you a promotion or raise without your having to ask for it or promote yourself?

Some people have been conditioned to wait for "gifts"; they believe that doing all the right things, performing well, and waiting to be recognized will bring the appropriate reward. This is not necessarily so. A far more useful technique, particularly in larger companies, is to find an intelligent, sensitive way to make your work visible. You may have to take the initiative in listing your accomplishments and requesting your own raise.

6. Do you believe that asserting yourself is being too pushy?

Here is a delicate balance, as well as a double standard: Behavior considered assertive for a man might be seen as aggressive in a woman. Generally, however, the better you are at your work, the more room you can carve out for being yourself.

7. Do you have specific long-term goals and a step-by-step process for reaching them?

"It is much more difficult to measure non-performance than performance."—Harold S. Geneen

8. Once you have a game plan for success, are you afraid to take risks and make mistakes?

"Some people try to softly tiptoe through life so that they can arrive at death safely."—Robert Anthony

9. Do you believe that to make it in the business world you have to behave like a man?

Your womanly side may be your best asset. Delores Danska, an award-winning television program manager, stated, "In my job, I need to bring out the best in my producers, which means being supporting, encouraging, and caring."

10. Do you feel you have to be a driven, type A personality to be a real success?

Achievers achieve because they combine ambition and ideals. They have a commitment and work to achieve it. None of these represent a personality profile or character type; there are many personality styles and types among achievers. Rather than trying to be more like someone who is an achiever, try to be more like yourself. Listen for how and what you want to do.

6

Work and Success: For Men Only

There must be more to life than having everything.

—Maurice Sendak

To know where you are going,
you must first know where you are.

What's with men these days? Some, especially male writers, are beginning to wonder aloud about the value of being immersed in a career, about allowing child rearing and vulnerability to be the exclusive property of women.

Real Men Don't Cry

A prominent man in his late fifties, very successful and highly esteemed, allowed himself to cry in his second consultation. He asked me at the end of the session if other people ever did that sort of thing in my office. A familiar face nationally, he had been a stranger to his own family and to his own feelings, which he was now allowing himself to know. He especially wanted to believe that his lifelong yearning for his father's approval and companionship was unimportant; fulfillment of this yearning had become impossible since his father's death.

A man's relationship with his father shapes his adult ideals of intimacy and work. A growing body of research indicates that boys begin searching for masculine models at about age three. Between three and five, boys withdraw from their mother and femininity and strive to become like their father [Reference 6-1].

Until recently, and still in some families, the father was a shadowy figure, uncomfortable with tender or expressive feelings and somehow difficult to understand. Boys rarely had warm, soft, tender, nurturing experiences with their father. Family researchers have found that fathers spent an average of thirty-seven seconds a day interacting with their infants during the first three months of life [Reference 6-2].

In the best circumstances, the father provides a confident, complete model of manhood and personhood, a composite of thinking and feeling and acting. Bonding with the father requires physical closeness and the father's acceptance of the child and his feelings; the child must feel unconditionally cared for. Unfortunately, the psychological absence of fathers from their family may be one of the most underestimated tragedies of our times [Reference 6-3]. One survey of 7,239 men revealed that "almost no men said they were close to their fathers." [Reference 6-4].

A small boy often interprets his father's absence from the house as evidence of his own lack of worth. If bonding does not take place, separation cannot occur. Separation occurs within the context of a relationship, not outside it.

Boys have always been encouraged by parents and by society to develop autonomy. In many cultures, arrival at the threshhold of manhood is celebrated with special ceremonies. Girls who have moved toward independence, in contrast, have frequently lost their family's support. To pursue their own endeavors, they have had to consider themselves *masculine* and deal with the anxiety of *going against the laws of nature*. Girls have even had to adopt male guises to fulfill their ambitions; for example, Joan of Arc cut her hair short and put on men's clothes before leading her army to victory, and Mary Ann Evans adopted the name George Eliot so her novels would be published. Ambition and expansiveness have frequently been deemed abnormal for women.

For millennia, Western culture has followed the patriarchal system: Men do things, and women serve men. In some patriarchal societies, men talk about things while women do things—all the farmwork, the craftwork, the trading, and the housework—and also serve men. (Wherever this pattern is found, conversation is predictably considered the highest of all human functions.)

With these differing roles, it is no wonder that boys and girls are raised differently. Many studies of *normal* families—I might add, not of psychiatric patients or *troubled* families—have revealed that both mothers and fathers emphasize achievement and competitiveness more for sons than for daughters [Reference 6-5]. Both parents tend to encourage their sons, more than their daughters, to control the expression of feelings, to be independent, and to assume increasing amounts of personal responsibility. Sons are punished more often and more severely than daughters. With their sons, fathers are strict, firm, and authoritarian. They are more likely to use physical punishment, and are intolerant of behaviors violating the traditional masculine stereotype.

With their daughters, fathers show greater warmth and physical closeness, they expect gentle, *ladylike* behavior, and hesitate to use physical punishment. Mothers tend to restrict and supervise their daughters more closely than their sons. Girls are pressured to be obedient, responsible, and nurturing, whereas boys are urged toward achievement and self-reliance. Boys are assigned chores that take them away from their mother and out of the house; girls are assigned homebound tasks that keep them in close proximity to their mother.

Boys are also raised to be more curious and exploratory than girls. A boy is expected to set off cherry bombs and wreck his room with chemistry experiments at an age when a girl may feel lucky if her mother even lets her bake cookies by herself. "You can't do that because you could hurt yourself," is a phrase heard far more often by girls than boys. They are expected to suppress fear, but girls are encouraged to yield shamelessly to fright and even to express their fears as a badge of distinction. The slicer-dicer horror movies of the last decade were most popular among dating teenagers. They gave the girls a chance to shriek, squeal, and hide their eyes while the boys could show their bravery by laughing and talking back to the screen.

Russell Baker, writing about men, summarized the *requirements* of manhood as utter fearlessness, zest for combat, and indifference to pain [Reference 6-6].

The Assumptions of Power

Many men collude in maintaining women in constricting, stereotyped roles. As boys, they had an intense and powerful emotional union with a woman, their mother. In this first relationship, power was centered in a female who seemed omnipotent. A man is uncomfortable with the unconscious recollection of his original weakness and helplessness, compared to his mother's boundless power. If this concept is a problem for him, he may attribute passivity, weakness, and inferiority to women. The man who is most afraid of a regressive pull toward early boyhood helplessness, is the one who rebels most against the power he perceives in a current *mother* figure (his wife or female boss). Internal issues remaining from childhood often provoke strong reactions.

Some men bring the madonna/whore dichotomy to their view of women. The madonna (often a wife) is idealized and admired, but the man is able to unleash all his sexual passions only with a woman he regards as inferior, a whore.

Men may actually prefer women for what they are not rather than what they are. Sharing life with an equal partner who has her own opinions, sees clearly, and has her own needs to satisfy is vastly threatening to some men.

Many couples live with the implicit understanding that the husband will make all the decisions and that the wife will function as an extension of his desires. She will act on her own initiative only in agreed-upon situations. When such a wife begins to recognize her own potential and autonomy, when she begins to feel like a *real* person, she challenges this assumption, often provoking major marital turmoil. Other similar assumptions that may rule a household are the husband's uncontested right to determine what the family will do about financial or vacation plans. He also determines the wife's responsibility; and if she takes an outside job it is simply added to her usual household workload.

Both men and women who want to achieve success comfortably need to free themselves from the traditional sex-role stereotypes. They must learn to integrate activity, aggressiveness, assertiveness, gentleness, serenity, receptiveness, creativity, and gratifying sexuality. If we hope to fullfil this aim, we may have to transcend the childhood models learned from our parents.

Women have traditionally been expected to seek affection and depend on and care for others; men are expected to be dominant, expansive, powerful, and apparently emotionless. Gentleness, tact, the easy expression of tender feelings, and an awareness of the feelings of others have not been behavioral standards for males in our culture. Yet the combined characteristics of both sexes produce the greatest success and the richest life. Both men and women can make effective use of ambition and aggression, and both can integrate assertiveness and independence with connectedness and concern for others.

Men suffer as much as women from gender-bound personality traits. If women have been limited in expressing their ambitions, men have been equally limited in expressing their sensitivity and emotions. But in the same families where females are encouraged to pursue their ambitions, males can express warmth, tenderness, and emotion and suffer no loss of masculinity.

Some men face another sort of role stereotype. Social obstacles often prevent them from seeking goals other than those expected of them, either personally or professionally. For instance, the man who chooses to become a nurse, a secretary, or a dancer may be ostracized, or have his masculinity questioned. Or the man who chooses work or friendships *below his class* may face disapproval from his family.

Being a Man

Wade was a depressed seventeen-year-old, referred for therapy because of a dramatic decline in school performance during the year—from grade *A* to grade *F* in all subjects—and impulsive, acting-out behavior. In therapy he described his utter helplessness and frustration with his parents, both ambitious professionals who demanded that Wade achieve grade *A* in every subject. They had enrolled him in an Ivy League college (as a legacy) two years prior to his high school graduation.

The following is an excerpt from some of our work:

Wade: I think about the past a lot. There is something about being home. I've disappointed my parents.

Me: How effective do you feel in getting your parents to respond and understand what you're experiencing?

Wade: I haven't gotten responses that make me feel good. I can't get their approval. Whatever I do, it's not good enough to really get their approval. It just hurts. There are a few things that I saw as accomplishment, but there is no change in their response. Like my grades . . . but they didn't say anything until I began to do badly. Unless I really get extreme—like extremely upset—there is no response. When I got failing grades, my mother got hysterical, and my father said we need to talk, and he took off a half day from his practice to take me fishing. It was great.

Me: Are there other extreme things you do to get them to respond to you?

Wade: This summer I went out with an Oriental girl. I was really hoping they would voice their opinion. It's hard to recognize what pleases my parents. One night I came in sort of drunk. I don't think they even knew. Both were away at board meetings. Then I regret what I do and end up feeling guilty.

Me: I understand how much you've tried to get their response and how—in doing things in an extreme way—you feel guilty and get the opposite of what you really want.

Wade: I can understand now, too, how much I've tried. And also how it doesn't work and how frustrated I am. I remember crying a few months ago because I was so upset, and my father told me to stop and to be a man.

Wade's imminent graduation and need for autonomy focused awareness on his unmet developmental needs and the inadequacy of his own self-regulation. We continued to talk about his efforts, about the intent versus the result, and how it did not work either to fit himself into, or to oppose someone else's position since both were external points of reference. I empathized with his frustration and pointed out that, in his efforts to get responses from his parents, he had given up his own internal standards.

During the fifth month in our twice-weekly therapy, I told Wade I would be away the following session. This was unusually short notice.

Wade: You are probably doing a presentation or something very important . . . I feel very shut down.

Me: What else are you experiencing?

Wade: I feel kind of bad, empty, not worth much. (He elaborated on feeling worthless.)

Me: It's as if you feel worthless because of our interruption, that I'll be somewhere else other than meeting with you.

Wade: That's right, and I feel empty.

Me: Empty can feel pretty bad.

Wade: It sure can. I feel that way a lot, though. Now I especially do.

Me: So it's your experience of me not being here that you take as meaning you are not worth much. It's your experience of not being effective in getting me to respond, as you want, that creates your empty, bad feeling. Your experience then, is created by you.

Wade: I never thought about it that way . . . It's not your being away, but what I made it out to be in terms of myself, and how I felt about myself that makes me feel bad.

He then talked of experiences with his parents that centered on feelings of isolation and neglect. We examined his feelings of worthlessness, depletion, and inadequacy, following episodes in which his parents didn't respond or sympathize adequately. Wade ultimately realized that his parents were caught up in their own needs, struggles, and concerns and that they were not an accurate mirror of him, even though he had always thought they were.

His point of reference changed from feeling good and effective only if his parents or I responded as he wanted, to an internal point of reference that allowed self-regulation and determination.

Self-Inquiry Quiz: For Men Only

1. What is success for you?

    "Nothing is enough to the man for whom enough is too little."—Epicurus

2. Do you have a clear definition of *external* success?

    This level of success is the easier one to define. The on-paper, external type of success includes money, material acquisitions, work accomplishments, titles, regard by associates, and friends.

3. Do you have a clear definition of *internal* success?

    This type of success isn't easily mapped. And it may be defined differently by men, by women, and even by each individual. The familiar model of male competition makes measurement of external success clearer. But internal success is measured against ideals, relatedness with important others, and comfort with oneself. This type of success involves connecting ambition with ideals and living up to your own standards.

4. Do you have specific long-term goals and a step-by-step process for reaching them?

    Having long-term goals can keep you oriented and organized; having step-by-step, short-term goals can help sustain enthusiasm and tolerate frustration. Short-term setbacks are an essential part of achieving success. An analogy is a toddler learning to walk, falling is not a failure but part of the process of learning to walk. If you have the end point, your purpose, clearly in mind, you can more easily keep setbacks in perspective.

5. Once you have a plan for success, are you afraid to take risks and make mistakes?

6. Is anything internal keeping you from proceeding with your plan for success?

When your head and your gut (what you think and feel) both agree, you won't go wrong. It is disregarding, deleting, or covering over one or the other that causes trouble. Your goals must be emotionally consistent with how you see yourself.

7. Do you feel you have to be a driven, type A personality to really succeed?

A passage in one of Schumann's piano sonatas is marked "As fast as possible," followed a few bars later with the admonition "Faster." The most outstanding characteristic of the superachievers I have known is that all of them love their work and their play. Rich is knowing you have enough.

7

Ambition and Ideals: Our Sense of Self

To him, being human was only an
excuse for not being perfect.

—Katherine Ann Porter

Nothing prevents our being natural
so much as the desire to appear so.

—Francois La Rochefoucauld

An esteemed trial attorney who had reached a high-water mark in her career made the following observations: "After you've advanced in your work, at some point there's no one else to give you good feedback besides yourself. If you're really good, they're either jealous or overly admiring, and there's no one more senior. I've run out of people to idealize, to look up to. At first, when I recognized that, I felt a little lost. The greatest favor another attorney did early in my career was when I went to him and said, 'How am I doing?' he said, 'Only you can tell.' At first, I got mad. Later, I realized how that remark helped me develop my own self-reliance and validation."

Our Innermost Design

Our *sense of self* consists of self-image and body image, personality and functioning, the organization of all our experience. It is all the qualities to which *self* is affixed: self-esteem, self-confidence, self-concept, what we feel, who and what we are. The concept of self and the experience of self serve as an internal point of reference and a center of independent initiative.

How Do I Become Real?

The classic children's tale *The Velveteen Rabbit* is a story of the development of a sense of self. The bunny, the Velveteen Rabbit, looked great on the outside, made of beautiful, shiny, rich velveteen. But on the inside he felt empty and hollow and knew something was missing. So he consulted with the oldest, wisest resident of the nursery, the Skin Horse. "How do I become real?" he asked. The Skin Horse responded, "Real isn't the things you are made of. It is what happens to you. When a child loves you for a long, long time, not just plays with you, but really loves you, then you become real."

Our basic sense of self is composed of our ambitions, the internal forces that energize us, and our ideals which give us a sense of who and what we are and what our goals are. With good emotional health, there is a dynamic link between ambitions and ideals that provides a sense of wholeness, the feeling that our life has meaning. Our skills and talents are the tools that help us achieve ideals and goals. The realization of goals—moment by moment, day to day, actual and abstract—creates self-esteem.

The channeling of ambitions through creative activity so that we might live up to our ideals is, in itself, nurturing. People with full and unimpeded ambitions and well-formed internal ideals, and a dynamic link between the two, find a smooth path through the world.

The sense of self is continually being refined and individualized in adulthood, with increasing internal regulation of esteem, confidence, initiative, and feelings. This internal point of reference predominates in healthy individuals, although others have an impact on us throughout our life. In narcissistic people, however, the sense of self is vague; mood and feelings of esteem and worth are chameleon like because they are determined by others. The sense of self is compromised when we abandon our internal point of reference and become so attuned to someone else's desires and feelings that we *lose ourselves*.

Throughout development, our self-concept gradually becomes less dependent on the responses of others; self-esteem becomes less vulnerable and more constant. A human being is never completely an island, but the internal regulation of self-esteem is a significant developmental achievement.

Most of us know, fundamentally, who and what we are. We have a sense of where a particular action falls in our life scheme. Our internal standards are our ideals. When we have any doubt about some action or decision, we can ask "Is it in my best interests?" For us, the big picture can be brought into focus at will; confusion is focused and managed. These guiding principles and organizing processes are the foundation of ethics in business.

The polar opposite of this process is impulsivity, the urge to put a thought into immediate action. Judgment resides in the space between urge and action. An impulsive action eliminates this space, and urge and action become fused.

The Development of Ambition and Ideals

To be true to our inner design, we must have an inner design—that is, ideals and goals, a sense of self to give focus, meaning, and organization to our ambitions.

Ambition develops over time as our needs, feelings, and experiences are mirrored by others. When our vigor and enthusiasm are accurately and empathically reflected by others, our ambition gains meaning and direction and our motivation acquires an end point. If a person's basic self is not consistently validated in childhood, or if it is criticized harshly and goes into protective hiding, emptiness, lethargy, and constriction appear where ambition and vigor might have been; the ability to value and affirm one's self fails to be internalized. The person who does not learn to regulate vitality and ambition is prone to overstimulation: A little is likely to feel like a lot.

A small child ventures out on the diving board and stops to look around. She looks in the direction of the lifeguard. She has not focused on the lifeguard because she is concerned about her safety; she wants to make sure that someone, preferably someone emotionally important like her mother or father, is watching her achievement. Her vitality and her wish to achieve, require mirroring at the moment she turns to see if someone is looking.

Children see themselves the way they think their parents see them. At least until mid-adolescence, we consider our parents to be accurate mirrors of ourselves. Children develop a cohesive, positive sense of self when their parents provide consistent, reliable, empathic responses that generally validate the children's own inner experiences and positive self-image. Children need empathy and affirmation, primarily from parents, to establish healthy self-esteem.

Adults can reexamine the basic assumptions established in childhood and define themselves accurately in the present. This is a process, however, not an event, and it takes time. The greater the transition involved, the more effort and time required.

Disorders of the Self

Disorders of the self, or narcissistic disorders, are the predominant neuroses of the last half of the twentieth century. One typical narcissistic disorder is faulty self-esteem, which creates the need to look continually to others and to the environment for confirmation and valuation of one's self. People who don't receive empathic responses from others may begin to devalue and criticize themselves and perhaps become depressed. Then, insisting on absolute control of others and the environment, such people become unrealistically harsh and demanding of themselves. They have not tuned into inner experiences to learn about themselves.

An individual with narcissistic problems typically feels empty and vulnerable to other people. Intense ambitiousness and grand fantasies often combine with feelings of inferiority and an over-dependence on the admiration and acclaim of others [Reference 7-1]. Narcissistic individuals are not able to regulate their own self-esteem because their own ideals are not clear. Instead of relying on an internal ideal, they depend on other people for self-esteem, self-worth, and happiness. These individuals are always vulnerable, because their point of reference is external rather than internal.

Most commonly, narcissistic people never feel good enough because there is no internal standard that defines good enough. They want to be perfect or to do things perfectly. But to set a goal of perfection is, in essence, to have no standard because perfection is unattainable. As a result, these individuals derive no satisfaction, no emotional closure from their pursuits. Nothing ever quite feels complete. One very wealthy man, in beginning analysis, tried to describe this feeling: "It's like having to leave every movie and every play before it's over."

Something Is Still Missing

There have always been patients who come for treatment with vague complaints, such as an empty feeling, depression, lack of motivation, dissatisfaction. These individuals often request treatment, not necessarily because of symptomatic behavior that interferes with their life, but because of dissatisfaction with life itself. Life seems purposeless, their achievements meaningless; they are lonely and unhappy with their relationships. The complaints of these often highly successful people are typically along the lines of "I've achieved everything, and something is still missing," or "My life is meaningless," or "I really don't know who I am." Their *nothingness* may focus on a variety of *somethings*, perhaps a perpetual quest for more money or the illusive perfect partner, perhaps an addiction to food, alcohol, drugs, another person, or work.

Problems with Ambition

It's Selfish to Want Too Much

Children's ambition can be stifled in two ways: (1) by parents' failure to mirror and affirm developing grandness in their children, good feelings about themselves, and expansiveness, or (2) more surely, by parents' direct criticism of the earliest glimmerings of ambition.

When Russell, a university professor, was growing up, his parents taught him that he should never have anything for himself, that he should dedicate himself to worthy causes and not succumb to the world's materialism. His parents constantly reminded him that it was wrong to want things for himself, that materialism was destructive, and that it was disgusting and terrible for him to want more. He received one toy for his birthday and one toy for Christmas. His parents became so enraged and punitive if he asked for more, that he quickly learned to be content with the little he got.

He reached the point of parroting his parents' views to his peers. He came to adopt his parents' attitude that other kids who had a lot of *things*, clothes or cars, were being phony and superficial and lacked real values. Moreover, Russell learned to be humble, meek, and colorless so that his parents would not ridicule him. He buried his grandiose fantasies and his expansiveness deep inside, where they remained alive, silent and secret.

The point here is not whether parents can afford what the child wants, but whether they understand the wanting. Russell's wanting was criticized rather than understood. Giving children everything they want is not warranted or even healthy, but parents should let children know that they understand how much a particular child may want something.

For Russell, the very act of wanting—a natural component of childhood—was reframed to make him feel frivolous, superficial, and stupid. Not only did Russsell not feel understood, but he came to feel that he was *bad*, and he eventually assimilated his *badness* into his self-image.

Problems with Ideals

Is That All There Is?

Narcissistic individuals are guided by the responses of others—by external points of reference—so they may not even know or have developed their true self.

A characteristic aspect of narcissistic pursuit is the idealization of what is greedily wanted but not available: the perfect body, wealth or expensive objects, exciting new places to explore, and new sexual conquests. Obtaining such things is narcissistically gratifying and provides renewable pleasure, but the charm wears off the new thing almost as soon as it's obtained. What's left is disappointment, boredom, and the need to escape into new pursuits. "Is that all there is?" is a question frequently asked by narcissistic individuals.

Guided by their wants rather than their ideals, the narcissistic see themselves as being so important that they can break rules or obtain special privileges.

Such individuals have difficulty regulating their own feelings, self-image, and identity and have to rely on external regulators. They depend on others to give them what they themselves are lacking. Their sense of self is fragile, and when their self-esteem is damaged, as it often is, they react in extreme ways. For example, they may become perpetual plastic surgery patients in an attempt to be forever young, they may exercise incessantly, or they may search endlessly for a partner beautiful enough to reflect what they wish they might be.

Although they may feel as if they are playing a role, narcissistic individuals often conform to what they think others expect of them. They are so sensitive to the wishes and moods of others that they do not feel they exist separately. Their words and actions may have nothing to do with their feelings. Instead, their activities are frequently motivated by the need to be seen and affirmed by others.

It is not the desire to do things perfectly (which is itself unattainable) that frustrates and motivates narcissistic individuals. It is the lack of a standard with an attainable end point, an ideal. Narcissistic people do not have a consistent, stable model of who and what they are, a clear internal standard of what *good enough* is.

For several years, I have served as director of a program dealing with eating disorders. Of all the girls and young women with anorexia nervosa whom I have seen, not one of them had an end point in mind when she began losing weight. Each felt at the beginning that losing "about five pounds more" would make her happy and allow her to feel good about herself. When the loss of five pounds didn't bring happiness, maybe "five pounds more" would. There was never an end point, and besides, the emotional goal could not be reached by physical means. Yet each one was making a valiant effort to be effective, to control her life, and to become a distinct individual.

All Alone (and Exposed) at the Top

Spencer, a thirty-eight-year-old executive, was profoundly depressed. He had left three major corporate positions just before, or just after, a significant promotion, the last being to CEO. Spencer was avoiding, in each instance, the fact that success would not fill his emptiness and emotional neediness. He wanted to keep hope alive, to feel that he would meet these needs with just one more step forward, that he could eventually be effective in filling his emptiness by himself, in his own way. When he was promoted to CEO, however, he immediately realized that this was the top of the ladder and that all his accomplishments still did not supply what was missing. He could no longer hope that whatever was missing would come with his next promotion.

Spencer was very critical of his colleagues and subordinates. Hardly anyone lived up to his standards, except occasionally some idealized person who seemed to possess near-omnipotent qualities. Those Spencer chose to idealize were usually very distant in his life or unknown entirely, such as prominent national figures.

As critical as he was of others, Spencer was still more critical of himself. Nothing less than perfection would do.

In therapy, Spencer recognized how frightened he had become at the times when promotion was near. He was afraid of being inadequate to the new position and felt that something bad was about to happen. Something bad always did happen: Spencer would quit. Each time he rationalized that he needed more of a challenge, that he wanted new horizons and a new company. Inside, he feared that once he got to a position where he was a boss without a boss of his own, he and everyone else would know that he couldn't do the job.

Spencer needed structure, rules, and standards to guide him. Without external structure and a boss to report to, he felt lost. He wanted to avoid exposing himself completely until he was absolutely certain of the results; he wanted to do things perfectly from the beginning. And Spencer never felt satisfied. His success brought him no joy. He merely felt relieved that he could keep looking for his next job, the one in which he would be able to prove his worth.

Spencer's intelligence and capacity for insight were extremely useful in therapy. We discovered which of his assumptions worked and which ones didn't and enabled him to change the ones that didn't.

The Conquering Hero

Charles, a thirty-seven-year-old advertising executive, had put his marriage and his work in jeopardy many times through his addiction to sexual conquest. He stated, "I'm not sure I've ever related to women as people or to people in general as people. When I'm with a woman, what overshadows everything else is the aspect of conquest. It proves to me that they like me, that I'm valuable, that I'm worthwhile, or they wouldn't let me get them into that type of situation.

"At times I desperately want to be accepted. I think that's what I'm looking for from another person: that I'm okay, that I'm attractive, that I have the power to influence them to do what I want them to do. They're just a vehicle. In business, the person is the vehicle I use for the same ends: acceptance, power, recognition."

I commented, "We can both hear how much you want to be able to give that to yourself, to feel content inside."

He added, "Yes, I realize that in business I've tried to figure out what someone wants me to do and to do it. I haven't figured out what and who I am. I need to sit back and perceive what I need to be, rather than try to mimic what I perceive that I need to be. I need to be me, but I'm not sure what that is."

Charles had felt shunned by his mother and had remained angry at her for being absent or inattentive to his needs throughout his childhood and adolescence. A hundred women since have paid for her inadequacies. In therapy, Charles began to recognize that, from his mother's point of view, she did the best she could. Charles's father had abandoned her, and she had two children to support with two poor-paying jobs.

Charles came to see how he had disavowed his accomplishments and successes with the feeling that others didn't really know who he was. This split between his false self and true self paralleled the split between his supercharged ambition and his fuzzy internal ideals and goals.

I Need an Escape Hatch

Narcissistic individuals may reduce their efforts to achieve full potential by not being totally involved in an endeavor, always leaving themselves an escape hatch in work or in relationships. They can then blame failure on a lack of effort instead of a lack of ability and avoid the pain of failing after really trying. In addition, there's something pleasing about succeeding without trying very hard, a magical confirmation of power and brilliance.

This cycle has been discovered among college students who won't study for exams. Failing is due to lack of study rather than lack of ability, but if they pass without studying, they must be truly brilliant [Reference 7-2]. On the other side of the same coin are the students who want to know everything perfectly in all detail. If they encounter a question they can't answer, they feel inadequate and anxious and mentally paralyzed.

When More Isn't Enough

Many narcissistic individuals can function without compromising their work, using their skills to make reality conform to and confirm their sense of omnipotence. For these people, the external rewards are great. Because their self-esteem is so dependent on others' acclaim, a powerful position and possessions, they are tremendously motivated to perform and succeed.

These narcissistic *success hunters* have high ambition and grand ideas of success [Reference 7-3]. They are usually contemptuous of moderate salaries and unsuccessful people. They have a drive to overwork and are constantly tense inside and intolerant of passivity. Unless challenging new adventures lie ahead, they are bored and dissatisfied. They cannot relax. They worry constantly about maintaining the flow of ideas and opportunities. They ward off hidden depression with increased activity, which verifies their worth and importance.

The motto of narcissistic individuals is "No matter how much I have, it's never enough; I want more." Recognition of this lifelong hunger for more, better, greater, is often postponed until mid-life. When attainment of wealth, possessions, and position do not alleviate the feeling of emptiness and the longing for self-affirmation, the illusion that worth and value can come from outside the self is shattered. At this point, many narcissistic individuals may plunge into extramarital affairs, risky business deals, or make other attempts to grab the *more* they are missing. It is to be hoped that they will eventually realize change must come from the inside and seek treatment.

These individuals seek wealth and status to cure the wound in their self-love and to defend them against feeling helpless, small, weak, and insignificant. They see strength and power in the accumulation of money. Their feelings of dependency and sensitivity have to be well concealed so no one else will see. Perhaps to reverse their feelings of dependency, they like to have others dependent on them. They often choose dependent, submissive spouses.

The Great Impostor

People who never experience themselves as whole, separate beings—who feel that they're nothing without their spouse, job, title, position, or other source of external confirmation—feel despondent when they have no definite sense of goals, competence, or direction. They require constant approval from others. Thus some narcissistic individuals have a crisis at the time of graduation from college. The structured learning environment has provided feedback and external regulation, and graduation leaves them on their own.

Other narcissistic individuals feel they must conceal their excessive ambition. They cannot accept a compliment; when they're praised at work or their accomplishments are publicly recognized, they may either disavow the accomplishment or react, paradoxically, with extreme embarrassment or with depression, feeling depleted and empty rather than triumphant. The problem is a fear of isolation, a fear that other people will withdraw their positive responses if the accomplishment is too great.

Because all performance includes the risk of making a mistake (and therefore making the performer appear flawed), people preoccupied with the risk of failure develop a special inhibition about their work. They avoid situations in which success isn't guaranteed. They need to be certain that they can succeed, and succeed from the very outset. Their expectations and ambitions are so high they often reproach themselves bitterly for failing to live up to them.

They may pursue their ambitions to a certain point, only to pull back just before the moment of real testing. They may withdraw their applications to prestigious schools, for instance, for fear they'll be turned down; they may leave their term papers incomplete or miss their final exams.

Very often, these individuals will suddenly lose interest in something that had engrossed them completely. That's because their interests are aroused more by the chance of some narcissistic gain—say by the promise of an illustrious career or the admiration of others—than by any pleasure in the work itself.

Narcissistic individuals may view their difficulties as evidence of some grievous basic defect in their makeup they are powerless to remedy. They may also resent discomfort, including the discomfort that arises when a task presents difficulties. Their enraged response is that it isn't fair that they should have to put up with such problems. They appeal to fate, await outside intervention, or look for tricks to make the difficulty disappear. They want magic, and when they can't get magic, they get mad.

At the same time, narcissists deeply doubt their own abilities. They may feel that they've gotten ahead in business or in their careers by fooling people and regard themselves as impostors. Paradoxically, a genuine accomplishment can be unbearably embarrassing; limelight is too revealing for those who fear that it will only show their shameful flaws.

Mirror, Mirror on the Wall

A thirty-year-old woman consulted me several years ago for symptoms of anxiety and sexual dysfunction, along with some physical complaints that turned out to be hypochondriacal. As soon as we began psychoanalysis, the woman mentioned that she had been a model and that she had appeared in *Playboy* in college, something she did not mention during the evaluation. She was an extremely attractive woman who dressed and moved somewhat provocatively.

In the first session, she began almost immediately to describe elaborate and vividly detailed sexual fantasies of what she imagined doing with me. She wanted me to be involved, to feel as she did. She changed positions, from lying down on the couch to facing me as if looking in a mirror, to command my absolute visual attention. She was very hurt when I did not respond exactly as she wanted.

Although I was concerned about the rapid development of her erotic feelings, I tried to encourage her to expand beyond these fantasies into discussions of feelings, of earlier experiences, of her thoughts. But when I asked during silences what she was thinking or feeling or what she wasn't saying, she would prolong the silence.

I suggested to her that she was afraid of letting go and allowing what was inside her to emerge. At first I thought her responses represented defensiveness and resistance to being in analysis, to having painful thoughts and feelings emerge. However, the woman had interpreted my recommendation that she say anything and everything that came to mind as my need for dominance. She therefore withheld more and more.

When she began mercilessly attacking herself and her appearance and talking of plastic surgery, I realized that we needed to explore how she experienced herself in my presence and to investigate her self-image and body image. Eventually she described how upset she was when, close to her thirtieth birthday, she saw some slight facial wrinkling; she was worried about losing her looks, her only source of affirmation. She had been embarrassed to tell me about this during the evaluation and the first several sessions. But now the woman acknowledged her hunger for admiration and praise and her shame and embarrassment on receiving it, something that happened often because she was very beautiful. Because she regularly discounted the responses of others, all the admiration she received did nothing to alter her concept of herself.

We came to realize that she had no internal image, or picture, of herself. Unless someone else was responding to her or unless she was in front of a mirror, she felt a void; she felt nothing inside. Her search for human responsiveness was centered around her sexual attractiveness and the responses it drew from men. I then understood why she sat facing me the way she did, demanding my absolute attention, demanding that I feel what she did; I understood that these demands represented her unmet infantile needs for mirroring, for response and affirmation to form, define, and soothe the self.

The Skin Horse, speaking to the Velveteen Rabbit, best summarized the development of healthy narcissism: "Once you are real, you can't be ugly except to people who don't understand. Once you are real, you can't become unreal again. It lasts for always."

Are You Helping Your Children
Develop Healthy Narcissism?

The following questions have possible application for spouses, lovers, and bosses, as well as parents.

1. Do you listen empathically?

    "Is anyone really listening?" This is a central question for most of my teenage patients; adolescents, especially, feel helpless when they believe that important people aren't listening. Empathic listening means listening from inside someone else's feelings and experience in order to appreciate their viewpoint. Sensitive listening creates an experience of effectiveness, one of the most basic human motivations. Not being listened to empathically and feeling ineffective may result in attempts to be effective in extreme ways: through destructive and risky action, through the use of drugs or alcohol, through various compulsions. Empathic listening can be developed by listening to understand, instead of to fix, criticize, judge, or advise. At times, simply restating what someone says demonstrates that you are listening and that you understand the person's point of view, even if you have a different one.

2. Do you have realistic expectations?

    Some parents create an excessive burden by setting unrealistic standards for their children, by bragging about their children's extraordinary talent or requiring unrealistic perfection. Most parents, of course, overvalue their children's efforts and this is healthy and normal, but parents who expect greatness with each effort are unrealistic and maladaptive. When the rest of the world inevitably fails to agree with the parents' extravagant assessment, the children will, of course, feel disappointed and resentful. Like parents' lack of emotional involvement, inappropriate overvaluation is difficult for children to deal with, and both represent failed empathy. Overvaluation may doom children to difficulty in completing projects that require sustained effort and delayed gratification. Outside the home, such children soon learn that the work necessary to complete a project, and complete it well enough to be praised, will result in an intolerable delay in the positive response they require from others.

3. Are you emotionally involved and consistently enthusiastic?

The absence of parents' emotional vitality and praise, or even the absence of one or both parents during important phases of development, is for children like looking into a mirror and seeing no image.

4. Do you allow your child to develop self-functioning gradually and appropriately?

Ashley had just completed high school and was preparing to leave for college when her bulimia became so severe that she had to be hospitalized. Her family was very well-to-do and respected; Ashley described them as all-American, "like a fairy tale." She couldn't imagine why she had any struggles whatsoever. She felt curiously inept, unable to function on her own. She mentioned that her brother and sister had both had trouble leaving home, too. Her brother had gotten into drugs, and her sister had failed her first semester at college. Gradually Ashley became aware of how much her parents had functioned for her, never allowing her to do things for herself. She had not developed her own independent functioning, and her self-concept was woven throughout with her conclusions that she was inept and inadequate. Her parents had tried to provide their children with more than they had had themselves, to shelter the children from the hardships they had faced. They had, indeed, provided a fairy tale for their children, a fairy tale Ashley was having trouble exiting.

5. Are you urging your child, overtly or covertly, to fulfill your own ambitions or to follow in your footsteps?

Another source of trouble is the family constellation in which the child becomes a major source of fulfillment for one or both parents. The stage mother is an example. A child may sense the neediness of parents who use the child's accomplishments as a way of feeling better about themselves.

6.   Is your child taking care of your feelings or esteem?

In some families, children are saddled with the burden of keeping the parents together or trying to make angry or depressed parents happy. The children are in some way aware of the parents' needs even when the parents may think they are successful in hiding their turmoil. These children are parents to their own parents; they are so attuned to the feelings and needs of their parents that they fail to develop an autonomous self-image. They become people-pleasers as adults, seeing their needs only in relationship to someone else's. They learn to seek guidance, direction, and initiative solely from external sources. Disregarding internal signals, they invalidate their own perceptions and creativity.

8

Work Addiction

I know well what I am fleeing from, but not what I am in search of.

—Michel de Montaigne

One of the symptoms of an approaching nervous breakdown is the belief that one's work is terribly important.

—Bertrand Russell

Work addiction is an unrestrained, unfulfillable internal demand for constant engagement in work and a corresponding inability to relax. A person with work addiction, a "workaholic," is incessantly driven, relentlessly active. Work is the one organizing and effective activity. For some work addicts, inactivity or activity other than work gives rise to guilt, anxiety, or emptiness. Some individuals view work as the only area in which they can establish and maintain their identities, feel effective, and enjoy feelings of importance, validation, and affirmation. Others may use work to counteract underlying feelings of inadequacy and ineffectiveness. In either case, the workaholic cannot rest.

Working passionately, long and hard, and deriving satisfaction, does not make someone a work addict. An addiction is something one cannot do without. The person addicted to alcohol or drugs cannot do without them. The person who cannot maintain comfort or a sense of worth without working is similarly addicted. People with work addiction have to work constantly, even on weekends, and during whatever vacations they permit themselves. For these individuals, however, the relentless pursuit of work and the attainment of material gain do not result in pleasure.

Psychiatrist Jay Rohrlich has listed some criteria for defining work addiction:

- Awareness of an inability to control the desire for pursuit of work, even if there is a conscious desire to do so.

- Withdrawal symptoms when not working, such as anxiety, depression, or psychosomatic illness.

- Medical problems as a result of overwork, including physical deterioration from drinking alcohol, smoking cigarettes, overeating, skimping on sleep, and being prone to accidents.

- A breakdown in psychological or social functioning as a result of excessive work, including neglect of children or destruction of a marriage [Reference 8-1].

Like other addictions, work addiction affects the workaholic's social life and restricts his or her personal freedom and happiness. In fact, excessive work can be a means to withdraw from relationships, to manipulate relationships by limiting one's availability, or to regulate relationships so that not too much is expected.

Individuals who are truly addicted to work do not find great pleasure in the work itself. Work is done to avoid feeling bad and is motivated by a desire to be effective, to experience mastery. Like other addictions, work addiction is an attempt to regulate one's feelings and self-esteem.

Profile of a Workaholic

The Dealmaker

Mike (the middle-aged dealmaker introduced in Chapter 3, the man who couldn't relax) was afraid that he would no longer feel useful or valuable if he faced no immediate challenge or risk. Whenever he completed a major business deal, he quickly got rid of the money so he would have to start working on the next deal without delay.

"As soon as I achieve something," Mike said, "I lose interest, like I don't need it anymore. I constantly create new challenges. I used to work my ass off to make a deal, and afterward I'd feel horrible—guilty, empty, inadequate—like I needed to blow part of it. Whenever something good happened, I'd wonder when something bad would happen. I'll make half a million on a deal but focus completely on the lousy thousand dollars that I didn't make. That keeps me from enjoying what I do make. Making money is fairly easy," he added, "learning to enjoy it is what's hard."

Mike felt that he was always running from something. He recognized that he was afraid of failing. He was even more afraid of losing his fear, because he might also lose his motivation to succeed.

Although wealthy and respected in his field, Mike felt empty and unfulfilled. Anticipation of the next challenge did not allow him to enjoy his current success. "The thrill is in the struggle, not the accomplishment," he said. "I fear enjoying the present. If I did, I'd lose my ambition. If I'm not constantly getting laid or doing a deal, I'm empty."

Mike's handling of money mirrored this difficulty. He'd spend recklessly on gambling and recreational drugs until he was broke enough to feel worried and challenged again. This pattern ensured his continued addiction to work.

As a boy, Mike was alone much of the time and entertained himself. Both his parents worked in a family business, so he saw little of them during the day; at night, they often entertained business associates and customers. When his parents wanted to be with Mike, however, they expected him to drop everything and spend time with them. Mike felt that he existed only as an extension of his parents' interests and desires and that they never responded to his needs. When they didn't want his company, he didn't exist. As a child, Mike felt abandoned and unneeded, much as he felt as an adult when he completed a deal. His life represented a continual effort to escape from those early childhood feelings.

Mike also explored the overwhelming sense of guilt he felt with every major accomplishment. This guilt related to his childhood desire to outshine his father and to have a closer and more exclusive relationship with his mother than his father had. Unconsciously, he was impelled by this guilt to quickly disperse his profits and start over again. Overwork had become a sort of punishment to relieve his guilt over doing well.

Work addiction varies from one individual to another and can only be defined by analyzing each individual's motivation and intent. Work addicts do, however, have certain things in common. Charles Garfield, a psychologist at the University of California at San Francisco School of Medicine, did a fourteen-year study of workaholics. He concluded that they are addicted to work itself, not to the results of their work. They tend to be motivated more by fear of loss of status than by any desire to reach actual goals or to make a creative contribution. He found that, as time goes by, workaholics grow increasingly unwilling to be creative or take even necessary risks, favoring predictability and certainty instead. Typically they burst into their career as an *up and comer* but level off in their late thirties to mid-forties. Concurrent with the end of their career advancement, they often develop psychosomatic disorders, cardiovascular disease, marital turmoil, alcoholism, or drug abuse. Workaholics demonstrate high stress levels on every major index of stress.

In contrast to work addicts, the group Garfield classified as "optimal performers" have "warm, outgoing relations and a good collaborative sense, both personally and professionally. They surround themselves with people who are highly competent and to whom they can freely delegate. They don't work for work's sake. They work in order to achieve results. They tend to be lower than the norm on all stress indexes."

The Workaholic Workplace

Many businesses tend to create a kind of pseudoworkaholism among ambitious employees. An "office ethic" develops in which all supervisory personnel are expected to demonstrate daily that their jobs are the greatest priority of their lives. The effect on employees' family life can be the same as that of genuine work addiction. Unfortunately, workaholic workplaces can be found in many fields.

Same Bank, Different Scenarios

Anita, age thirty, was a pretty, soft-spoken bank executive with a gently humorous manner. She had worked her way up to a lower-middle management position in the regional office of one of the nation's largest and most aggressive banks. It employed many women in the middle-management ranks but very few at the more exalted levels.

Every weekday Anita got out of bed at 6 A.M., fed her nine-month-old son, breakfasted *on the run* with her husband, dressed in what she called her "lady banker's uniform" (tailored suit with soft blouse), began the commute from her suburban home to the child-care center and then to the office. Anita consistently arrived at work at 7:45 A.M., fifteen minutes before working hours officially began, and nearly always worked until 7 P.M. At any given moment, Anita's division was expected to complete several major and highly visible projects, each of them immensely time-consuming and each with a stringent deadline.

Despite her eleven-hour days, Anita's work practices seemed to match those of the "optimal performer" rather than those of the workaholic. She was warmly cooperative with peers, considerate of subordinates, and enthusiastic about her projects. She was also a loving and patient mother.

Anita's husband, an ambitious lawyer, would pick up their baby at the child-care center on his way home from the city so he could have some "time alone with my son." Anita would arrive home at 8 P.M. and have dinner with her husband, even if it was only *take-out* pizza. She then played with the baby for half an hour before putting him to bed. This *personal time*, however, was frequently interrupted by work-related phone calls from other managers at Anita's bank, calls nearly drowned out at Anita's end by her son's loud sobbing, which began whenever the telephone rang. Once the child was asleep, Anita and her husband would spend the remaining two hours until bedtime completing paperwork from their offices.

On weekends, Anita always worked four to eight hours per day at home on bank business. Her supervisor, Jennifer, worked even longer hours and expected Anita to do the same so that all the impossible projects would be completed on time, the division would *shine* for the higher executives, and they'd both perhaps earn promotions.

Anita longed for an on-site day-care facility at the bank but had no hope that one would be started before her son reached school age. She had expected to enjoy a dual career as a mother and banker, but her "banker's hours" made her nearly a stranger to her baby.

Sean, age twenty-eight, worked directly under Anita's supervision at the bank. His wife Nora stayed home to care for their daughter, who was one month older than Anita's son. Although Sean was warm and loving with his wife and daughter, he also found himself staying at the office well into the evening. Nora grew increasingly dissatisfied with her isolation, feeling she'd been left to care for their child alone.

Nora wanted to discuss Sean's long hours, his constant absence, his unavailability to her and their daughter, but he was rarely there to talk with. When he was home, he either fell asleep after dinner or shut himself into the den, poring over paperwork. Finally Nora walked out in tears, leaving the baby with her husband. In a deliberate attempt to force Sean to pay attention to her, she phoned him from a friend's house, telling him she would divorce him unless he promised to quit his job and find one with *normal* working hours. She wanted him to share in the responsibility of caring for their child and to go out with her and have some fun on Saturday nights. Sean immediately gave a month's notice and began job hunting, specifying at every interview, "I'll give you forty hours a week, a full forty hours of serious work, but I won't give you a second longer. My wife and daughter mean too much to me."

Before his month was up, Sean was offered a higher position at another bank. The situation at Sean's worksite was known to the personnel officers at other local banks, and former employees were considered desirable catches who'd been tempered in the very heart of the fire.

The Compulsive Achiever: Pursuit of Self-Esteem

At the bank where Anita and Sean worked, employees adopted workaholic behavior in the hope of professional advancement, a specific external goal. In contrast to pseudoworkaholics, who are pressured by external forces and pursuit of a concrete aim, many genuine work addicts are propelled by the wish for admiration and the pursuit of self-esteem. Immersion in work may be their compulsive attempt to reverse feelings of worthlessness. Enslaved by the drive to prove themselves powerful or even just adequate, their attention is constantly turned toward new sources of attainment and acquisition. Even when they've reached their vocational or financial goals, compulsive workers remain dissatisfied. Something is still missing; they want more.

People whose parents wouldn't or couldn't give them confirmation and approval for their childhood achievements often suffer in adulthood from an intense drive to attract as much response and admiration as possible, from as many sources as possible. This unrelenting ambition, the need for approval and validation, is the basis for many work compulsions.

Even remarkable success may not confer much enjoyment. Each accomplishment may lead only to a let-down feeling or even a depression, as if the real goal lay in pursuing the challenge rather than actually overcoming it. When a goal has been met, work addicts feel neither joy nor relief, and the excitement of the moment lasts merely a moment. The echoes of the applause have barely died before compulsive achievers begin to feel empty again. They need to find, instantly, a new goal to strive for, a new admirer to impress.

These are the narcissistic individuals described in Chapter 7; they have no internally regulated sense of self-esteem, and their point of reference is always someone or something external to them. They seek the admiring approval of others and hunger for affirmation [Reference 8-2]. They seek powerful, admirable people to mirror them and reflect their worth in order to feel complete, whole, and valuable.

They may be driven by the desire to be idealized by others. They're not interested in warm, intimate relationships but crave the dazzled approval an audience gives to an actor or actress. They feel alive only when they're receiving the confirmation of an admiring audience, whether it is employees, clients, lovers, or spouses.

For individuals who can't regulate their sense of self internally, work may become a central organizer in the same way that heroin is the central focus shaping the daily activities of the drug addict. One woman, a specialist in her professional area, used her work to repair the profound deficits in her self-esteem: "My work reassures me," she said. "When I feel overwhelmed, I turn to my work, which I know well, and I feel calmed. I became an achiever because it's something I could do that would exist in time and space and become objectively real. My work gives me pats on the back." She described how work lent continuity and stability to her life. With disruptions in her personal life, she immersed herself even further in her work to reestablish her internal sense of order. She didn't remember her parents ever holding or calming her; when she became upset as a child, she'd retreat to her room to furiously engage in her childhood version of "work."

Few work addicts are seen in treatment. Often they and others consider themselves successful as long as their accomplishments follow an ascending scale, and they receive substantial gain for their achievements. The tragedy behind these successful, hard-working, and aggressive people, is their relentless need to escape from their feelings of guilt or inadequacy. Attainment of a goal often brings a feeling of deprivation: Since love can no longer be earned by performing well, reaching a goal is deeply unsettling. Arriving at any goal threatens to crystallize feelings of unworthiness, non-productivity, and guilt.

Without therapeutic treatment, this basic scenario is re-created throughout the work addict's life. Although the names of the characters change, the same psyche is forever writing the script.

A work-addicted woman was described by her friends as follows: "She is so ambitious that one cannot help but think it is overcompensatory. I can't imagine her relaxed and trusting anyone. She is remarkably neat, proud, well-groomed, efficient, depend-able, and service-oriented. Sometimes in her enthusiasm and self-confidence, she does not realize that she has offended or used others. She is a person who tries to excel in everything she under-takes. As a person who never experienced failure or difficulty, she is not very sympathetic toward other students and at times is inconsiderate of them. She is obsessed with the idea of personal success and has spent her entire career obtaining it." [Reference 8-3].

Success based on perfectionism, relentless personal demands, and feared loss of love can provide external rewards, but only at disproportionate internal cost. Success is often an anticlimax for work addicts, who consistently feel frustrated by the small amount of gratification that accomplishment brings. Feeling nothing but disappointment, they may belittle an accomplishment, sensing that nothing can measure up to their grandiose ideals; anything they do is doomed to fall short.

Persons with a narcissistic addiction to work may feel a kind of boredom and uncertainty about their occupational identity. Work is valued only to the degree that it satisfies the deep desire for admiration. Because the needs fueling this desire are insatiable, workaholics are left with a constant gnawing feeling of failure and emptiness, together with an often inaccurate sense of inadequacy.

Some individuals with narcissistic problems are able to engage in active, sustained achievement as long as admiration consistently flows from others. They may seek a mentor—an older, admired, experienced adviser—who emanates the warmth and support necessary to sustain motivation. When narcissism is only a minor problem, this relationship and the confidence accumulating from accomplishments can be internalized to become a part of the individual. This bestows increasing independence from the need for applause.

With pathological narcissism, though, work may be superficial, with a lack of substance behind the glittering performance. Young geniuses who never fulfill their promise are examples, as are the people whose position, responsibility, and sphere of influence diminish gradually over the years. Recognition of this downhill trend may be difficult at any particular moment but quite clear over a decade or two of performance.

Using work to regulate self-esteem is itself problematic. A goal of perfection ensures defeat and disappointment. Perfectionists feel that if they're found lacking in any way, they're bad people, unlovable and insupportable. This all-or-nothing attitude turns a single mistake into a devastating event, as though every error committed points to some basic flaw. For perfectionists, merit is based purely on performance, not on the intrinsic value of a whole human being. Thus, no matter how well perfectionists perform, they cannot change their negative internal view of themselves.

As soon as work addicts succeed at something, they begin to doubt that they could do the same thing again. They can't enjoy their success for very long because of a gnawing fear that any moment they may lose their business or position. Then they need praise all the more intensely, to be reassured of their wholeness and ability.

Dancing For Daddy

Beth had been promoted to coordinator of the public relations division of a major corporation, a significant advancement in the accelerated career of this bright, engaging thirty-three-year-old woman. She worked twelve- to sixteen-hour days, feeling anxious and uncomfortable if she was not doing something *productive*. Even on weekends, she felt the urge to work, and guilt about relaxing. Her superiors praised her diligence, loyalty, and care. She enjoyed doing tasks with a clear and precise goal and relished having the structure to determine what *good enough* actually was, of having an end point to each task and praise for its completion. "Just tell me how to do it and I will" was her operating style.

After six years of zealous work, Beth was promoted to the managerial position she'd long desired but never actively sought. Here her desire to achieve and move ahead was countered by her fear of being exposed as inadequate, if she had to initiate and structure work for herself or for others. Pleasing others, working tirelessly, and attaining—with perfection—goals set by others, were not qualities she could use to inspire and manage others.

Beth faced an anxiety-provoking dilemma. She began to feel that her accomplishments were insufficiently appreciated and recognized by her bosses, but veiled her feelings of anger and worked even harder. She consistently felt inadequate and berated herself for feeling hostile toward her superiors and for not achieving more. No matter how much she achieved, she could never satisfy her perfectionistic ideals.

As a child, Beth experienced little overt warmth, love, or acceptance from her parents. Throughout her childhood, she tried desperately, although in vain, to win their affection and praise through perfection and desire to please.

Beth's father was very demanding, and he constricted the range of his daughter's interests to traditional feminine pursuits, extolling the virtues of a secretarial career. Despite Beth's unmistakable promise as a dancer, her father would not allow her to take a summer dance workshop for which she'd won a scholarship. But Beth's mother supported her daughter's wishes and took a job to pay for her transportation to the dance retreat, where Beth worked on her technique with utter dedication. Upon completing her rigorous training, Beth performed for her father. After a flawless, gifted rendition of a lengthy and difficult ballet, she turned to her father, expecting his praise. His only remark was "Don't you know any ballroom steps?"

Beth was first hurt, then angry. Only later, in therapy, did she recognize the intensity of the rage she felt toward this icy, perfectionistic father. She'd literally danced faster and faster for him, awaiting the applause that never came. In treatment, she was finally able to see her father more objectively, recognizing that he'd projected his own sense of inadequacy onto her and criticized her in place of himself. He had been more engaging and loving until Beth reached adolescence, when he withdrew. Her budding attractiveness as a young woman evidently made him uncomfortable, and he didn't quite know how to relate to his little girl when she wasn't little any more. Beth had concluded, unconsciously, that she was inadequate and unattractive, because the first man she loved apparently didn't see her as attractive or lovable at all. However, by all standards she was strikingly attractive.

Because Beth considered herself flawed and *bad*, she feared unconsciously that any man she'd come close to would see how she *really was*. She had a pattern of unsatisfactory relationships, including two broken marriages. Both had begun with a joyous honeymoon period, filled with idealism and hope. But the joy inevitably faded as Beth discovered each man's "fatal flaw"; both husbands transformed into critical, insensitive, self-serving people with only their own best interests at heart.

Beth's difficulties with her self-concept and self-esteem arose in part from her relationship with her mother. When Beth was a young girl, her mother interacted energetically with her—but only until Daddy came home, when all focus abruptly shifted to him. Beth's mother couldn't pay attention to her daughter's interests and needs because she felt unable to say no to the father, who demanded to be the center of her attention. She and Beth both believed that to oppose Daddy was to enrage him, a folly to be avoided at all costs.

Explaining her experiences to herself, Beth concluded that it was she who was not good enough or adequate enough to elicit the responses she needed from both parents. She escalated striving to be good into striving to be perfect. When this didn't work, she became depressed with a sense of chronic inadequacy. She restrained her assertiveness and retreated emotionally, dancing still faster, striving in vain for perfection. If Beth had stopped working for even a moment, she would probably have realized how angry and driven she was.

When she re-created with other important men her earliest relationship with her father, she was trying to right a traumatic wrong. Each man was unconsciously selected for certain characteristics; they were all older, handsome, intense, absorbed in their careers, hard-working, bright—and emotionally unavailable. Beth was trying to make her relationship with her father turn out right; each new edition of her father would seem at first to be caring, loving, admiring. But in attempting to master the hurt she'd endured passively at an earlier time, she only succeeded in replicating it through her choice of men. Beth was frustrated by the endless repetition of failed relationships and by the feeling that she was alone and unsupported, as she had been with her mother when Daddy came home.

Part of her problem lay in identifying with a mother whom she saw as limited, inadequate, passive, deferential to her father. She incorporated this identification into the way she saw herself, and she couldn't accept any information to the contrary. No amount of success would erase her unconscious vision of herself as incompetent. Her compulsion to work represented an attempt to reverse this vision, but Beth wasn't able to recognize the source of the problem until she entered therapy, because she had deleted it from her consciousness.

With treatment, Beth finally recognized and resolved those aspects of herself that had been so inaccessible to her. She could hold an accurate mirror to her self, her work, her womanhood. She became even more successful and finally happy in her career and enjoyed herself in her free time. In a letter about three years after her therapy ended, she described finding her "soulmate," contentment in a new marriage, and happy involvement in her career.

When the Workaholic Faces Mortality

Sometimes it appears that fulfillment and happiness lie in the attainment of a certain goal: making a million or more dollars, buying a certain house, getting a raise or promotion, earning a degree. Someone who is fortunate enough to achieve such a goal must then decide whether the goal is the answer. A degree, money, or an important position may not improve low self-esteem. That the emotional issues have to be addressed directly to find the answers is often one of the harsh realizations of middle age. The hope for "just a little more time" begins to fade when the number of available tomorrows becomes roughly equal to the number of yesterdays.

Addiction to work is frequently a way to fill emptiness and assuage loneliness. Changing a work pattern raises the question of what will make one feel full and complete. Relentless work may be an indispensable part of one's identity, the source of esteem and nurturance.

Those addicted to work sometimes suffer a depression in middle age, when they have to face the reality that future challenges and expansion will be limited. The limitation may be in the domain of work itself, or physical illness may remind us of our powerlessness in the face of ultimate mortality.

The Impostor at Work

The impostor phenomenon describes those who feel like fakes despite outstanding business, academic, or professional accomplishments. The sense of having fooled everybody persists, despite the objective evidence of their achievements. The young doctor in Chapter 4, who felt like a "quack" when he had to lecture at his alma mater, was suffering from the impostor phenomenon.

People who feel like impostors may work incessantly, fearing that if they stop, slow down, or relax, all their basic inadequacies will be exposed. One study discovered that a number of women who suffered from work inhibition in established careers felt like impostors [Reference 8-4]. They were sure they were missing some critical virtue and imagined they were inadequate. Worse yet, they were certain their success resulted not from having skill and knowledge, but from being born to do their particular job. Few of these women were able to enjoy their success; it made them feel too powerful, controlling, and competitive, and they viewed competitiveness as taboo.

Many of these women felt conflicted about surpassing their mother, who seemed to them weak, passive, and "only a woman." In short, these women felt inferior because they were women. They downplayed their success in several defensive ways: They attributed it to accident, they worried that they'd be discovered as impostors, or they disassociated themselves from their achievements in a variety of ways.

Roland was a young physician board-certified in family practice. Despite a booming practice and the apparent respect of his colleagues and patients, his anxiety level was dangerously high, and he could never relax. He had accepted so many referrals that he was physically unable to keep up. He was afraid that if he refused a new patient or a referring physician's request, his practice would suffer and his referral sources would dry up. If his waiting room was less than packed, Roland panicked and resolved to build his practice even more.

He feared his patients would discover that he was an impostor, that he didn't really know as much medicine as they thought he did. Despite his having passed the rigorous examination for board certification and despite his ample continuing education, he still felt inadequate and worked harder and harder to try to escape his sense of unworthiness.

Eventually Roland could no longer sustain the pace of his twenty-hour workdays, and he began taking amphetamines for extra energy. Facing a state medical board review, prompted by a concerned colleague's report, Roland entered intensive treatment. There even more problems were revealed. Roland had not only become addicted to amphetamines to sustain his energy but also used painkillers and sleeping pills to relax and ease the depressing crash that follows an amphetamine high.

Roland's treatment consisted of a brief hospitalization for detoxification, followed by an intense therapy. For almost two years, twice a week, he made the two-hour drive to Houston for two back-to-back psychotherapy sessions. Finally he was able to resolve the unfinished business from his past and settle into a comfortable work and family life. He has now developed, in addition to his practice, an educational program for impaired physicians.

Work Addiction: Self-Evaluation Questions

Change begins by looking at things in a different way. Consider the following questions in relation to your work and your feelings about your *work identity*.

1. Do you have a specific time when your work life stops and your private life begins each day? Each weekend? For vacations?

2. When you leave work in the evening, do problems, projects, calls, appointments, and meetings follow you home and erode your private time?

3. Has anyone close to you ever accused you of being a workaholic?

4. Have you become creative in rationalizing your excesses, perhaps by convincing yourself that success demands a dedication bordering on obsession and fearing failure if you do anything less?

5. Can you not seem to stop replaying conversations at work, reassessing decisions, and reexamining work details?

6. Is what you do who you are? Is your identity as a person so closely linked to your work identity that it is difficult to enjoy an activity not connected with work?

7. Do you take setbacks, feedback, or criticism of work projects personally?

8. Are you still trying to prove your worth to yourself, or someone else, by what you do? Do you believe that only unending effort will demonstrate your true value?

9. Are you doing what you do for someone else's response, or for your own benefit and satisfaction of your own ideals?

10. Is work an escape? Does it allow you to fill a void or get out of doing something you regard as unpleasant, such as meeting family obligations or facing family conflicts?

Some Remedies for Work Addiction

- Establish a clear boundary between your work life and your private life: each day, each weekend, and for designated vacation periods. If you feel guilty or vaguely uncomfortable with taking time off or relaxing, consider reframing the time, even the play, as a necessary component of your work. In order to be maximally effective when you are at work, making time for a private life and for play is crucial. I so enjoy my work that it would be easy to extend my day beyond 6:00 P.M., but my secretary knows that she should not accept late appointments. I return calls on my car phone on the way home; when I am home, I am 100 percent present. Setting and respecting this boundary allows me to be 100 percent present for my patients during the day. I do not plan any meetings or accept any positions that require me to be away in the evenings. I want to be at home with my children in the evening and do not wish to have any regrets about missed experiences with them when they are grown.

- Even though you may enjoy and feel rewarded by your work, play is equally important. Creativity, which can be nurturing in itself needs time to ferment, develop, and expand. You may even find it useful to set aside a brief time at the end of each day to allow closure of work activity, to have an official transition time that puts a period at the end of the sentence of each day so that time off is really time off.

- Establish your own game plan on a daily basis, as well as the *big picture* on a yearly and career-long basis. Keeping a journal may be useful. Writing down your thoughts, feelings, plans, and timetables regarding work can clarify things and may provide a basis for reflection and comparison from year to year.

- Distinguish the feedback, criticism, and setbacks on work projects, as relating to the work itself, the task you've performed. Try not to hear them as a personal attack or personal invalidations.
- Develop your emotional, interpersonal expertise as well as your technical expertise. Both can be finely tuned. Consider, for example, when different listening positions may be most effective. At times a colleague or employer may need your empathic ear; at other times an objective, even confrontational position may be needed.
- Know the difference between thinking, feeling, and imagining, as opposed to acting. Physical action is not the only form of doing something; thinking and contemplating are active forms of *doing something*. This distinction may seem obvious, but it is not clear in the minds of many people. For example, a patient may come in and want to know what to "do" about her depression. There is no immediate thing to *do*; we must begin by understanding and resolving the emotional issues that underlie the symptom. The patient's own failed attempts to approach the problem actively, to apply willpower and the like, provide ample evidence that another approach is required.
- Reassess the amount of time you spend talking about your work with family and friends, and the amount of time you spend associating only with friends from work or people in the same line of work. Obviously people who care about each other are interested in all the things that are important to the other, including work. But, being caught up in *war stories* may represent an inability to establish boundaries for work or an overinclusive identity with one's work.

9

Why Managers Fail and Succeed

Wisdom is learning what to overlook.

—William James

Tell a man he is brave and you help him to become so.

—Thomas Carlyle

The effectiveness of any business is determined by the leader's personality, the extent of the leader's expertise, the adequacy of the business plan, and the human and material resources needed to carry it out. And, of equal importance, the ability of the administrative structure to the requirements of the task [Reference 9-1]. What concerns us here is the leader's personality.

Personality Styles of Leaders

The leader's lack of technical knowledge, conceptual limitations, or incapacity for administration or an improper fit between personality and administrative style may all create problems for an organization. However, an extreme personality style forces the organization to adapt in ways that may affect its success [Reference 9-2]. The three most common extreme personality styles that can create problems in an organization are the narcissistic leader, the authoritarian leader, and the emotionally isolated leader.

The Narcissistic Leader:

Because narcissistic individuals are often driven by an intense desire for power and prestige, they may assume positions of leadership and authority. They are usually hardworking, highly intelligent, talented, and capable in their field. However, individuals with more pronounced narcissistic needs may dramatically compromise their creative potential and that of their organization.

Extremely narcissistic individuals may be excessively self-centered. Their overvaluation of themselves may manifest itself in grandiosity, which serves to cover their feelings of inferiority, and their overdependence on external admiration. They may be emotionally shallow, intensely envious, and deprecatory and exploitative in their relationships with others.

One of the most professionally devastating features of narcissistic individuals is their inability to evaluate themselves and others in depth, partly due to a lack of capacity for empathy and a difficulty in connecting emotionally with other people. Their need for affirmation and feedback demands that they surround themselves with individuals who will confirm their view, praise, and idealize them. True judgment of both personality and business is therefore difficult.

Seller of Illusions

A man I'll call Mason founded a company based on direct sales of personal products. Over only two or three years, he signed up many thousands of direct-sale members nationally. His company's rapid growth was due primarily to Mason's own charismatic appeal and to his ability to attune himself to his sales force's grandiose fantasies of unlimited wealth.

In order to study such an individual and the phenomenon of his success, I attended the company's national meeting during the year of its most startling growth. It was an inspiring and emotional event for all those who attended. Their sense of unity centered around the expectation of unlimited financial opportunity.

The plans for expansion seemed to me particularly grandiose at the time, even considering Mason's rapidly rising fortunes. He spoke of building an entire town, a college, a medical center, a small universe with his name stamped on all of it. Equally remarkable, as I observed on examination of the corporate structure, was that he would not allow the formation of a functional board of directors. He made all of the decisions and selected as subordinates people who "shared the vision," who literally idolized him. This very narcissistic leader had created a system with no checks and balances, and he had no way to receive any input or opinion from anyone other than those who agreed with him.

Some ten months after this national meeting, the organization was bankrupt.

Mason's reach had far exceeded his grasp, for all the reasons mentioned above. Tens of thousands of direct marketers across the country simply could not understand how or why the bankruptcy had occurred so quickly. The main reason was that Mason had surrounded himself with yes-men and individuals shrewd enough to play to his narcissistic needs. More honest and critical members of his staff were pushed away to become silent and dissatisfied opposition or to leave the organization entirely.

Mason's ability to judge people in depth and to appreciate true human values was a critical (and massive) blind spot; his view of others was based on their ability to reflect his own opinions and views. He surrounded himself only with people similar to himself, like standing in a hall of mirrors.

In the short run, Mason's grandiosity and expansiveness could be transmitted throughout the organization as a charismatic excitement, bringing an initial spurt of productivity. In the long run, however, his pathology brought about the organization's rapid deterioration. Although many of the characteristics that Mason demonstrated may exist to some degree in other situations, his personality and style illustrate dramatically the fatal weaknesses that may take much longer to develop in other organizations and with other leaders.

Narcissistic leaders require submission from their staff, as well as their love and idealization. They crave unconditional, repetitive expressions of admiration, which may become a requirement for communication with them. Their tolerance for unavoidable, everyday frustration is low. Meanwhile, the wish to be admired for personal attractiveness, brilliance, and charm exists alongside an intolerance for the success of others, if it overshadows or threatens the narcissist's own. They may become resentful of the most creative or productive members of their staff. When a younger colleague develops professional autonomy, a previously supportive narcissistic leader may begin to devalue or undermine the colleague's work.

The Authoritarian Leader

Some leaders have an obsessive-compulsive personality that translates into an excessive need for order. They must always be right and always in control.

These traits make for efficient organizational functioning. No one ever doubts that there is a leader who is in control, which can be very reassuring. But if these traits are extreme, the inordinate need for orderliness and control may reinforce the bureaucratic components of the organization and encourage decision making on the basis of regulations and mechanized practices. An overly rigid bureaucracy may interfere with the creativity, expansiveness, and autonomy of decision making, which is especially likely to cause problems at times of rapid change or crisis.

The Paper Tiger

After graduating with honors from an Ivy League college, Mara was hired as associate editor of a national magazine. The salary was modest, but the job seemed to offer tremendous opportunities. On Mara's first day at work the editor who hired her, took her to meet the owner of the company. His name was listed as publisher on the mastheads of the four magazines the company issued every month.

Mr. B. remained seated at his giant, polished desk as Mara was introduced, and he then asked the editor to leave. Alone with the young woman, Mr. B. looked over her resume and transcript with a sneer, then stood up to speak. "I see you're an educated woman," he said. "Well, to me, you're just a paper tiger, I'll tame you soon enough! You've got your fancy degree and I've got a seventh-grade education, but I'm forty-seven years old and I've already got more money than you'll make in your whole life."

A few months later, Mara was performing her job competently enough that the editor arranged for her to receive a raise. At this point, Mr. B. swooped into the editorial offices during the frenzied final afternoon of editing, just before the corrected galleys were due at the typesetter, to demand that Mara drop her work and run his personal errands for several hours. This apparently was a longstanding pattern in which Mr. B. tried to force the staff into missing their deadlines. They would then have to put in unpaid overtime to catch up, or he could unleash a barrage of criticism on them the next day for failure to meet the deadline. The editor, accustomed to this behavior, was silent. When Mara protested, Mr. B. only laughed at her and repeated his "paper tiger" epithet.

After the third *deadline day* interruption in as many months, Mara spoke to the head of the secretarial pool, a formidable woman who was greatly feared by her subordinates. Her perfectionistic criticism of their work was constant, and she had a caustic response to even a minute's tardiness. When Mara asked if the pool could spare the most junior typist to run Mr. B.'s errands on deadline day, the head secretary responded, "This office worked perfectly well before you came, young lady, and it'll work perfectly well after you leave. Any changes made here will have to be made over my dead body."

Both Mr. B. and his head secretary operated with similar authoritarian personalities within an authoritarian organizational structure. Although Mr. B. had won great financial success, he was so envious of those who had obtained the education he lacked, that he felt compelled to attempt to humiliate them. The head secretary resisted any changes in her normal routine and guarded jealously the modest power of her position. The self-esteem of both Mr. B. and the head secretary rested on the fear and submission they evoked from others and the control they were able to exact. Paradoxically, they had come to love being hated, as if being hated was an emblem of their power.

The Emotionally Isolated Leader

These leaders isolate themselves from other executives in the company, frustrating the appropriate dependency needs of executives and workers. One result is various *pairings*, or the formation of small groups for mutual support and understanding. Each of these subgroups may have its own agenda and ideas, creating particular difficulties for each corporation.

An adaptive evolution in this situation is a manager or executive who acts as a warm and compassionate buffer between the cold CEO and the rest of the company. This more open and responsive person functions in a nurturing capacity so workers and managers feel listened to. Sometimes the buffer actually supports the organizational structure rather than splitting or undermining it.

Subordinates' predictable response to an aloof, isolated CEO is the development of fantasies about him or her. The distance between the CEO and the employees is filled with all sorts of notions about the CEO, simultaneously an idealized version and a critical, judgmental, and stern version.

An Arabian proverb says that every man in his life should be able to plant a tree, write a book, and have a child. Translated in terms of an executive's functions, the planting of a tree might represent productivity and building new things; the writing of a book, the creation of new ideas and knowledge; having a child, the development of an organization's human resources through the encouragement of individual growth and the development of gratifying relationships in the process of productive work.

The Most Common Managerial Problems and Some Possible Remedies

The following is a distillation of several studies of management and managerial success and failure. Although there are real, external reasons for managerial failure or difficulty—including massive reorganization after takeovers and the realities of discrimination due to age, sex, and race—managers fail most often for reasons they themselves create [Reference 9-3].

These reasons include excessive narcissism and self-interest, an inability to get along with subordinates, the fear of action and of failure, and a failure to adapt to change and rebound from setbacks. With only slight modifications, the context of the following remedies can be changed to any executive function, including being an employer with one employee (and even to being a parent).

Excessive Narcissism and Self-Interest

Individuals with an excessive need for positive feedback and a preoccupation with themselves quickly alienate colleagues, superiors, and subordinates. Others with strong narcissistic needs may require the enthusiasm and idealization of others. If you fall into this category, you may try the following:

- Reframe statements about personal glory and accomplishment as if they are organizational glory accomplishments.

- Use the words *we* and *us*, instead of personal words like *I* and *me*. Caution: For this to work, the change in terminology has to reflect a change in attitude. You have to become an authentic team player.

- Instead of demanding recognition and affirmation from colleagues and subordinates, develop other ways to address these needs. Other groups and endeavors outside your professional arena, as well as your family, may better meet these needs. If expanding your scope isn't enough, seek therapy.

- You must be able to be wrong all alone and be successful as part of a team.

- There is a thin line between self-absorbed narcissism and charismatic leadership, often bridged by thinking systemically of the group or organization rather than "I", and supplying to others the very feedback most wanted by yourself: affirmation, recognition, praise.

Inability to Get Along with Subordinates

Authoritarian leaders may have an especially difficult time inspiring others, creating a sense of loyalty, and establishing cohesive teamwork. Many experts in the field view poor interpersonal skills as the single most frequent factor in the failure of managers, especially early in their career. This is a crucial area. Some guidelines to follow are:

- Develop the ability to listen well. Invite feedback and criticism, then listen carefully, attentively, without interruption, and without the need to feel defensive.

- Remain empathically attuned to subordinates. Listen to them, to their experiences, and realize how they may hear what you have to say. Anything you say is already in the context of a superior-subordinate relationship, thus, they may be inclined to hear it more critically or harshly than you intend.

- View conflict and differences of opinion as something welcome and inevitable rather than as something bad that must be quashed.

- Involve subordinates in decisions to develop a *we* and *us* feeling. For group cohesiveness, they need to consider themselves part of the group effort. Elicit new ideas and cooperation.

- Give them credit for their work, and subordinate credit for yourself to the credit of the group.

Fear of Action and Fear of Failure

Some executives have difficulty putting themselves on the line, their ideas, or their position. An emotionally isolated leader may retreat just when he or she most needs to proceed. Fearing failure or significant criticism, such a leader may lack commitment or fear action. The underlying assumption of such managers is that their inaction prevents mistakes in management. In actuality, this practice may hasten the leader's downfall.

- Accumulate as much data as possible, but plan a time when data collection will stop and action will begin. Some individuals will study something so exhaustively that they bypass deadlines needed for action.

- Separate, as much as possible, personal assumptions and fears of failure from the organizational task at hand. Recognize that inaction is a form of failure; know when action is required. A ship is safe in a harbor, but ships aren't made to sit in harbors.

- At times, it may be useful to consult with someone outside the system who can be objective and observant.

Failure to Adapt to Change and Rebound from Setbacks

Life is a developmental process; so is the life of an organization. What worked at one stage may no longer work. A once-successful management style or strategy may have to be changed as an organization grows and evolves. Flexibility of thought and action is especially important for managers in companies that have restructured or been acquired. It is essential that they not be rigid or cling to old management styles in a rapidly changing environment.

- Be sure your management style and approach fit with the organizational task and your level of responsibility. For example, the individual who moves from a creative or entrepreneurial task to the management of people doing similar tasks needs to adopt a different approach to work.

- Acknowledge a failure, and request understanding and help in rebounding from it.

- Do not become defensive at criticism or feedback, but welcome it; cooperative input is vital in a rapidly changing environment or company. Don't try to conceal failure or blame it on others. The way one handles failure is an issue that may make or break an advancing career.

Creative Criticism

If you want to know how you're doing, you might ask subordinates to evaluate your performance in an anonymous questionnaire. You may be uncomfortable with such direct and explicit feedback, but it can be immensely useful. Subordinates are uniquely situated to experience, observe, and evaluate their bosses.

The areas of evaluation might include leadership, organization, crisis management, facilitation of cohesiveness, and even inspiration. Since the evaluations are confidential and anonymous and since no pay raise or promotion depends on them, you might not wish to share them with anyone else.

Being able to give such feedback, knowing that a superior is interested and that their comments may be effective, helps workers feel more involved in their company.

Problem Solving

A systematic method for reviewing and solving problems can be remembered by the acronym SOLVE:

S   State the area of the problem as specifically as possible.

O   Outline the problem in as much detail as possible: where, when, how, who.

L   List alternatives. Write down the first ten solutions that come to mind without analyzing them. Then select the three best solutions, which are the ones that recognize your limitations (and don't create them) and that organize a focus.

V   Visualize the consequences. This visualization should incorporate a good bit of your interests, abilities, personality style, and values with your problem-solving approach. The alternative that feels best—the most comfortable—may be the best. Plan a strategy to achieve the specific goal. Gather information from experts if necessary, but develop your own plan.

E   Evaluate the results after a full effort at problem solving. If there has been a failure, evaluate the most common causes of failure: a wrong fit between one's work and one's abilities, interests, and personality style; too scattered a focus; an absence of commitment; confusing discomfort about being in unfamiliar territory; and hidden barriers, such as a conscious goal in opposition to an internal model.

Remember: There are few true emergencies. Unlike coaches, you have as many *timeouts* as you need. Whenever you sense that emotions are rising and objectivity is needed, call a timeout. A coach will call a timeout when a key player seems to be angry and may respond impulsively, when the team is in jeopardy, or when it needs a change of pace or strategy. Simply removing yourself from an overwhelming situation for a brief time can be important, so you can calm down and become objective.

Section II

Money

10

Money Meanings and Madness

A man's treatment of money is the most decisive test of his character—how he makes it and how he spends it.

—James Moffatt

When you're rich, they think you really know.

—Tevye, in *Fiddler on the Roof*

The word *money* has an incredible number of synonyms. For instance, *Webster's New World Thesaurus* notes that money is "(a medium of exchange) gold, silver, cash, currency, check, bills, notes, specie, legal tender, Almighty Dollar, gravy, wampum, shekels, dough, long green, coins, lucre, folding money, wad, bucks, hard cash, bread." *Roget's Thesaurus* adds several less common monikers for money: roll, jack, rhino, blunt, dust, bawbees, brass, dibs, mopus, tin, salt, chink, oof, spondulics, pile, pin-money, doit, stiver, rap, mite, farthing, tester, groat, mint, and plum, among others. And appropriately enough, Rodale Press (publishers of organic gardening guides and natural foods cookbooks) lists in *The Synonym Finder* these additional synonyms: chickenfeed, peanuts, small potatoes, cabbage, lettuce, spinach, kale (and several other natural foods), plus simoleons, mazuma, pelf, scratch, loot, and do-re-mi.

The Last Taboo

The objects that usually collect the most slang synonyms and euphemisms also arouse our strongest and most confused emotions. In this regard, money is clearly in a class with sexual acts and excretory functions.

Some folks call it loot, some folks call it honey,
Some folks call it bread, but everybody calls it money.
But I can't get enough
Enough of that long green stuff . . .

—Chester Arthur Burnett
(Howlin' Wolf)

Terminology aside, the reality of money is itself complex. Does it represent present value, downside risk, a stream of payments, future value, potential gain, security, freedom to buy things when needed, cash flow, assets, debt?

A therapist once wrote, "Money questions will be treated by cultured people in the same manner as sexual matters, with inconsistency, prudishness, and hypocrisy." The year was 1913. The therapist was Sigmund Freud. Over three-quarters of a century later, many of us can talk comfortably about sex yet remain embarrassed if we have to deal openly with money. We have been raised in a culture that is fascinated with money but that considers personal discussions of money, fees, and income inappropriate in social situations. Money may be the last taboo [Reference 10-1].

Money is treated in some families as secretly as sex is in others. When children are given little real information about such "secret" matters, the vacuum of actual fact is rapidly filled by fantasy and myth. Just as children pick up all sorts of distorted and value-laden misinformation about sex, they also accumulate myths about money; for instance, the feeling that money, or a desire for it, is dirty or bad. Children who continually hear how troublesome money is and who never hear anything positive about it, are getting confirmation of this fantasy. Children who are never allowed to handle money lack information about what money really is.

Naturally, the myths that children learn affect their attitudes toward money once they become adults. Miserly parents, for example, often produce children who are either scrooges or spendthrifts.

Parents are often secretive about their income. A poll of 20,000 people revealed that half had never discussed finances with their parents and that almost two-thirds of the parents had never revealed their income to their children [Reference 10-2]. Among the people polled, 57 percent felt it wise to conceal their income from both family and friends.

Children in such families never develop a realistic picture of money to replace that widespread early-childhood fantasy that their parents are incredibly rich and are simply withholding money or toys out of sheer meanness. One of my patients recalled being very curious about how much money his father made. He asked on numerous occasions but never got an answer. The unspoken message was that money is a deep, dark secret that makes people so uncomfortable they cannot discuss it openly.

It Must Be Very Bad

Sharon, a young professional woman just discovering the financial realities associated with beginning a practice, was reflecting on her own conflicts and questions about money. She indicated that her mother and father were always worried about money when she was a child, so she was also worried and confused. She never knew quite what was the matter, but she knew that her parents were frightened about debts, money inadequacies, and the uncertain future. She would snoop through the drawers of her father's desk in an attempt to figure out what was making her parents so concerned. Her parents' attitude about money and their reluctance to pay for even small things worried Sharon a great deal; she was sure they must have a very large problem. This experience carried over into Sharon's adult life. If she had financial problems, she would cut expenses, including food purchases, just as her parents did, until things evened out.

Sharon saw much later that her parents were always concerned about money because her father frequently overextended himself with substantial investments and large purchases. Despite his substantial income, the family was always financially stretched. Sharon now recognizes significant discrepancies, such as her mother's purchase of a $50,000 ring and her father's overspending to the point that, not only could they not travel, but they had to worry about monthly necessities.

Her parents continue to try to alarm Sharon about finances by talking about all the taxes they owe. Her mother goes over the will with her periodically to indicate the proper value of all their possessions.

Children sense their parents' attitudes toward money: their comfort (or discomfort) in dealing with it; the importance and symbolism they bestow on it; their comfort in talking to the children about it; how obtainable and sufficient it seems; and how they regard people who are richer or poorer than they are. Children fashion their attitudes from these observations. The parents' ability to empathically perceive and discuss their children's point of view, as well as their own, is as important here as it is in dealing with any other aspect of life. Children gradually learn the limitations of money, the pleasure of getting and having it, and what money will buy (and what it won't buy), as well as experiencing the consequences of their own effort and work.

Children often conclude that things treated secretively and uncomfortably are taboo. Their unconscious equation of money and evil can create a lifelong legacy of discomfort. Even when children grow up and know better intellectually, they may still subscribe to that archaic emotional equation. One of my patients is a forty-four-year-old venture capitalist who said it bothered him to devote his entire day to making money since he felt that money was the root of all evil. His ideas were contradictory; he consciously wanted to succeed, yet despised and unconsciously feared one of the products of success.

The Reality and the Symbol

The Reality

Money has two basic meanings. The first is purely realistic: Money is a medium of exchange. Everyone needs money to purchase essentials, material comforts, and other important tangibles, along with such intangibles as *lifestyle*. Money is a unit of agreed-upon value that is exchanged for goods, services, or time. Money is money.

When we look at money simply, we begin to see the complexity of the meanings that have become attached to it. As a store of value, it represents one's work, but it is not the work itself or even the internal value of the work. It's intrinsically bound to work, however, and is an important symbol of the work one does. For instance, a physician's income may symbolize the many years of education his or her work requires and the status it confers. People who are bored with their job commonly figure the price of a luxury purchase in terms of the hours of tedious work that the price tag represents. ("Hmm, that dress equals nine hours of pounding on a typewriter.")

In reality, money in itself can't make dull work enjoyable or creative. It can only make it tolerable.

The Symbol

The second aspect of money is its symbolic value. Perhaps more than any other facet of contemporary life, money carries massive emotional meaning. Only food and sex compete with money as magnets for such strong and diverse feelings.

This second function of money is difficult to grasp. Although society does add some metaphors of its own, money's symbolism is very subjective. It's woven into our personality, out of our own life history, sensitivities, experiences, possible internal conflicts, emotional needs, and our basic sense of self. Some of its meaning is unconscious, outside the realm of intellect, reason, and logic.

Money may represent self-esteem or the esteem of others, power or impotence, innocence or sophistication, fear or security, love, control, dirtiness, freedom, status, sexiness, immortality, or a host of other things. The issue of money may quickly spark insecurity, panic, lust, envy, guilt, depression, or ambition. For those who are insecure, competitive, or prone to worry or fantasize on a grand scale, money is always a reliable object to focus on.

The more money symbolizes our unfulfilled needs and desires, the less it satisfies us. When our unconscious motivations oppose our conscious intentions, we face serious threats to our well-being. The inappropriate use of money, the inability to acquire money to one's full potential, and the inability to enjoy the use of money are only a few of the consequences.

The Self-Made Bear

Joseph was a sporadically successful stockbroker whose erratic career had corresponded not to the ups and downs of the stock market, but to his own succeed-and-retreat pattern. He said, "I don't feel worthy to make money. I don't feel good enough."

Joseph indicated that one of his current difficulties was that he tended to undercut his own commissions. He said that he lacked the final closure instinct with every customer.

"Price doesn't sell stocks, stories sell stocks," he believed. Joseph's stories usually centered around his lack of enthusiasm for his work. He felt that, because of his failing marriage, he didn't have any way to get charged up after talking to his clients; making cold calls was especially depleting. Joseph's marriage did not provide him with emotional refueling, nor did any success in his work or relations with his customers. He had felt emotionally depleted for some time before he entered therapy.

Joseph felt bad about making money when it was so "preposterously easy," before the stock market crash. He had made so much money from some accounts that he didn't feel he had worked for it.

Another aspect of Joseph's difficulty may say a great deal about the value of seeing real, tangible, immediate results for one's work. In Joseph's previous firm, he was paid on the same day he sold a block of stocks or bonds. The relationship between work and reward was immediately obvious. In his current firm, on the other hand, he would turn in his commission slips for reconciliation at the end of the month and be paid the first week of the following month; the time span between a sale and the monetary reward was thus a month or more. Joseph needed a more immediate response to keep up his excitement.

What Money Does and Doesn't Buy

Money can be a potent catalyst for ambition and work, or an obstacle to them. But what money really means to each person is seldom clear. Its *magic* arises from our unconscious needs and perceptions. The way we handle money may symbolize fears or beliefs that have nothing to do with finance itself.

Net Worth

Society tends to encourage the use of money as a measure of human value. Thus the pursuit of money may come to seem more important than the pursuit of life.

Contradictory ethics make the issue of money very confusing. On one hand are the altruistic, selfless, humanistic, self-sacrificing values of the Judeo-Christian ethic, which teaches that the odds of a rich man getting into heaven are less than those of a camel getting through a needle's eye. On the other hand is the acquisitive, individualistic ethic of capitalism, which is predicated on money. In our society, therefore, money is both worshiped and condemned. People with a great deal of money are regarded with awe and esteem; those who openly lust for money are considered tasteless, vulgar, even disgusting. We may simultaneously view money as secular (evil, taboo, the all-or-nothing of early childhood) and divine (good, omnipotent, the magic of early childhood).

Although money may not bring happiness, the lack of it causes vast unhappiness. Carl Sandburg once wrote, "Money buys everything except love, personality, freedom, immortality, silence, peace."

Wealth and money may create their own pathology, according to Lewis Lapham in *Money and Class in America* [Reference 10-3]. Money may also be the attempted cure of pathology.

We often confuse what money is with what it can do. *How much money is enough?* can be answered only by identifying tangible goals, only by clearly seeing what it can do and knowing what you want.

Freedom

Money, a tangible commodity, doesn't buy intangibles, such as freedom. Yet at some point, no money does mean no autonomy. Money doesn't buy internal freedom, but it certainly can purchase external freedoms, especially from those tasks that others are hired to do.

Many people fantasize that limitless wealth would solve such problems as daily boredom, a sense of emptiness, and feelings of deprivation left over from childhood. In short, people imagine that money will compensate for their lack of internal freedom. But when they contemplate the amount of money they would need to *buy happiness*, they frequently fall prey to envy and greed. Paradoxically, the more money that comes in, the less satisfying it is. Some people continue trying to accumulate more no matter how much they have. Others may recognize, finally, that what they really need more of isn't money at all.

> *When should one change his mind*
> *And jump the fence for the dollar sign?*
> *It's a sad thing, it's a bad thing, but so necessary*
> *That this cold world holds your values*
> *To become monetary.*
> *Now, what is success?*
> *Is it doin' your own thing, or to join the rest?*
> *And if you truly believe, should you try over and over again*
> *And live in hopes that some day*
> *You'll be in with the winners?*

—Allen Toussaint

In our society, we usually have to grapple alone with our individual conflicts about money. We rarely examine or resolve its personal meanings. Even hiring a financial adviser usually does not address the emotional issues that influence the way we make, save, spend, save, invest, and enjoy our cash.

When money represents power to an individual, it can be used in an effort to compensate for feelings of inadequacy and helplessness. But in the end, a symbol is only a symbol and not the real thing. Many people become disillusioned in midlife when they realize that whatever wealth they've acquired has not brought them the freedom, happiness, self-esteem, or emotional comfort they expected. When confronted with the symbolic meaning of money and the realization that they have not purchased happiness, people often consult with a therapist. They need help coping with disappointment or disillusionment over what the success doesn't mean, what it cannot change, or what it cannot do.

People also sometimes feel guilty about being paid to do things they really enjoy, even when their work is highly valued by the person paying for it. They feel virtuous only when they hate their work or when their tasks are rigorously demanding or intolerably boring. Such people, when extra money comes in unexpectedly, may spend it quickly on a whim. People who win a bet, for instance, often rapidly lose an equal amount. For such people, an increase in income may be accompanied by feelings of disillusionment or guilt.

Love is a Verb

I don't care too much for money,
Money can't buy me love.

—John Lennon
and Paul McCartney

Perhaps the thing that money symbolizes most commonly is love. Children who do not receive enough love to nurture their growth and sense of internal value may, as adults, attempt to compensate for a poor self-image with an abundance of money. Money becomes the currency of caring, of adequacy and worth. The child's need for something intangible and uncontrollable, like his parents' unconditional love, has shifted to a desire for something concrete and controllable.

Money can be accumulated, but love can't. Money can be dealt with directly and tangibly, asked for, manipulated. Cold, hard cash can be used to satisfy a craving for warmth. It's easier to obtain and manipulate money than to acquire an elusive and intangible sense of worth.

I said, "Tell me baby, face to face,
How could another man take my place?"
She said, "Money honey, money honey,
Money honey, if you wanna get along with me."

—Jesse Stone

Your parents don't like me because I am poor,
They say I'm not fit to be seen by your door.

—Traditional ballad

And Cupid is always a friend to be bold,
But all of his arrows are pointed with gold.

—Glen Ohrlin

If you've got the money, honey, I've got the time.

—Lefty Frizzell and Jay Beck

Money can't buy love, get that through your head!
'Cause it's gonna be lonesome on a certain side of your bed.

—Roy Brown

The emotional meaning of money frequently spills over into apparently nonemotional arenas. For example, requesting a bank loan may evoke a fear of personal rejection rather than the impersonal suspense appropriate to a business transaction. Buying money from a bank is different from buying any other product from any other kind of seller. Borrowers are often so relieved to have their loan request granted that they accept any conditions the bank dictates instead of negotiating for the most favorable terms. It's hard to do business well when feelings of personal acceptance or rejection accompany every deal.

Chapter 11 (no pun intended) deals with compulsive spenders and compulsive nonspenders. Both problems are based in the same issue, the equation of money with love.

Power

Almost everyone equates wealth with power and aims for both in fantasy and work. The process of equating wealth and power starts in childhood. Very small babies have a great deal of power; their cries swiftly bring food, comfort, cuddling, clean diapers, or whatever they need. Healthy, beloved infants rule their world.

Small children are less mighty than babies. They are still relatively helpless, but they no longer have infinite power. However, they come to believe in the omnipotence of all grown-ups (especially their parents) and try to reestablish their own power by identifying with the adults around them.

The ubiquitous fantasy of immense wealth—and thus of unlimited power and freedom—is a feature of our childhood desire to restore infantile omnipotence. The basic aim is to acquire not just power but an uninterrupted positive self-regard. Power and worth can both be represented by money. Money becomes a yardstick of achievement, indicating the degree to which power and respect have been attained, making worth tangible and countable. When money symbolizes power, it's associated with control, order, and responsibility.

Your mother she's an heiress,
Owns a block in St. John's Wood.

—Nanker Phelge, as sung by
The Rolling Stones

The rich are different in some ways, and their children face problems and benefits different from those of children from families with less abundant financial resources. Once vast wealth has been acquired, it takes on the symbolism of status, social importance, and often competitiveness. It can also shelter children from the normal process of learning through frustration and error. Philip Slater, writing of wealth, points out, "One of the main reasons wealth makes people unhappy is that it gives them too much control over what they [don't] experience. . . . Learning and growth are very difficult with wealth because they depend on experiences in real life, and wealth enables one to buy out of life." [Reference 10-4].

Psychiatrist Frank S. Pittman III studied children of the rich and concluded that money was, at best, a mixed blessing [Reference 10-5]. He discovered that, although many more rich kids are high achievers, a significant number of rich kids are functionally incompetent.

Could I Have Made It on My Own?

Children with trust funds, in particular, may be crippled by the knowledge that their future living is guaranteed and therefore they need not do anything. Moreover, those who inherit or receive money from trusts at age eighteen or twenty-one do so at a time when they have not yet developed their own full identity [Reference 10-6].

Inheritance of money at an early age may therefore disrupt the consolidation of identity and autonomy and undermine motivation and ambition. On the positive side, inheriting wealth allows a moratorium before full commitment, a time to establish satisfying lifework [Reference 10-7]. In *The Republic*, Plato indicated that those who inherit wealth are often less interested than others in making money and can pursue more important matters.

John rose to a top managerial level in the multinational corporation that his father founded. The division John headed had done extremely well under his guidance. One day he spoke of his decision to continue in the family business: "There are advantages in so many ways, it would have been stupid for me not to have gone into the family business. But the one thing I'll never really know is if I could have made it in some corporation other than my family's."

Individuals who have gotten rich on their own are often competitive in their family life as well as their business and may be impatient and intolerant of anything less than remarkable success in their children. Many of the super-successful fathers of rich kids became rich by ignoring their family and their own emotions in the single-minded drive to make money.

People who create wealth sometimes try to make up, both to themselves and their children, for what they themselves did not have earlier. However, giving a child all that the parent did not have may disrupt development of the child's mastery and self-esteem.

The Principle, Not the Money

Rebels are those who seem to thrive during economic downturns or when the odds are most strongly against them; for them, adversity is a challenge and obstacles are a stimulus. One study of the personality traits of successful *maverick* entrepreneurs concluded that their independent urge had roots in childhood [Reference 10-8]. Their emotionally charged relationship with a father who constantly criticized or competed with them developed into an attitude of defiance and a compelling need for independence and success. These same attitudes also disinclined them to submit to any authority (such as a boss), and they would often get fired, thus explaining in part why they became independent entrepreneurs. Another motivating factor, especially among minority and female entrepreneurs, was discrimination. Most of the successful entrepreneurs were not motivated by money but by the desire to build a successful and esteemed company or organization. The passion to achieve allowed these individuals to focus on a goal and pursue it to a successful conclusion. Another study of successful entrepreneurs found that the key motivator was not acquiring money or love, but acquiring respect and admiration [Reference 10-9].

What Does Money Mean to You?

The following three pages are designed to help you reflect on your feelings about money and perhaps to crystallize some of the things money means to you. After you fill out these three pages, set them aside and come back to them in approximately a week. Actively raising these issues will stir your conscious and unconscious mind. Therefore, during the week, you will undoubtedly continue working on these exercises in various ways, including while you are sleeping and dreaming. These exercises may look or feel somewhat different when you reassess them.

Money Exercise

List the following for yourself:

1. My current income:_____

2. My anticipated income for the next five years: _____
    _____
    _____
    _____
    _____
    _____

3. The yearly income it would take for me to be happy financially:_____

4. What I would like to do with additional money:_____
    _____
    _____
    _____
    _____
    _____
    _____
    _____
    _____
    _____
    _____
    _____
    _____
    _____
    _____
    _____

Money Exercise — Page 2

Spend three minutes writing every word, phrase, image, feeling, and experience that the word *money* brings to mind, and define what it means to you.

Money Exercise — Page 3

Spend three minutes writing anything and everything that comes to mind about your childhood experiences, attitudes, and ideas regarding money. Include what money was, what it wasn't, what you heard from your parents, your fantasies about it, how much you thought you'd have when you grew up, what you thought you'd do with it.

11

Understanding Money Symptoms

*The price we have to pay
or money is sometimes in liberty.*

—Robert Louis Stevenson

*The cost of a thing is that amount of life
which must be exchanged for it.*

—Henry David Thoreau

A financial adviser once observed, "Many people don't seriously want to make money, or they wouldn't keep making the same errors in their investments." He suggested that investment mistakes arise from a lack of clearly established goals. For some individuals this may be true, but for others, psychological barriers keep them from making, keeping, or enjoying money. No one consciously intends to lose money or to make bad deals, yet some people may have an unconscious need to lose money. Naturally, these losses create frustration and a sense of futility, especially after arduous conscious efforts to make money.

When we are able to recognize the emotional entanglements that prevent us from making reasonable money decisions, we can often confront and conquer them. The emotional problems most common in money acquisition and management fall into three categories: autonomy struggles, fear of wealth, and risk taking. Money addiction, a related issue, is the topic of Chapter 12.

Autonomy Struggles

Various money symptoms fall into this category: compulsive spending, competitive spending, compulsive shopping, compulsive bargain hunting, revenge spending, compulsive refusal to spend, and autonomy worship.

People who fear autonomy may reveal their phobia in various ways, such as wanting someone to take over and make decisions, refusing or being reluctant to assume full responsibility for certain aspects of one's life, or creating crises (including financial crises) from which they must be rescued. The fear of autonomy may also manifest itself as its apparent opposite, *autonomy worship*, featuring the person whose life is governed by a driving need for independence from other people's demands.

All of us have mixed feelings about autonomy and have dealt with them at some time in our development. But unresolved problems with autonomy can create financial havoc in adulthood.

Having somebody else take over and make important decisions may mean, emotionally, that somebody loves and cares about you. If you are good at handling money or are financially independent, you run the risk of forfeiting someone else's taking care of you. Women are especially likely to struggle with this issue. Psychologist Adrian Berg stated, "Women for whom financial care equals love will see their own financial competence as a disastrous loss of femininity." This problem also extends to men.

Please Take Care of Me

Bob, a young geologist, became interested in investing some of his money after a promotion left him with some extra cash for the first time in his life. He discussed his situation with a neighbor and soon received a phone call from the neighbor's friend, who wanted to offer some "investment advice." This friend of a friend enticed Bob into buying into a limited partnership that owned 250 movies to be shown on cable TV, offshore oil platforms, and home video cassettes. Bob bought in for $17,500, some of which he borrowed. Not until he'd laid down the cash did he learn that the movies he'd purchased were old Z-grade features, unpopular with audiences, poorly marketed, and utterly worthless as an investment.

Examining his important and expensive lesson, Bob discovered his underlying wish to be taken care of. "I unquestioningly trusted the neighbor's friend who brokered the deal," he said. "I was essentially telling him, 'Please take care of me, I'm a novice investor.'" Bob examined the assumption that had worked well for him in his original family, his job (in state civil service), and his marriage: If he worked hard and did all the "right" things, he'd be treated well, be looked after, and have his needs met. In the world of finance, of course, this assumption simply didn't apply.

By recognizing that his assumptions had lost their usefulness, Bob was free to choose another, more rational path. He decided to learn about investments instead of relying on "free advice"; he took courses in money management and consulted a professional financial planner about the more complicated areas of finance.

Compulsive Spending

Some people spend money to fill their loneliness and emptiness and to contain anxiety, in much the same way that other people compulsively eat or drink. None of these behavioral attempts to ease emotional pain has any permanent effect, however, because they don't address the real cause of the distress. The pleasure of spending may actually eclipse the pleasure in the items or services purchased. For example, the seemingly unlimited spending that a charge card offers (equaling emotionally unlimited love) is especially tempting, even if the items impulsively purchased with a flash of the plastic seem useless once they're out of the bag at home.

Proof of Worth

Barbara, thirty-eight, was recently divorced with custody of her two teenage children. She lived on a fixed, barely adequate salary and small child-support payments. Nonetheless, she went on frequent spending sprees. When she felt lonely or depressed, she would purchase an extravagant item or two. One day she bought a $250 silk blouse, a $175 silver key ring, and some $825 diamond earrings. These were hopelessly out of her grasp economically, but feeling worthless and devalued, she used the external compensation of "high-class" purchases to create the illusion of her own worth. Barbara's emotional needs were so great that neither reason, nor willpower, nor a budget, nor credit counseling, nor a financial planner, succeeded in changing the pattern. Only in psychotherapy was she able to understand and resolve the internal conflicts and the emptiness that hitchhiked on the issue of money.

A compulsive spender may also be driven by a sense of inferiority. Some people compulsively spend their way into self-inflicted poverty so someone else will have to take care of them. Their return to dependent status usually reinstates a relationship with a relative or friend which seems outwardly to stem from economic need, but is inwardly rooted in an emotional need for nurturance.

He'll Rescue Me

Shannon, a twenty-seven-year-old, unmarried woman, came to therapy with Bert, her forty-year-old, cocaine-abusing boyfriend. She was depressed and intensely confused about their relationship. A wealthy man, Bert essentially kept Shannon as his mistress, although he was currently unmarried. He dated her exclusively and supported her in many ways.

Shannon described her depression and discontent with her life. She felt ready to break away from this boyfriend to be emotionally and financially independent, but she was frightened because she did not know who she was or in which direction she was going. She described feeling empty inside, angry at those who had not done things for her. Her desire, her compelling urge, was to spend money—usually on expensive food, wine, jewelry, and clothes. The desire was not for having the items themselves but for spending the money. The act of spending gave Shannon a feeling of worth and pleasure, but it was only a temporary high.

Shortly after the first two evaluation sessions with this couple, Bert decided that therapy, especially couples therapy, was not for him. Having to come and talk about their relationship was the impetus Bert needed to go his own way.

When Shannon and Bert parted, she felt an intense urge to "go into a store and get something new—even some little thing like a silver bracelet or T-shirt—but just to buy something new." She ended up charging $600 to buy a shirt, jacket, belt, shoes, and earrings at a store where she and Bert had shopped. She said, "I wanted to go in there and believe that I could still go and spend money. At the moment that I was purchasing those items, I felt powerful and confident. A few moments before that I was feeling depleted and completely without power. When it first hit me— what I had done—was when they gave me the sales receipt. It was like reality hit then. I was nervous about it then and still when I came home." She described imagining that Bert would think she looked fabulous in the outfit and that he would have to get her out of the bind.

Shannon's compulsive spending had the intent, at one level, of reestablishing the relationship with Bert. She stated, "I had to get back with him to get him to bail me out. If everything else failed and I had to go back to him, I would just have to go back." We further discovered that she had spent just enough so Bert would have to help her out; juggling her credit cards, she could manage by herself a maximum of $500.

Shannon regarded her spending as an addiction. Sometimes, instead of going home to face being alone and feeling depressed, she would try to think of things to buy. At other times, when another person was not around to enable her spending addiction, she would create a situation of risk, of unworkable financial disaster, and figure out how to get out of it. She felt sneaky and guilty, yet excited and powerful, about this risk-taking.

Competitive Spending

Red-hot spenders with a flagging sense of self-esteem are trying, publicly, to buy their own worth. Competitive spenders use money to measure social prestige and compete by outspending others in their social group. They spend money, not for enjoyment of what they buy, but for the acclaim or admiration of others, and they require an audience to witness their lavishness. They may make a great show of picking up the check for guests at an expensive restaurant or may give money to organizations that publicize the larger monetary gifts they receive.

For generations, the paunchy, aging, overgenerous "sugar daddy" with a young girl hanging on his arm has been a familiar cartoon figure in virtually every men's magazine. He's an object of ridicule not only because of his irresistible urge to spend in public but because his choice of what (and whom) to spend it on guarantees that he'll be repaid in the false coin of insincere flattery and feigned sexual attraction. He's considered comical because he's attempting to buy something that is far superior when it's free.

Compulsive Shopping

Some people are addicted to shopping binges. Compulsive shopping is a specific form of addiction, a pattern characterized by a compelling urge to buy items, usually clothes. There is usually no real need for buying but rather an acute awareness of an empty feeling and an emotional craving for connectedness with someone [Reference 11-1].

Compulsive shoppers never have as much spending money as they *need*. They spend everything they make, sometimes going deep into debt, as if there are no boundaries or limits.

I Never Had Plenty

After her parents' early divorce, Brittany found herself with several sets of parents in a very extended family. During Brittany's early childhood, her mother felt especially sorry for her daughter, mostly out of guilt about the divorce. Projecting her own emotional needs onto Brittany, her mother gave her things to make up for the lack of an intact household. Brittany's father, on the other hand, was strict and restrained, both emotionally and financially. Brittany's small allowance from her father was constantly (and secretly) augmented by extras from her indulgent mother, aunt, and grandmother and later from her guardians.

When Brittany wanted to buy something, she could intuitively find the soft spot in one or another of her many parental figures. At the same time, however, none of these people really made Brittany feel like a special person, an individual. They were indulgent but not demonstrative; all of them were more comfortable giving Brittany things instead of attention, empathy, or physically expressed affection. She felt consistently depressed and wished someone would hold her, hug her, wrap her in their arms.

Only through extreme behavior could Brittany get someone to respond to her and make her feel real. As a girl, she repeatedly ran away from home, hoping someone would come after her. She felt alone and lonely. Simultaneously, she wanted her own space, but that space never seemed clearly outlined and distinct to her. She felt either smothered and encroached upon or lost in boundless nothingness.

Brittany learned to spend all the money she had, as this practice was certain to bring her more money. Her need thus took the form and substance of money; it was tangible and real, something people gave her to show their love. She never learned to tolerate the frustration of delayed gratification or of choosing between two possibilities, and she never learned that money could be saved for future use. She developed little capacity for imagining the future; she didn't need to.

As a freshman in college, Brittany felt depressed and bewildered, longing for the unconditional love that she'd never possessed. She sought to possess tangible things to make her feel better. "I'd feel empty, frantic and frenzied, and would feel an urge to get something new, something more," she remembered. "I never thought I had enough, I never thought I had plenty. I would jump up and run to the mall to buy clothes."

Brittany's excitement and pleasure from the act of spending far exceeded her actual need for or enjoyment of the purchase itself. Her charge cards gave her relatively unlimited spending power, and she would borrow from her several "mothers" with no intention of repaying them. She was remarkably attractive and found that men were willing and eager to buy things for her and loan her money. She chose to buy things that she imagined would enhance her beauty and desirability, such as clothing, jewelry, and beauty treatments. Spending money as if there were no limit made Brittany feel that she could have anything and everything she wanted; it was the same blissful, powerful feeling she had when she went on eating binges.

She'd feel happy and hopeful as she bought a new outfit, something new and different that no one had seen her wear before. She really hoped that her new clothes would change her, that each new purchase might bring the answer to her insatiable hunger. "I need something tangible," she explained. "I can hear but not fathom the concept of love. If I can touch or grab it, it's something." She favored big, bulky clothes in sensual fabrics, which stimulated her skin and made her feel "outlined" and thus more real. But the good, hopeful feelings that new clothes brought lasted only until she wore the clothes the first time; as soon as the price tags were gone, so was the feeling of happiness.

In addition to denying her emotional poverty with spending binges, Brittany had a rich fantasy life involving unlimited wealth, power, attractiveness, and response from others. She tried to fill her emptiness with food and compulsive sexual activity, in addition to shopping. Like purchasing clothes, sex was immediate, focused, not at all vague. And it brought her affirmation about what a superb sexual partner she was. She described herself as always giving, always listening, not seeming to have needs of her own but always pleasing her partner. She hoped to someday find the magic partner, the one who would give to her. She was, understandably, quite popular, but neither her ever-new wardrobe nor her sexual generosity attracted that one magic person who would forever make her feel good.

When she was younger, her mother would buy her clothes whenever Brittany felt bad. Later her guardian, Marian, would take her shopping and buy her as many as a dozen outfits in a day. "We'd buy whatever I wanted," Brittany recalled. "Marian set some limits—for instance, no more than $3000 for me on a trip—but if I really wanted something, I'd beg her and she'd say okay." When Brittany asked Marian for spending money, her guardian would tell her "Just take the highest bill from my purse." Both Marian and Brittany enjoyed reading mail-order catalogs and meticulously planning, matching, and ordering items. When Brittany asked Marian's husband, Pete, if he ever got frustrated with Marian or with her for spending so much money, he answered, "No, I married her knowing that she would do that, and I want her to do it." One day Brittany asked Pete for $10 for gas money, and he handed her a $50 bill.

It seemed that everyone in her disconnected family participated in keeping Brittany from discovering her own boundaries.

No limits were set for her, so she never discovered the limits to her. Little wonder that she longed desperately to be held, hugged, and embraced. She craved not only this tangible, undeniable demonstration of love but also the feeling of having her physical boundaries defined by an embrace.

For Brittany, clothing was a concrete way of being held, just as food was a symbolic nurturing, and she binged on both in an effort to regulate her moods. Her family encouraged her in this: Her mother and then her guardian bought clothes to comfort her until shopping became for Brittany a souvenir of mothering comfort. Spending money was a way of giving to herself, of feeling reconnected to a mother who gave her "love" in a similar manner. Brittany's clothes were a fashionably tailored version of her earlier security blanket and carried the same emotional magic.

Compulsive shopping represents an urgent attempt to confirm that parents or spouse are giving of things; spending money becomes an emblem of love. At a deeper level, it is a demand, even a retaliation, that insists the parents or the spouse pay for not giving needed emotional responses. Thus compulsive shoppers are not unlike small children who steal from their mother's purse to get something tangible from her.

The parents of compulsive shoppers often view things and money as the currency of caring, as a way of expressing love. Frequently, this is how their own parents expressed love. The pattern for compulsive shopping often begins in adolescence as parents attempt to alleviate their guilt for leading busy and involved lives away from home, or as they try to maintain an emotional bond with their children. They may give cash or credit cards to their children as a means of enhancing dependency.

By the same token, adolescents may overspend in an attempt to get even with neglectful parents, as well as to fill an emotional void. The overspending serves to attract the parents' attention, albeit punitively.

The following is a typical sequence of impulsive buying:

1. The urge to buy usually occurs after a rift in a relationship with someone important. The individual who is vulnerably reliant on the responses of another experiences this disruption as an internal emptiness.

2. He or she feels the urge to fill this emptiness with something real, tangible, concrete.

3. He or she narrows the focus of what is immediately wanted, perhaps to clothes.

4. The impulsively bought item is usually self-enchancing, as clothes are, to make one attractive and desirable.

5. The individual loses sight of the big picture, of what can be afforded, what is needed.

6. The impulsivity constricts focus, so the thinking is "If I don't get it now, it won't be available."

7. Justification of the purchase inevitably ends in "I just want it, to hell with anything else."

8. Consequences—such as affordability, budget, payoff, and debt burden—are not considered.

9. Afterward, when the items are in hand, the individual feels guilt or shame.

10. Only then is affordability considered, but the individual often requires help or rescue by someone and the reestablishment of a dependency bond.

Compulsive Bargain Hunting

Some bargain hunting also involves compulsive spending for the sake of the bargain rather than the desire for what is purchased. The penguin character in a "Bloom County" comic strip felt compelled to take advantage of the *bargain* offered on late-night television and ordered not just one slicer-dicer-ricer machine but a dozen cartons of them.

For many bargain hunters, the act of purchase represents a battle with the seller, a narcissistic illusion of triumph. The item is bought, not out of need, but in an attempt to defeat and outsmart the seller; thus fulfilling a need to feel special or favored. Edmond Bergler, who has analyzed a number of bargain hunters, found that they have in common a constant need to outsmart others; yet, by their behavior they unconsciously provoke feelings of disappointment through their apparent defeat of others, perhaps repeating a childhood disappointment [Reference 11-2].

The bargain hunter aims at one level to outwit the seller in order to get something (an unconscious substitute for the love or attention that would have been squeezed or cajoled from others in the past) for a bargain price or for nothing. Getting things for less than others might, as if one has been treated in a special way, is accompanied by a feeling of dominance or superiority.

One example of extremism in bargain hunting occurred during the era when savings banks offered "free gifts" with every new account. In one extended family of four middle-aged sisters, these "free gifts"—ice chest, thermos bottle, barbecue implements, and desklamp—were rotated from sister to sister every Christmas and birthday. The sisters had been impoverished during childhood and considered their adult relationship "close, giving, and warm." This was less a case of compulsive spending than of compulsive refusal to spend, even though the real costs in terms of the time and inconvenience of opening and maintaining half a dozen minimal bank accounts were probably higher than the actual value of the gifts.

By saving money, compulsive bargain hunters may be saying that they can survive and compensate for deprivation in other aspects of their life.

Revenge Spending

Lisa was a self-confessed "catalog addict." Coming home from work, she looked forward to browsing through the pile of catalogs the mail carrier dropped on her porch daily (they wouldn't all fit in the mailbox). She preferred ordering her purchases by mail to shopping in person, explaining to herself that catalog shopping used less of her valuable time and offered lower prices than the department stores. In addition, she often couldn't remember what she'd ordered from which company, so when the packages arrived they seemed more like presents than like purchases, giving her Christmas every day.

Lisa was most likely to actually order rather than just "window shop", immediately after a quarrel with her husband, Jack. The couple quarreled frequently, and many of their arguments centered on money. Lisa considered Jack tight-fisted and selfish, and Jack viewed Lisa's spending as irresponsible.

Lisa could not tolerate arguing as long as her husband. He seemed to draw energy from his anger as the argument went on. When the quarrel had gone on too long for Lisa, she would simply withdraw, not conceding, but simply bowing out and postponing the outcome for another day. Going directly from quarreling to defying Jack by ordering, gave Lisa distinct pleasure. It was her way of saying "My desires count too," or perhaps "You ought to send me a dozen roses after that fight, but since you're not going to, I'll just send myself a new dress instead."

Although she was aware that she often spent money unnecessarily, Lisa had no conscious desire to change the pattern that continued to afford her the pleasure of revenge. Spending money was an indirect way of expressing her present anger at her husband and her unresolved past anger at her parents.

During her childhood, she'd received a weekly allowance somewhat lower than other neighborhood children her age. Her parents had grown up during the depression, and although they had become fairly comfortable financially, they continued to worry about their financial future. They explained to Lisa that they were "saving it for your college education" or "saving it for our retirement," explanations that seemed to Lisa like thin excuses for withholding the things she wanted now. They also demanded to know exactly how she'd spent each week's allowance, and they maintained strict control of larger purchases, such as clothing and toys, by buying things for Lisa but not with Lisa. "When you make your own living, you can buy what you want and do what you want," her mother told her. "Until then, what we say goes."

In adolescence, rebelliously impatient to separate from her parents and their control, Lisa first engaged in revenge spending with the money she earned from summer jobs. She enjoyed buying her own clothing, jewelry, and cosmetics in styles and colors her parents found "trampy." Her parents loved classical music and had insisted that Lisa take piano lessons for four years; they finally gave up in the face of her stubborn refusal to practice and her deliberately nerve-shattering renditions of their favorite sonatas. Just after high school graduation, Lisa's summer job gave her the money for her most cherished (and expensive) purchase yet: an electric bass guitar from a pawnshop. On it she played rhythm and blues, the music she preferred. Even when she was an adult, just picking up the guitar evoked pleasurable memories of her adolescent self, of using her own money to assert her right to be herself.

Women may be more likely to enjoy revenge spending than men. The limits on assertiveness that women often learn in childhood may keep them from carrying an argument to its conclusion, and their premature withdrawal from conflict often leaves unexpressed issues and residues of anger that will later (or almost immediately, in Lisa's case) be expressed indirectly. Furthermore, during adolescence, girls' behavior and appearance are usually more closely supervised than boys'. A girl's choice of *trendy* or *sexy* clothing, jewelry, and cosmetics is often in direct opposition to her parents' more conservative tastes and fears that their *baby* will present an unvirginal image.

If this interaction is conflictual, it may produce a rebellion that persists into adulthood and contribute to an association between buying clothing and freely expressing adult sexuality.

Even after the advent of the women's movement, many women have a genuine need to assert and reassert their entitlement within their marriage. A husband's hobby equipment may seem to him, no matter how expensive, more justified than his wife's least costly small luxuries. As a boy he may have received any "educational" or developmental toy he asked for, while his mother made sure he knew that she was sacrificing her own desires to buy things for him. He may continue to assume in adulthood that men are more entitled than women to spend money on themselves, even when a wife contributes equally to the family budget. Thus a husband may actually be "tight" about his wife's spending and loose about his own, and his wife may feel a compulsion to spend more on herself when she feels that her husband is invoking these unfair limits on her freedom.

Men, too, engage in revenge spending. A man may buy himself an expensive piece of recreational equipment, or even deliberately blow some of his paycheck at a bar to express anger at his wife—especially if he's angry because she's just bought something for herself. Unconsciously, he may be trying to exact revenge for the childhood deprivation he experienced from a withholding mother. Or he may be seeking indirect revenge on a withholding or disapproving father when he indulges in some long-desired and not really affordable purchase, minutes after a fight with his male boss.

In both men and women, revenge spending differs from competitive, *show-off* spending. Revenge spending is often carried out very quietly and privately as a form of secret self-indulgence, a gift to oneself from a "secret admirer."

Compulsive Refusal to Spend

I Can't Part with My Good Friend, George

Stephen made enough money as an accountant to maintain a good standard of living, but he was overcome by such an inner fear of economic insecurity that his ability to spend money comfortably and reasonably was deeply inhibited. He tried to combat his fear by combining a minimal, subsistence level of spending with a maximum rate of saving. Still, he didn't feel satisfied and continued to worry about his finances beyond any realistic point. This pattern had afflicted him for most of his thirty-four years.

Stephen's life and pleasures were equally constricted. He was cautious about dating too much and especially too extravagantly. He spent considerable time hunting bargains and used much of his free time repairing his own home and car so he wouldn't have to pay someone else to do it.

He occasionally deprived himself of things he needed, which he could certainly afford, and he actually regretted each dollar he spent, as though it were a departed friend whose loss he actively mourned. Stephen drew his satisfaction from actual contact with money, bank books, deposit slips, and other symbols of his supposed security. Unconsciously love hungry, consciously money hungry, Stephen had interpersonal relationships that were equally spartan and isolated.

As a child, he lived a strictly regimented life. His parents made liberal use of directives and punishments to make him feel guilty if he didn't respond exactly as they wanted. They would reward him with money for good deeds, good grades, and other outstanding adherence to the family doctrine. Money, the reward he learned to elicit quite effectively, came to represent the love, affection, and security he desired. As an adult, he rewarded himself for outstanding work (such as cleaning his entire house himself) with a bag of chocolate chip cookies, a rare "extravagant" expense. He equated spending money with losing control and feared it. Stephen hoarded his feelings as carefully as his money.

The Consummate Conservationist

Will's problems were similar to Stephen's, but in his case they actively impeded his career. An expert technician whose income placed him securely in the comfortable middle class, this *perennial bachelor* was, by age thirty-seven, easily able to afford a large house in a good neighborhood. But Will could not bear to pay utility bills to make his house comfortable, or to buy clothing he needed for work. He had trouble keeping up with the latest developments in his fast-changing field because of his reluctance to pay for the electricity required to read the magazines and pamphlets dealing with his field of expertise; he often remained in his office after work to use its electric lights. He painstakingly sorted all his trash for composting, recycling, and burning (he warmed his house by burning household trash in his fireplace) and paid no garbage bills at all; he had to explain to city sanitation officials why he required no garbage service.

Pleased with his victory over the city "busybodies," Will decided to work on his water expenses. He gradually reduced his personal hygiene schedule, bathing less than once a week. He wore the same shirt and underwear a week at a time to save laundry costs, and he owned only one suit, which he wore to work day after day, year after year, until it wore out.

Will found a sort of social life as a Scout leader, teaching young boys his skills at recycling, repairing, and "making do" with almost no resources.

Although Will performed very competently at his job, he never won advancement. In fact, instead of being promoted, at age forty-three he was sidetracked entirely. After he cut back to bathing every ten days, his bosses quietly removed him from the central workspace (and the central work flow of his company) and gave him an office of his own so that he could work on his own projects.

The Cheapskate

There is a classic story about a dedicated cheapskate. The man invited a couple to a posh restaurant and encouraged them to order lavishly. When the check arrived, he announced that he had forgotten his wallet. The couple, who had known this man a long time, were not surprised and indicated that they would take care of the check. Their friend added, "Be sure to leave a very nice tip, because they know me here."

Dedicated cheapskates have established a style of very carefully holding onto things—not only money, but also love, sympathy, and compassion. They have probably felt shortchanged and deprived themselves, and perpetually feel insufficiently nurtured. They feel that they have little to give because they have been given so little. This position incorporates both dependency and hostility, "I want to be taken care of now because nobody ever took care of me before", and a particular kind of entitlement, "I shouldn't have to pay now because people owe me".

Being a cheapskate is only one of many ways to mortgage the present to achieve retribution for the past. Remembering the past and the injuries that were inflicted then is the only way to keep from spending more responsibly now.

Autonomy Worship

Paradoxically, among those who love money most are those who are abidingly and obsessively interested in personal freedom. Called "autonomy worshipers" by psychologist Jay Goldberg, these deeply dependent people carefully arrange their lives so as to avoid responsibility, schedules, demands, or anything else that might restrict their independence [Reference 11-3]. For some, money buys freedom; they acquire it to ensure autonomy. For others, money (and its pursuit) is shunned entirely because of its potential for encroaching on freedom.

Autonomy worshipers, who buy freedom with cash, believe that the more money they can accumulate, the greater the distance they can place between themselves and their dependency needs. Autonomy worshipers who disavow the importance of money, accumulating only enough to meet their immediate needs, reveal the underlying emotional charge that money carries for them. People can, indeed, give up freedom by fitting into a mold cast by others, but they can also lose freedom by compulsively fleeing from any external demands. In both cases, the demands and not the individuals design the outcome. In neither instance are the individuals free to create, pursue, and enjoy goals of their own shaping. The point of reference remains that of some other person, of some parental ghost from the past.

Your Money or Your Marriage

Money is often a major issue in marriage, a vehicle for such common themes as the autonomy and the separateness of the marital partners. One couple, Preston and Sarah, kept separate bank accounts and separate budgets in order to distinguish their income and expenses and to "preserve their individuality." Nonetheless, conflicts arose out of their opposite points of view about money. Sarah said, "I am working so I can spend this money." Preston said, in contrast, "I'm working so I can save and invest this money." Whereas Sarah believed in enjoying her money and saw it as a means to an end, Preston saw money as an accumulation of his personal worth, value, and self-esteem. For him, money was the concrete evidence that people (including himself) could believe in him. But having cash and spending it is what made Sarah feel valuable; in fact, she competed with her mother and sisters to see who could spend the most. Predictably, Preston complained when he found in the trunk of Sarah's car a brand-new pair of $80 shoes that she had bought six months earlier. Preston felt panicky and worthless when there was no money in the bank. His sense of worth and his confidence were tied to having real, tangible, financial evidence of his value.

For Sarah, the value of money lay in letting go of it; for Preston, the value lay in keeping it. Although the obvious conflict in this marriage centered around money, the underlying conflict lay in the self-valuation and self-esteem of each partner. When these issues were examined in couples therapy, Sarah and Preston were able to detoxify their money conflict and discover other ways to meet each other's emotional needs. Money did not resolve either one's emotional issues; it only pointed up their basic need for self-affirmation.

It is not uncommon for two people who have some doubt about their lovability to have money struggles within a marriage. Typically, they use money in equal but opposite directions. One will be a spendthrift trying to buy love and admiration and the other a tightwad who creates, through the accumulation of money, the security lacking internally or in relationships.

The need for care and love often expresses itself in money issues. Another patient treated money as though it were a magical token of value, esteem, and affection. He had never asked for a raise at work but simply hoped his boss would care enough to give it to him spontaneously. This hoped-for expression of the boss's "love" never materialized, and the patient had to take his destiny into his own hands.

Fear of Wealth

Changing Internal Models

Bad Kid Makes Good

Bryan had an astonishingly small income, considering his position as a reputable attorney specializing in a complex area of law. In one of his psychoanalytic sessions, Bryan complained about the pressure he was getting from his wife to bring home more money for essentials.

He recognized that he was negligent about his billing and fee collection. He didn't bother to collect on his accounts until he had trouble paying his own bills; he often waited until the bill collectors harassed him. He fell behind in the payment of psychiatric fees.

His best and only motivation was panic at external pressure. "If there is no one pressuring me for money, then there is no need to make money," he said. "I work only under pressure." Indeed, Bryan's practice was structured so that he continually had to meet externally imposed deadlines. When no deadlines loomed, he had difficulty concentrating on his work.

Bryan wanted somebody else to direct, guide, and motivate him, yet when somebody did (in response to his passivity, pseudo-helplessness, or failure to meet a deadline), he felt intruded upon and "crowded," as though someone else was taking over his life. For Bryan, work and achievement were complex issues.

A major source of Bryan's problem was his experience with an overly involved and controlling mother. She seemed to take credit for all his achievements. As a boy, he felt so dominated by her that the only way he could distinguish his own mastery and avoid becoming an extension of her was to not achieve. His parents were most pleased with him when he looked good to others and was the best in his class, so he discovered that he could assert his individuality by constantly being "bad" and getting into trouble.

He felt a great thrill of mastery when he met his unconscious goal of publicly embarrassing his parents. Once as a teenager, when Bryan's parents had gone to dine in an elegant restaurant, he secretly followed them and went through the restaurant wearing tattered clothes, carrying a tin cup, and begging for money. The manager threw him out, dragging him past the table of his astonished parents.

This pattern was constant throughout Bryan's life. Once, after earning a large fee for a case, about $250,000, he fantasized about giving half of it away and spending the other half instantly. Getting rid of it quickly seemed a remedy for the anxiety he felt. Bryan recognized in analysis that he wanted to retreat to a more familiar, comfortable (yet limiting) model, the "bad kid" who was needy rather than successful.

This image had been established in childhood when his bad behavior drew constant criticism from his parents instead of the love and affirmation he craved. Feeling loved only when he conformed to his parents' desires and interests, Bryan spent his adulthood alternating between the conformity that brought love and the "badness" that brought a sense of autonomy, control, and individuality.

Foolishly spending half of his large fee represented Bryan's childhood wish to break free of demands and responsibility. Giving away the other half of his settlement would have repeated another childhood scenario. As a child, Bryan intuitively recognized that his mother was depressed (he later learned she'd been addicted to amphetamines in an effort to relieve her constant depression), and he gave up part of himself, his emotional independence, in order to remain enmeshed with her and relieve her depression. Throughout his childhood, Bryan let his mother do things for him that he could have done for himself, so she could feel needed and valued. Eventually, with his enduring dependency on his mother, Bryan came to view himself as inadequate and incapable.

Money was the symbol of Bryan's autonomy—something he desired and feared simultaneously. With analysis, his inability to acquire or enjoy money commensurate with his professional skills was resolved, and he became able to bill and collect for his full professional worth.

Guilt over Money

Work Is No Sweat

Raul, a psychologist in therapy with me, was troubled by a consistent pattern of not being able to set or collect his fees. He recognized that the ways he discussed his fees with patients precluded any possibility of collecting them. He would actually talk patients out of paying on time or in full.

The most successful son of a large blue-collar family, Raul discovered that he unconsciously believed his parents and family didn't really value his work. It wasn't manual labor like his father did. "Just sitting in an office and not doing hard work that makes me get dirty and sweaty is so different from anything I ever grew up seeing or believing. It's like work has to involve some suffering, the need to sweat. Somehow, I'm not supposed to enjoy my work." He came to recognize that he'd been compensating for enjoying his no-sweat occupation by avoiding payment for it.

Raul still wanted his father to admire everything he did, including his work, and this desire kept him tied to his outmoded attitudes. By freeing himself from these attitudes and openly mourning the lack of parental admiration, he was able to recognize that work is work, with or without hard labor. He came to value his own point of view and his own desires and began to find rewards within his own domain.

Risk Taking

Fear of Risk

Engineering Rejections

A writer once remarked, "I've written any number of articles, and even one book. But I can't bring myself to send any to a publisher, because I'm afraid they'll be rejected." He brought on himself what he most feared, rejection. Ambivalence about money and its acquisition can bring about similar immobility. Individuals may be afraid to do anything with their money for fear they'll choose the wrong thing.

It's (Almost) a Deal

Darrell, an entrepreneur, described how he loved to find and research deals in limited partnerships, land syndication, and real estate purchases. He would find out about all aspects of the investment. At the moment of decision, however, he'd inevitably back out before committing a cent. Despite his substantial means, Darrell's only investments were in savings accounts; he had never closed a single deal. He was disgusted with himself for settling for financial mediocrity instead of attempting even the most calculated of risks.

Darrell could only imagine the bad possibilities. He couldn't imagine any positive outcomes to his hopes and fantasies. With this viewpoint, his actions seemed logical: By backing out of every deal at the last minute, he avoided the negative consequences he expected. In his belief system, the best that could happen was the avoidance of the negative. To even imagine any positive possibilities, his outlook had to be expanded to consider a full range of potential outcomes, including some good ones. Only then, could he realistically appraise any financial situation and place it in the realm of business, not emotion.

A story told by a financial researcher, Andre Sharon, illustrates another aspect of the fear of risk [Reference 11-4]. A patient came for psychiatric treatment of a costly and frustrating pattern in his personal investments. He was a successful senior partner in a major Wall Street brokerage firm. In his position, he constantly heard "investment stories." Of the many tips and bits of inside information he received daily, he'd act on one and ignore the rest.

Over the years, this man noticed that the one stock he'd buy out of the entire group tended to be the only one to drop sharply; the stocks he ignored would consistently do well. Rather quickly, his psychiatrist pointed out that he had a strong puritanical streak, following the traditional ethic of working very hard for whatever money he made. Because he'd gotten his investment tips without working for them, he could take only the worst risks among them. By making sure he only lost money, he managed unconsciously to deal himself the punishment he felt he deserved for trying to make "easy money."

The psychiatrist was able to provide this man with an immediate solution. Going through the motions of working for his reward by researching each prospective investment would let him feel that by his research he'd earned his reward; thus he would not have to feel guilty about making money. This "research work" would allow him to avoid his usual mistakes and actually make money on his investments.

The Don Juan of Risk

Another kind of investor is the _Don Juan of risk,_ someone who fears risk so much that he or she creates it over and over, ostensibly in order to master it.

Phobic individuals can engage in at least two basic behaviors. One is avoidance. For example, someone who is afraid to ride in elevators may try to avoid using them. The other course is to ride an elevator scores of times to try to master the fear. Of course, neither behavior is likely to be effective, because each is only a behavioral attempt to reverse a basic fear that elevators represent. A ghost of some much earlier, long-forgotten terrifying event or consequence lurks behind the elevator's doors.

Don Juans of risk will seek high-risk, speculative investments, or take ill-advised risks with money, job, or life, in order to challenge fate and emerge victorious. They're like mountain climbers who are secretly afraid of heights: They're more dangerous (both to themselves and to others on their ropes) than mountaineers whose fears are reasonable and specific to the dangers of each climb. Climbers with a height phobia are liable to choose the riskiest, flashiest route, instead of the most prudent, and to dissolve into helpless panic in a crisis. Don Juans of risk are equally dangerous in the financial realm, to themselves, their family, and their business associates.

Compulsive Gambling

Serious, compulsive gamblers wish to control fate, to feel "chosen." Whether they succeed or not, they experience a particular exhilaration, a flow of adrenaline, from taking a risk—from going to the edge and not falling off. Their hope, their exhilaration, their optimistic illusion is the process and the quest. Serious gamblers are intoxicated, addicted, and cannot stop. Even if they lose, they don't stop. Instead, they wait for more magic so they can "win back their losses." Each win may be experienced as a victory. Dostoyevsky captured this feeling in his novel *The Gambler*:

In five minutes I accumulated 400 gold pieces at roulette. I should have left at that moment, but a strange feeling came over me to challenge Fate. It was the wish to give Fate a punch in the nose and show her my tongue.

Compulsive gamblers often feel the greatest impulse to gamble after periods of stress. Their feelings of helplessness and vulnerability are countered by their exercise of power and the risks they take in gambling.

When Losing Is Winning

One man described regularly losing several hundred to several thousand dollars per single poker session. The son of a wealthy financier, he had inherited all his money. At age sixty-two, he knew that his time was limited; he had already had a quadruple bypass and was in failing health. As his health worsened, his poker losses became larger and more frequent.

Referred by his cardiologist for management of stress and anxiety, he preferred to talk about how angry and disappointed he was with his life. We discussed his compulsive gambling. The loss of several thousand dollars a day would not noticeably affect his lifestyle for years to come, but he wanted to tell me why he needed to lose so much money. Almost all of his motivation was conscious. He was striking a blow at the past by losing the money inherited from his father, and at the same time a blow at the future by losing the money his children would otherwise inherit. He didn't want his children to be the recipients of his wealth, partly from anger at their ingratitude and sense of entitlement and partly from knowing how his inheritance had robbed him of ambition and mastery of any meaningful work. He could never have equaled the wealth accumulated by his father.

His heart surgery forced him to confront his mortality. He had always believed, somehow, that his wealth could buy him immortality.

Some Personal Observations on Gamblers

On a family vacation a couple of years ago, I had an eye-opening experience. We were on a cruise ship for part of our vacation and it was the first time my fourteen-year-old son had seen casino gambling. It intrigued both of us, and we decided to form a partnership for gambling. He couldn't participate actively, being underage, but he sat behind me as my "consultant," where he could directly view the action of the blackjack table and whisper strategy and directions in my ear. I was surprised to see that his gambling skills far exceeded my own.

This was a wonderful opportunity for him to learn some principles of business. We decided to capitalize our venture at $50, $25 each. We knew we might have losses that could disillusion or stop us. We set aside some "bounce-back money," aware that the most common reason for the failure of small businesses is inadequate capitalization. We also decided that, no matter what our winnings were, we would never risk more than $25 per night, half our initial investment.

We gambled for approximately an hour and a half each of six nights on the cruise. We had agreed on when we would hold, when we would ask for another card, and when we would place more than our minimum bet. The value of having already established these principles became abundantly clear once we were at the table and in the throes of impulsivity. On the two or three occasions when we abandoned our principles, we learned important lessons that served to firmly reestablish loyalty to our rules.

At the end of six evenings, we had seen about thirty people at our table come and go. Amazingly, only two or three of them actually came out ahead. We were, happily, ahead about 300 percent. We made the following observations about those who did not win and especially those who lost spectacularly: (1) They had no consistent principles or standards; (2) those who appeared to have some standards abandoned them with sufficient emotional stimuli, such as a big win, a big loss, or a sustained streak of wins or losses; (3) emotionally motivated behaviors always lost, including anger at losing, overstimulation from winning big, and greed; and (4) they had no established end point for loss or gain.

One evening an older woman looked at me indignantly when she saw what my son and I were doing. She said, "I suppose you're proud to be teaching your son how to gamble?" I responded cheerfully, "No ma'am, I'm proud that he's teaching me."

Are You a Compulsive Shopper or Spender?

1. Do you go shopping to escape feeling bored, empty, angry, or scared?

2. Do you want to spend money to feel better after a setback or disappointment?

3. Do you use shopping or spending in a way that creates conflicts for you, or between you and others?

4. Do you spend impulsively and wish later you hadn't bought the items?

5. Have your spending habits created chaos in your life?

6. Do you buy things with your credit cards that you wouldn't buy if you had to pay cash?

7. When you shop or make a purchase, does your mood change— for instance, do you feel euphoric or anxious?

8. Do you feel you're doing something taboo, dangerous, or defiant, by shopping or spending?

9. Do you think extensively about money that you have, don't have, wish you had, or owe, and still go out to shop?

10. Do you have to compromise your life or leisure to adjust to your shopping debts?

11. Are you able to fully enjoy what you purchase—or do you feel bad, guilty, ashamed, or embarrassed about your purchases or simply never wear or use them?

12. Are you making purchases to enhance your self-esteem? Would you still buy the items for yourself or your family, even if no one saw you in those items?

If you answer yes to any of the above questions, you may be using money or shopping in a symptomatic way—that is, to regulate your feelings or esteem. If so, your spending may be in control of you, and you may need to address whatever it is you are escaping from.

12

Money Addiction

Money is the root of all evil, and everyone needs roots.

—Unknown
(at least, unadmitted)

I don't know what I want, but I want it now.

—Ditto

I want money, that's what I want!

—Berry Gordy and
Janie Berger

An inability to relax and enjoy leisure or luxury may be a component of money addiction. Money addicts' passion for acquiring currency is equaled only by their inability to enjoy it.

I Need Money!

Kerr, a highly accomplished professional, consulted me when he ran out of wall space. He had just received a coveted national award for distinguished contributions in his field, recognition as one of the three best in the country. He placed this award in the only space remaining on his wall. The walls of Kerr's office, as well as his trophy case, were now completely filled with awards and medals.

In addition, his goal of being in the top half of 1 percent of the national money earners in his field had been met for the past several years, as had his goal of making more every year than he had the previous year. His annual earnings had reached $500,000. He had fully funded his retirement plan, paid off his home and ranch, and accumulated savings enough to maintain his lifestyle without working. But as he hung the new plaque in the last vacant space on his office wall, Kerr realized that he felt empty, that something was missing.

Kerr became increasingly despondent with the recognition that he was not happy, had never been truly happy, and that now the hope of fulfillment through continued achievement and award could not continue. There were no higher awards to achieve; there was no one who had accomplished more to pat him on the back and encourage and admire him. He had done it all.

Kerr readily acknowledged that his self-esteem and internal regulation depended on money acquisition as well as the admiration of others; he also realized how little affected he was by all of it. No accomplishment satisfied his ambition longer than temporarily. He wanted "more," but the "more" he got was never enough. When he ran out of wall space for "more," Kerr finally had to confront his *illusion* that "more" would be enough. As a result, he despaired and became depressed.

Proof of (Net) Worth

Some individuals equate financial worth with internal worth, self-esteem, and self-confidence. People who feel empty inside—whose value and self-esteem stem more from the response of others than from internal reference—may pursue external validation through wealth, applause, or admiration. Ultimately, they face the frustrating realization that great financial worth does not, after all, equal great self-worth. At this point, they may face up to the futility of their equation, and a depression may occur.

The distinction between financial worth and an internal feeling of worth is highlighted by the realization that money can't be expected to fill emotional needs or resolve ancient conflicts. Some individuals do manage to maintain a lifelong illusion that money will some day equal happiness and self-validation; they continue to look for "the big deal" or to feel that it's only a matter of "a little more time" before they make enough money to buy their own self-worth. Those who accumulate considerable wealth may have to confront the fact that money won't buy happiness; still others use their money to shore up their sagging self-esteem by surrounding themselves with admirers.

Becky was thirty-four and owned an insurance company. "When I was growing up, no one believed in me," she recalled. "My folks never believed I could even graduate from college. Money became the only way I could compare, the only way someone would believe in me. It's proof, undeniable, concrete evidence! The only way my parents seemed to believe in me as a child was when they could see concrete evidence that I could run faster than other girls my age or make better grades. I've spent a lot of time and energy showing them that I've made it. I wanted more than anything for them to be proud of me. I still do. And now I feel the same with my husband."

Some money addicts commit themselves deeply to frugality and refrain from spending money. Others have a compulsion to spend freely. Red-hot spenders can never admit that they can't afford something; they overspend, overpay, and overtip. They're wildly conspicuous consumers, even though, out of the public eye, they may be quintessential misers. Self-doubt and insecurity, coupled with a drive to demonstrate their worth, make them buy more than they can really afford. They must prove that they can afford any product or investment they want. Needless to say, these individuals are easy prey for any skilled salesperson selling goods or investments.

Individuals with poor self-esteem may feel driven to pursue money. They may have many admirers, followers, acquaintances, and associates. What they have few, or none of, is true friends. They may feel that they don't need intimate friends and may, instead, prefer to surround themselves with people who will praise them and function as extensions of themselves. Since they feel incapable of internally regulating their own self-esteem, they may feel depleted and lonely unless they receive constant positive input from others. They insatiably seek more money, more success, more fame, more power. A deep emotional hunger for "more" may be rooted in emotional deprivation during early childhood. Success and money acquisition hold out the hope of self-validation, of *feeling good at last.*

Benjamin Franklin stated, "Money never made a man happy yet, nor will it. There is nothing in its nature to provide happiness. The more a man has, the more he wants. Instead of its filling a vacuum, it makes one."

A Million Isn't What It Used to Be

Edmund, the commodities trader introduced in Chapter 4, had imagined for most of his life that once he acquired a net worth of a million dollars he would feel secure and "good about himself." He worked and saved diligently to reach his goal, but he eventually entered treatment with all the symptoms of a major depression: a depressed, irritable mood; sleep difficulties; decreased energy; poor concentration; diminished appetite with a twelve-pound weight loss, and waning sexual desire. In therapy, examining the causes of his depression, he reconstructed the following scenario.

At an early age, Edmund secretly promised himself that he would beat his father and his favored older brother by making more money, by being the first person in the family to be worth a million dollars. Surely his parents would then give him the love, esteem, and respect he felt was missing.

His depression occurred decades later when he actually met his financial goal. In his fantasies, money represented esteem and love, and acquiring a vast sum of money was supposed to allow him to revise his poor opinion of himself. He was terribly disappointed to discover over the years that only his financial statement was improving, not his happiness, contentment, or feeling of self-worth. When he did reach the magical million-dollar figure, his disillusionment became depression. Money was only money, and

Edmund was still the same "inadequate" person he had thought he was since childhood. In fact, he now felt absolutely hopeless, since his one last chance to reverse his chronic depression was revealed to be only a fantasy.

In therapy, Edmund finally looked objectively at himself, at the way he'd developed a depreciated view of himself, and at his unconscious equations involving money. He discovered how the events of his childhood had planted the seeds of both his achievement and his depression and had motivated his behavior for four decades. He had his million, and he discovered he was free to choose what to do next with his life. He had finally released himself from the path chosen by an unhappy eight-year-old boy.

The Addictive Process

Effectiveness (mastery) is the most basic human motivation. The desire to be effective, to be a cause, and to experience pleasure at being a cause has been demonstrated in earliest infancy and exists in varying forms throughout life. The experience of ineffectiveness thus has serious repercussions, and individuals address those repercussions in a variety of ways. Money is one such antidote to the experience of ineffectiveness.

To an extent, sometimes a very large extent, money is effective, especially in an external arena. In emotional algebra, love and esteem become equated with money, fame, prestige, and power. The abstract is defined by concrete emblems of status, which are more tangible and seem more real. The addictive quest for money may be fueled in part by the individual's unconscious assumption that he or she is ineffective without some obvious source of control and power, which are certainly present in money.

Many behaviors can have a compulsive quality without someone having to say "I am addicted." For example, some individuals, after many years of training for a profession or a business career, spend much of their time trying to beat the stock market. Some are motivated by an addictive kind of grandiosity: "I know enough to beat the market" or "I can look into the future."

Addiction is a process, a quest for something tangible that can regulate (for a time) mood and self-esteem. The things one can be addicted to are endless: money, work, sex, alcohol, drugs, another person. Each has its own side effects and consequences. The process is the same. Of the many things people are addicted to, work and money are the most justifiable and socially approved.

Greed and Competition

Drug or alcohol addiction, in an extreme form, may result in criminal activity, a willingness to do anything and everything to obtain more of the addictive substance. Similarly, the extreme form of money addiction is manifested in greed, a willingness to do anything and everything to get more money. Some people become powerfully addicted to money.

In the financial community particularly, but not only there, money is regarded as a magical substance. The magic is not really in the acquisition of the money but in all the things having money implies, what other people can see. The trappings of wealth serve as signals of worth and value and affirm the importance of the person who possesses them.

It takes two people or two entities to create and maintain the notion that money measures worth. Someone has to have the money, and someone else has to judge that person to be more valuable because of it. This is a trick that we play on ourselves, whichever side of the illusion we're on. We think that money will make us valuable to others and to ourselves.

Some people are able to confront this illusion. Those who do may reflect upon themselves and their important relationships and come to concern themselves less with what they possess.

Pride provides a great impetus for competition and money acquisition. The high of making big money and big deals motivates more winning and even greater risk taking. Scrully Blotnick, a research psychologist, points out that young competitors on Wall Street are driven not so much by greed as by pride, and a fear of being classified as inadequate or second-rate; they begin to measure themselves against a relative scale rather than absolute standards [Reference 12-1]. Possessing or earning a million dollars a year is not enough if a competitor earns two million. The compelling drive to outdo their rivals gets some individuals into trouble.

Driven individuals set their financial sights ever higher; relative rather than absolute standards may cause them to lose their own anchor. Just as the anorexic girl wants to "lose five pounds more" and persists in losing "five pounds more" until she is on the brink of death, these individuals may be driven to make more without ever feeling fully satisfied that more is enough. For some, trying to measure up to a relative scale may mean losing sight of the boundary between legal and illegal, ethical and unethical.

The extravagances necessary to acquire wealth are sometimes as profound as the extravagances of wealth. Consider the advertisement that ran recently in leading magazines, headed with the words "What Does a Rolls Royce Cost?" The answers include the following: "The years without a holiday," "The school sports days you never saw," "The friendships you had to leave behind," "Risking your health for the health of the business," "Late nights in the office when your contemporaries were in the pub," "Missing your children's first steps into the world," "Demanding excellence in everything you do." The ad concludes that a Rolls Royce costs "more than most are prepared to give."

This dark side of excellence reveals itself when self-esteem becomes overly linked to demonstrable success and when internal principles are violated in pursuit of money.

How Much Money Is Enough?

Does money do our will, or does it drive us? Even very large amounts of money do not settle money issues in our heads.

Every society idealizes some thing or idea. We see distinctive idealized symbols for different societies, at different times within the same society, and among different individuals. In our society, the idealized power accorded to money is an echo of the virtually universal childhood wish for unlimited wealth. Children form this fantasy in response to feeling small, helpless, unskilled, and un-employed in an overwhelming world. The fantasy of limitless wealth repairs littleness and helplessness. This fantasy, perhaps unmodified, exists in varying forms in adults, as fantasies of having unlimited wealth, winning the lottery, or inheriting money from a previously unknown aunt.

Money is both a symbol and a reality. It is superstition with a considerable basis in fact. Money can do many things; it can create respect for those who have it, relieve many forms of suffering, and prolong life. It also represents ever-renewable promise, and people sometimes place monetary value on such abstractions as happiness. We often wish to endow something intangible with substance and form, to create a materialized hero, a recognizable villain, a pal-pable reward, an answer, the hope for change.

When I have been a guest speaker or conducted a seminar on the subjects of work, money, and success, I have sometimes asked the audience to play a game called "Top Secret." I provide all members of the audience with a large index card. Promising anonymity, I ask them to write (1) what their current annual income is and (2) what they feel their yearly income would need to be in order to ensure happiness and contentment with no more money problems and with the freedom to have and do what they please.

Inevitably, people feel they would need to make twice their current annual income to be happy and free of worry. This is as true of someone who makes $25,000 a year (and would like to make

$50,000) as it is of the individual who makes a million dollars a year (and feels that about two million dollars would be enough). In discussions afterward, many people admit that they have applied this same principle in reality through one or more *doublings* of income. If you doubt this result, go back to the self-quiz at the end of Chapter 10 and review your answers.

I suspect that some individuals who assign abstractions to money—such as unlimited happiness, health, power, and esteem—never have to confront the fact that money is none of these things. They either never establish a money goal so they can see what the possibilities are, and are not, or they continue to raise their sights so that their goal is never reached. Others may stop short of their goal in order to maintain the fantasy and avoid being confronted with what money might not do.

Withdrawal and Detoxification

We usually think of losses as involving the death or departure of people we love. When a relationship ends, the loss is not only of the actual relationship with that person but also of the future relationship, a loss that may be even more painful than the actual loss. Along with the end of the relationship, we must mourn the loss of the hope the relationship carried with it.

One of the ways we maintain the hope of attaining romantic dreams, the illusion of power and freedom, anything and everything we want, is by clinging to the illusion that money will bring all of this and more. If one attains just enough money, the hope for more still exists. More money may mean happiness, invulnerability, security, even a kind of immortality. This illusion stalls the mourning of the loss of an earlier self or of unfulfilled expectations. The quest for money, with its magical promise of more, better, and ultimate happiness, replaces the mourning of what was and, even more painfully, of what might have been.

The passion for money acquisition may come at the time when we most need to turn attention away from mourning former states of the self. Many patients consult me when their illusion of what money or work or success may provide has failed. At age thirty-five or forty, sometimes at fifty or during a divorce, the hope for more and better begins to fade. If someone's goal is a net worth of a million dollars or some multiple of that, and the goal is reached, that person must confront the reality of what money is and what it isn't. That person must come to grips with the symbol versus the reality.

Midlife is a time of impending or threatened loss of beauty, perpetual energy, vigor, and potency. Money may seem to be the magic that will reverse all these losses. The less developed the inner core of identity, the greater the person's reliance on attaining possessions. The weaker the inner core of identity, the greater the allure and magic attributed to money. Individuals who reach midlife with some unfinished business in forming their own identity may therefore increasingly seek an identity in work or in money. At midlife, even individuals with a strong sense of self will naturally and inevitably reexamine the meanings of work, love, money, and success.

Significant confrontations follow the internal compromises of "if only" and "with a little more time" and "when I make more money." Mourning the loss of the fantasy about what money will do may be the most disappointing aspect of remarkable success.

13

On "Suckers"

Some people will believe anything if you whisper it to them.

—Louis Nizer

*There are some frauds so well conducted
that it would be stupidity not to be deceived by them.*

—Charles Caleb Colton

All of us, at one time or another, have been suckers. But some people are suckers repeatedly. And most instances of being suckered can be avoided.

The Need to Believe

Saul, age fifty-six, was an investment victim but not a typical investment victim. He was a sophisticated money manager and had worked on Wall Street for twenty-two years prior to his current prestigious position with an investment firm. He had, however, lost $94,000 in the previous year to a platinum commodities scam.

Saul was quite impressed with the crafter of the scam, who talked in an informed way about commodities and buttressed his position with quotes from leading financial periodicals. He presented "no-risk" silver commodity contracts with a virtual guarantee of 30 to 40 percent returns within five to six months.

Why are even *Wall Street types* susceptible to the same scams as people with much less financial and investment sophistication? "Sucker lists" are developed from the names of those who fall for such scams, some of them more than once. The North American Securities Administrators Association in Washington, D.C., estimated that in 1987 investors lost $40 billion to scam artists. These losses occur despite an increasingly sophisticated public, alerted to con artists by television, books, and newspapers [Reference 13-1].

The reason scams work is that inside even the most sophisticated people is something that can be described only as the need to believe. Deep down, we would all really like to believe that we have found Aladdin's lamp, the ability to be given whatever we wish. Scams work because we are all susceptible to the fantasy of magical powers bringing immense return, of being "the lucky one," of running across someone who will let us in on something wildly lucrative that few other people know about.

Fate Loves Me

Melanie was quite wealthy and came from a background of immense wealth. She became very excited when she talked about a "hot tip" concerning a purported takeover stock. She was able to maintain her excitement and analyze her motivation at the same time: "I'm investing in hope, keeping hope alive. It's like I'm saying 'Fate loves me.' Reality, if I'm right about this stock, responds to what I want, rather than being resistant as I throw myself against it."

I suspect a similar dynamic applies for the hordes of people who enter sweepstakes. Even though they may know intellectually that they won't win, for the cost of a single stamp, a sweepstakes offers the hope of winning. Other grand illusions can be purchased with a one-dollar lottery ticket. Melanie herself indicated that she could understand someone gambling addictively when the usual ways of getting money offered no particular hope of accumulating either great wealth or just a little extra money.

Melanie also described the appeal of gambling on football games. Her bets had a specific end point, the game on Sunday, with a definite outcome. Perhaps most important for her was the community of peers created by others betting on the same game.

This sense of unity is an example of the many pseudo-families Melanie created all her life to counterbalance the lack of cohesiveness and connectedness in her own chaotic family. As a child, she felt ineffective in obtaining emotional responses from her parents. Because of her vulnerability and sensitivity, Melanie was susceptible to not getting affirmation, love, and bonding with others in the usual ways. Her gambling behavior and stock market gambling offered affirmational bonding. If the stock did well, a whole group of people brought together by the broker would benefit. If it didn't do well, Melanie still had the experience of being together with a group of people. To her, this was more important than the actual money she made. She said, "It's like the guys at the ice house who get together and celebrate on Monday night, if we've won a big bet; it's a communal thing."

She elaborated further: "It's like fate loves me; fate is not ill disposed to me. If I win by a miracle, when there are insurmountable odds, fate is really smiling on me. It's so mixed up with exciting fantasies. And you feel so clever if you win, like at gambling, even if it is luck. And you get to explain your strategy and the reasons for your predictions when you pick a winning team. If I do well, I can alter for a moment my repudiations and self-hatred from a drab woman to a savvy reader of sports or the market. You hate yourself, though, if you didn't bet one time or if you buy the one stock that didn't fly—like you missed out."

The Chosen One(s)

There is a particular appeal in getting "inside" information. It creates the sense of exclusivity. Especially for those who have a hidden (or sometimes not so hidden) desire for specialness, the wish to be chosen and not be excluded is very powerful. To be included in such a special group may not seem possible on one's own, by one's own efforts.

I'll Prove My Worth

Skilled salespeople, whether they are selling goods or investments, soon learn to spot those who must prove their worth by being able to afford any product or investment they want. Self-doubt and insecurity make them candidates to buy more than they can afford. Usually wanting to be liked and admired, they may feel embarrassed to tell the stockbroker that they really can't afford to purchase his or her current recommendations; they begin scrambling for funds as soon as they hang up the telephone. These individuals may also succumb to a salesperson who insinuates that they can't really afford an item.

These spiels are understandably hard to resist, playing not only on greed and anxiety, but on intimidation. Various ploys include making you feel embarrassed if you cannot come up with an amount of money, intimating inadequacies if you have to consult a spouse, attorney, or investment advisor; even quietly suggesting a lack of intelligence by suggesting that perhaps you do not understand the program, and thus need to go over the figures again. One script contained the following: "Maybe we should go over the numbers again because perhaps you don't understand the program. Smart people have known about it for years." The final pitch is to instill a sense of urgency, as if not acting now would mean missing the train.

Three Types of Suckers

The public is offered an unending variety of investments. Many are incomprehensible and exotic-sounding, and a completely informed position is a rarity. Even making an informed decision and consulting a trusted adviser is no guarantee of success. But other factors make some individuals more vulnerable than others.

The Fact of Being Chosen: The Chosen Sucker

These investors seem more susceptible to scams that convince them they now have a chance to get in with the *smart money*. They see others making big money and feel that such deals are reserved for the *big players*, people they read about. When a scam artist offers them a chance of their own, they have an illusion of quick wealth and a desire to be chosen. They can be helped rather quickly to convince themselves that the illusion is true.

One young professional woman described how she had lost $28,000 to an investment fraud. She had heard of an investor who was doing extremely well and called to ask if he might consider her as a client. She went to his office and was immediately impressed with its opulence and the technical paraphernalia, including a ticker-tape machine and computers. She felt grateful to be "playing with the big people." She later found out that she had ignored warning signs. If she had done some homework, she would have discovered that he was not associated with the brokerage firm he claimed to be, and that he had no successful track record in his investment arena. Recognition of these warning signs would have shattered the illusions that she wanted to keep and even cherished.

A Passive Position and an Active Hope: The Passive Sucker

A psychologist who works with investors and commodity traders observed that the most significant finding among those who had been defrauded was a belief that what happened to them was beyond their control. This passivity with their money was pervasive throughout the transactions. The defrauded individuals decided, on the basis of little information, to write a check for a significant amount and turn it over to someone they did not know. They would examine more carefully the references of an office secretary, who would make less in three years than the amount of the one investment. These investments were not viewed as making a conscious choice but as turning over money to someone who would then take care of them and their money.

Impulsivity Without Anticipating Consequences: The Impulsive Sucker

These investment victims combine impulsiveness with either an inability to consider consequences or a disinterest in doing so. They are usually shocked to find themselves in the middle of a scam, simply because the possibility never occurred to them. Investment sellers capitalize on this trait by setting immediate, all-or-nothing deadlines: "This offer will probably be completely subscribed by tomorrow. If you're not in by then, its gone."

People who have been cheated once are no less likely to be cheated again, partially because they want to get even or make up losses. This phenomenon occurs repeatedly with gamblers and, in many instances, with investors.

The desire to be chosen, to be taken care of, implies a particular suggestibility and vulnerability to con artists, who specialize in creating illusions. When people with such a desire find themselves defrauded or when their investment sours, they are shocked, because they do not consider the possibility of a rip-off.

The ability to create an illusion is present in every successful seller. A successful, scrupulously honest bond trader once told me, "Actually I don't sell bonds. I sell stories. It's important to me to include everything I know in the story, but I always know that it's the story I am selling."

For Love or Money

Some investors own stock more for its emotional value than for its investment value. A survey conducted by Chicago's Center for the Study of Investment Behavior indicated that almost half of the 47 million Americans who own stock in publicly traded companies or mutual funds hold only one issue or mutual fund [Reference 13-2]. The most likely reason for holding that one issue is emotional: the individual works for the company, used to work for it, inherited the investment, or has some other specific emotional attachment to it. Stockholders like these are in essence saying "I am a loyal person." One individual surveyed, an attorney, said that selling the shares given to him by his grandparents at his bar mitzvah "would be like selling a memory." Statements and dividends from that company remind him of his grandfather.

Shareholders who have strong sentimental ties to stocks recommended, for example, by their father, view selling the stock as a repudiation of their father's judgment. One individual indicated that selling stock would be like violating a tradition, describing the special link with the past that stock ownership provided.

One investment adviser estimated that about 80 percent of his clients had some sort of emotional attachment to their securities. Some were positive attachments that prevented sale of the securities; but some individuals wanted to rid themselves of all their current holdings to sever emotional ties, as in a divorce.

An article in the *Wall Street Journal* of March 24, 1988, was titled "Victims of Investment Scams Seemed Condemned to Repeat Past Errors." In this article, Martha Branningan wrote about several firms that compile and sell "sucker lists" of people known to buy by telephone; such people are profiled according to their investment tastes as well as their gullibility. It might seem that someone burned by one fraud scheme would be doubly wary with future investments, but Branningan discovered that many people repeatedly fall prey to investment scams.

Some Very Brief Therapy for Suckers

- Ask yourself why you are the lucky one. All of us wish that someone would hand us something. But if an offer is too good to be true, it usually isn't true.

- There is no way for everyone to know about all the investment instruments and options. I once heard someone say that he recognized the possibility of either becoming an expert on all the wines in the world or becoming an expert at dealing with wine stewards. He chose the latter and has enjoyed wine ever since. Doing your homework, being in an informed position, and not being a lazy investor may mean knowing the person and the company you're doing business with, their track record, their references, and how they are regarded professionally.

- Victims of scams do not see themselves as lazy, impulsive, or suggestible (nor do con artists). They are not objectively aware of their wish to be taken care of. They see being taken advantage of, often repeatedly, in a passive way, as if they had no control. They often want to get even and make up their losses. Sit back and examine as objectively as you can the investments you have made and honestly appraise their results, every investment you have made. Look at the trend, the patterns, the losses, the gains, the net, the areas of strength. Sit back even further and look at your illusions to see how they match your records.

- There is a space between urge and action in which judgment resides. Create and maintain that space, fill it with homework, an investment game plan, and consultation with experts.

- Don't invest in something you don't understand.

- Don't listen for what you want to hear. In listening to a pitch about a stock or a deal, we want to hear how well it will do. The seller knows we want to develop a fantasy. But keep the big picture in focus, the worst case as well as the best case, the midrange of reasonable expectations. Listen for what isn't said; consult someone who isn't inside the fantasy that you and the seller have created. An analogy in my clinical practice is the young woman who described her troubled relationship with her father: "He loved the picture he painted of me. And he painted his own picture, the 'perfect' me. He never saw the glasses, the allergies, the corrective shoes, or even the anorexia nervosa until I was almost dead."

- This may be the most difficult: the illusion that somebody is going to take care of us. It is the hardest one to let go, and it is the most adult. We all pay for our illusions. It's good to know exactly what they cost.

Section III

Mastering Work and Money Problems

14

On Change and Progress

*Just because everything's different
doesn't mean anything has changed.*

—Irene Porter

*One's destination is never a place,
but rather a new way of looking at things.*

—Henry Miller

An older student went to his mentor and said, "I have been to see a great number of teachers, and I have given up a great number of pleasures. I have fasted, lived a celibate life, and stayed awake nights seeking enlightenment. I have given up everything I was asked to give up and I have suffered, but I have not been enlightened. What should I do?"

The mentor replied, "Give up suffering." [Reference 14-1].

An Assortment of Caveats, Observations, Hunches, and Humble Opinions

1. You'll never do anything important that will feel comfortable in the beginning. Uncertainty in doing anything new is to be expected. Feeling anxious does not automatically indicate incompetence or inability. Comfortable is not a place you begin.

    An example illustrates this anxiety. In learning to swim, at the moment of being on the edge of the pool about to jump in, you

271

feel anxiety. At that point you can either proceed despite your anxiety or back away and abandon your task, an immediate and effective treatment of the anxiety. The anxiety is a signal that you are moving ahead; you must proceed despite your anxiety in order to master the task. At some point you have to *jump in*, have the new experience, because some things can't be done theoretically. You can't learn to swim by figuring it out on paper or in your head. The only way to deal effectively with the anxiety about jumping in is to do it, and eventually become comfortable with it.

Anxiety is often assumed to be bad; some monster or some danger is about to emerge. But anxiety may also be a signal that you are proceeding, that you are in new territory, beyond where you've been before. Remember your first date? First speech? First day on a new job? You can either retreat or proceed despite your anxiety.

2.   On internal ideals and external goals:

- Develop objectivity about your ideals, your internal model of who and what you are, the unspoken assumptions on which you operate.

- Clarify your external goals. The clarity and consistency of your principles and goals can then be called on at times of emergency or confusion to help bring the big picture into focus.

- Be certain that there is a fit between your internal and external goals, that what you want to accomplish is consistent with your ideals. This consistency can provide an organizing structure and direction to your ambition.

- Recognize unacknowledged ambitions, which may conflict with conscious ambitions. For example, the woman who sees herself as an unselfish caregiver may find it difficult to compete with a colleague for a promotion. Her external goal of gaining money and power may not fit with her internal model of being a loving and nurturing person.

3. Anything important requires a commitment to going forward despite discomfort. One of the great philosophers of the twentieth century put it most simply:

Try not.
Do.
Or do not.
There is no try.

—The philosopher, of course, was Yoda, in *The Empire Strikes Back*

4. Know what reaching a goal will do. It is important to know what achieving a goal will do in order to distinguish clearly what it will not do. For example, reaching a goal won't undo the past, won't make other troubles go away. Monetary wealth will do many things, including providing pleasure, luxury, and financial security, but it may not make your marriage better. A common mechanism for keeping hope alive is stopping short of a goal so there is no need to confront the illusion that reaching the goal will provide all the hoped-for solutions; this is a common manifestation of success phobia.

5. Know who you are doing things for. It is not uncommon for adults—even well into their adulthood—to be doing things for their parents or to oppose their parents. Conformity and opposition imprison equally.

6.   "What is in my best interest?" is a question that should always be in the background and, at times, the foreground. Asking this question is just another way to assess the *big picture* at a time when you may be focusing on details.

7.   For an end point, ask yourself "What is good enough?" The pursuit of perfection is the result of not having a standard of what *good enough* is, of not establishing an end point. For perfectionists, failure may even be a relief, ending the relentless and impossible pursuit of perfection. Perfectionists have to assume that something will go bad sooner or later, and failure ends the suspense. In a system of negative expectations, the only mastery is of how, where, and when the failure occurs.

Playwright Neil Simon said, "Money brings some happiness. But, after a certain point, all it brings is more money."

8.   Align financial goals with your internal model. The financial goals should be attainable, consistent with your internal standard and your external goals.

9.   On resolving emotional issues: Coming to the end of your past isn't enough; you have to have a purpose, a dream, in order to have hope.

10.   Just having a choice can make choosing the same thing feel very different.

11.   To get what you always wanted in the past may not feel as good as you expected, because it's no longer the past.

12.   What we decide to accept undergoes a change.

13.   The past may not be the best or the most relevant context in which to understand the present. The model of understanding must fit the situation, one's style, and personality type; it should be consistent.

Recently I attended a board of directors meeting in which we considered particularly troubling dissension within the corporation. Two executives had banded together to bring a dispute they were having with the CEO to the attention of the board. They promptly embroiled the board in their dispute, and it became obvious that two camps were forming. A spirited and lengthy debate occurred. At one point, a psychologically minded member of the board made the observation that a very destructive process was occurring, in which the entire board might be unconsciously seeking to undermine the organization's progress. The organization had had a prolonged start-up period and was now enjoying rapid success; he suggested that sabotaging that success might be the dynamics at the root of this dissension.

This theory may seem very plausible viewed from an unconscious and historical context, knowing how processes that individuals are not aware of can operate in a group both consciously and unconsciously. I made the observation that a historical context, although it may be true and applicable, is not always the best context in which to understand the present. This statement from a card-carrying psychoanalyst got the board's attention. The current context, I continued, was that a simple breach in the administrative structure had occurred and that we had been caught in the symptoms of that breach. The breach was abandonment of the principle that machinations between the chief executive officer and operating executives had to be worked out in the CEO's office, with his decision being final. Allowing this dissension onto the board's agenda had undermined the administrative authority of the CEO. Our unconscious motivations and the group process of the board of directors were not relevant in the current context.

We were able to adjourn and be on our way home within five minutes.

14. You can become rich because of an inferiority complex.

15. Between an urge and an action lies a potential space in which judgment resides.

16. The capacity to endure uncertainty is the essence of growth.

17. Succeeding is not an event or an act, but a process.

18. Not only can we change, but we can choose how we change.

19. Insight and understanding are internal change; external change is a step in and of itself.

20. Mourning the fantasy of what might have been is more difficult than mourning what actually was.

21. Growth and change involve their own mourning. You have to relinquish a past position in order to move ahead.

    Handsome, bright, and very charming, Steven had always enjoyed easy relationships with equally attractive and engaging women. Now, during his subspecialty training as a physician, he had become ready to make a commitment, even to have a family, but he was deeply conflicted about closeness and exclusivity with a woman. He had entered analysis because of an inability to achieve full intimacy with one individual; for a long time, part of his style was to be involved with several people.

    As he went through analysis, Steven discovered the underlying reasons for his self-imposed barricades, was able to develop a special relationship, and fell deeply in love. As he began to make plans for marriage, he mourned the loss of his freedom to attract others, the freedom to be with others sexually, and the tremendous gratification from the positive feedback he got.

22. The only familiar territory is behind us. Danish philosopher Soren Kierkegaard said, "Life can only be understood backwards, but it must be lived forwards."

23. Growth and change are hard. The only thing harder is not growing or changing.

24. Our experiences are always consistent with our theories. Most often, we attempt change by changing our experiences, which may only result in new editions of the old experience. For example, people often marry someone just like the parent with whom they still have the most to work out. There are other ways to repeat the same process, although the content (and some of the characters) may be different.

It is well known in medicine that, at least 40 percent of the time, change is caused by the idea of a pill and not by the pill itself.

We become what we believe ourselves to be. We construct the events of our life and give meaning to them. Thus it is vital that we know our theories well.

On Changing Careers

It is remarkable that so many people in the United States stay in careers chosen so early in life—possibly at age twenty—usually at least before age twenty-five. The career decision made at such an unripe age is supposed to last over the next four decades. How can one possibly know, with such limited experience and at such a tender age, what will hold his or her interest for a lifetime? Some, fortunately, do; others don't but are able to use a career to organize and develop their interests and the synthesis is harmonious. Others recognize that they did not or could not know and, after years of compromise and perhaps denial, realize that they need to change. One study indicates that at least 45 percent of us have missed the target, are chronically dissatisfied with our choice, and want to switch careers [Reference 14-2].

Consider the following if you've been contemplating a job or career change:

1. Have you achieved enough? That is, have you known what it's like to be successful at your current job or career so you can make an informed decision?

    An analogy makes this point. For many years, as a small part of my professional time, I served as a consultant for The Institute for Rehabilitation and Research, working with people who had become physically disabled in adolescence or adulthood, often as a result of an accident. Not surprisingly, some of these individuals considered suicide as an alternative to lifetime disability. Instead of trying to convince them not to kill themselves, I indicated that I could understand their feelings about the overwhelming change in their life. Suicide was at least one way they could control something about their life, especially when fundamental body control was out of reach.

    I recommended that we work together to understand their options and that they work to achieve their full capacity, even though it was at a different level since the onset of their disability. Only by achieving full potential at their current capacity could they make an informed decision about whether they truly wanted to live, or not live, as a disabled individual. I told them that I would understand entirely if, after achieving full capacity and being able to make an informed decision, they decided to die; I would respect that decision. As yet, no one has decided to die after going through full physical and emotional rehabilitation and achieving his or her fullest capacity.

2. Distinguish temporary frustration from permanent dissatisfaction. Be wary about confusing dissatisfaction, disillusionment, or a "slow period" with terminal disillusionment. Before you can distinguish temporary from permanent, you may need to

put two or three years into your career. This may seem like a very long time, especially if you are accustomed to instant everything. Keep in mind that choosing the wrong career may be every bit as easy as it was the first time.

3. Distinguish internal dissatisfaction from job dissatisfaction. Internal struggles and unhappiness are often blamed on a job (or a marriage); people want to change the perceived external cause, rather than look inside. Sometimes people even create job-related struggles to externalize unhappiness or conflict and pose a ready remedy: The way to get rid of the problem is to leave it.

Adjusting to Rapid Changes

Success may threaten some people because it pushes them out of their optimal range of processing and organizing. New experiences, especially considerable success, may force individuals to operate outside their model of themselves, and of the world with which they are familiar. But change creates stimulation and interest if it is divided into reasonable doses.

An extreme example of the inability to cope with sudden change is the athlete who turns professional at age twenty-two after graduating from college. Suddenly undergoing astronomical changes in lifestyle, income, and contact with the public, he commonly becomes stressed and overstimulated. Some turn to alcohol and drugs in an attempt to regulate feelings and control overstimulation.

Some individuals with self-esteem problems are threatened most by overstimulation and are thus frightened more by success than by failure. Too much of something—praise, speaking in public, even a promotion—dangerously energizes and excites those who have difficulty with internal regulation and are not able to soothe themselves.

People who have difficulty adjusting to the changes that success brings may have difficulty saying no. Stimulated and made expansive by success, they may feel there are no limits to what they can do in business or in related fields. They may confront their limits only with a crashing failure.

15

Mastering Problems with Achievement

Either I will find a way or I will make one.

—Sir Philip Sidney

Success is not a place at which one arrives
but rather . . . the spirit with which one undertakes
and continues the journey.

—Alex Noble

The two most consistent aspects of the human condition are the will to change and the fear of change. The will to change can be a powerful motivating force; the fear of change can make us resist achieving the very goals we're consciously pursuing. Overcoming the resistance to change—even the resistance to knowing ourselves fully—is one of the most challenging aspects of my psychoanalytic practice. When we become consciously aware of our basic assumptions about ourselves, our lives, and our internal standards for living and relating to others, we often find a fresh, different way to look at ourselves and our world. We discover new options for our lives and opportunities to change them for the better.

Our Basic Assumptions

Although we're rarely conscious of them, our basic assumptions deeply affect our lives. We act on these assumptions, however, and the results of our acts seem to validate the assumptions. We're then caught in an endless cycle. For instance, people who assume they're inadequate often act inadequately, by being cautious not to expose themselves or withdrawing from a full commitment. They subsequently gather feedback from themselves and others about their actions, feedback that reiterates the concept that they're inadequate.

Understanding more objectively the emotional model from which we operate can be very important. This model—our belief system and our presuppositions about ourselves—determines what we can and can't, will and won't, do. The process is analogous to having a computer and computer program. Only the data relevant to the program are accepted by the computer; everything else is rejected as invalid or as "noninformation." People who have a fixed assumption about themselves dismiss as invalid any information or feedback to the contrary ("He just doesn't know" or "If she only knew how I really am").

Some of our assumptions were formed during an earlier time in our lives. Continuing to apply them to our current lives may prevent us from reaching our full potential for comfort, happiness, achievement, or relatedness with others. Conflicts may arise between the goals that we consciously and rationally seek and the expectations derived from early life experiences.

Learning to recognize the set of assumptions that guide our behavior and determine our perceptions is difficult. When we are operating within a set of assumptions, they don't seem like assumptions, merely *the way things are*. But learning to recognize our assumptions is important. They can limit our ability to think flexibly, give us false information about what is or isn't possible for us, and channel our thinking. A fuller awareness of what we're assuming frees us to choose other assumptions, rather than being stuck in one system.

This book has examined some of the basic presuppositions and unconscious emotional equations involving work and money. The process of elevating these meanings and assumptions to awareness and then scrutinizing them may catalyze a different way of looking at things. We may then consider alternatives that were not even imagined before.

We all fashion a destiny out of our own fantasies and assumptions about ourselves. Personal myths and assumptions, conscious or not, can imprison us. Those we cannot recall consciously, we reenact. Those who do not know history, it is said, are destined to repeat it. Personal history cannot be changed, but by understanding it, we can free ourselves from its grip. We define the boundaries of the domain within which we can achieve and orchestrate our life experiences and achievements to fit with our expectations.

Our perceptions of the world, along with our perceptions of ourselves, determine to a major degree our experiences and choices. We create a model of the universe based on our experiences, and this model becomes a private and individual reality, our unique point of view. If, for instance, the model includes stereotyped sex roles for men and women, then the stereotypes are internalized and we adopt the role mandated by the stereotype. For some adult men and women, the changes in society that have weakened external constraints on sex roles may not be enough. They may also need to overcome personal, internal constraints based on earlier developmental experiences.

Although the objective world may contain multiple alternatives, our own models of the world and of ourselves determine which of those alternatives we see as available to us. Internal models may not allow us to recognize or shift to new, more current, more creative ways of thinking. We must evaluate ourselves and our models in the context of our unique life experiences and self-concept.

Emotions and behavior, too, are personal creations. The responses, feelings, and events in our lives are personally generated and perceived. We may create penalties for or impediments to our success, or we may perceive even significant obstacles as merely steps to realizing our vision.

The perception of any actual event is the emotional creation of the person perceiving it. Each person sees and interprets events in a highly personal way, usually using the template of earlier experiences and previously learned systems of thinking and response. The residues of these experiences include those carried to current times from earliest childhood.

When siblings discuss their mutually shared memories, they're often surprised to discover strikingly different perceptions of the same event. Two siblings may have very different perceptions of the same parent. For example, two brothers who had entered psychotherapy at about the same time compared notes on their childhood. One brother described their father as cold, obsessive, distant, and authoritarian. The other brother described their father as warm, spontaneous, and supportive. Of course, they were both right, each was describing his own experiences, memories, and perceptions of his father, which constituted his own psychic reality.

Psychic reality is the way external reality is perceived and processed internally, by someone and the way it's woven into a fabric of total life experiences. From a very early age, we interpret, transform, alter, and symbolically represent—and thereby create— our perceptions of all that we experience, and we integrate these perceptions into a cohesive internal world.

All of us, at various times in our lives, make commitments. Although the process may be automatic for some, others are very aware of the process, perhaps more so at times of pronounced change. An example is deciding to give up an unwanted behavior, such as smoking, drinking, or binge eating. When we hear someone speak of giving up a certain behavior, we know, instinctively if the person will be successful. Someone who says "I need to," "I want to," "I should" "I ought to" will never be successful for long. The person who says "I'm going to do it" is serious. He or she has made the commitment.

Those who have made the commitment to do something, have relinquished the fantasy that someone else will do it for them or that it will magically happen. They have moved from a passive position of wish fulfillment to an active position of responsibility. *Stopping smoking* becomes an active decision, made each time they desire a cigarette, until not smoking becomes as automatic as smoking was previously.

Once you're inside a commitment, you'll know it. Any new development or obstacle that gets in the way will only be another step toward reaching your goal. If you aren't committed, any number of things can arise that will serve as sufficient reason not to proceed.

Several years ago, two anthropologists were chosen to live in ape colonies as identical as possible. The two anthropologists were chosen because of their remarkable similarity in personality, philosophy, and education. They both entered an ape colony to live and observe for a year. When they emerged to compare results, rather than the similarities they expected, they found remarkable discrepancies. The first anthropologist, after an initial period of transition, was able to achieve harmony and oneness with the ape colony. He was accepted by the apes and integrated into the colony, resolving the issues of aggression and achieving intimacy. The second anthropologist never got beyond the social periphery of his colony. He struggled constantly with the issues of aggression, conflict, and trust, never resolving any of them or achieving harmony or intimacy with the apes.

The anthropologists puzzled over these results for months until they finally found one difference. The second anthropologist, the one who was never more than an outsider, had a gun. He knew that if things got tough, he could escape. This knowledge colored his perspective and interactions from the beginning, although in a subtle and unconscious way. The first anthropologist had no gun. He knew from the beginning that he would either make it or not, on his own. He had no "out." He was committed.

Understanding your own assumptions and unconscious goals will help you know exactly what you've succeeded at. You are always succeeding, even if the overt result is a failure. Every behavior is motivated. Even if you fail at something, by understanding the motivation you will know which specific goal you have reached successfully.

What Is Success?

There are as many definitions of success as there are human beings, but several kinds of general, overall success are evident. One type of success is the development of warm and intimate relationships with both men and women. Another area of success is the development of skill or professional expertise. Success for some includes productivity in the home as a mother or a father.

Successful people are not devoid of conflict but are able to handle it in a healthy, constructive way. They are able to express themselves appropriately, even in the face of external constraints, because they know themselves fully and feel comfortable with themselves. They experience independence and vitality, balancing their external achievements with their private life. Their self-esteem remains intact or fluctuates only moderately, regardless of external circumstances, providing a solid foundation for ongoing growth and development.

Charles Garfield studied 250 highly successful men and women to determine what characteristics they had in common that distinguished them from less successful individuals. The following traits emerged:

- Foresight combined with effective, thoughtful planning.

- A drive to constantly improve on previous performance.

- Feelings of self-confidence and self-worth.

- A desire for responsibility and control.

- Interpersonal skills (communication, salesmanship).

- Mental rehearsal of upcoming events and encounters.

- Internal motivation with little need for recognition or praise from others.

- The confidence to take creative risks (instead of clinging to a comfortable area).

- Use of feedback and criticism for changing.

- Full ownership and acknowledgment of their own ideas.

In any situation where achievement and success are in question, both men and women have an ambivalent, underlying feeling of anxiety. (The specific anxiety involves different issues for men and women.) For both men and women, however, success may usher in anxiety about loss of dependency, increased responsibility, capability, and loss of the gratifications gained from previous roles and levels of attainment.

Our concept of success changes with the stage of our lives, as well as the culture and period we live in. In his novel *Siddhartha*, Hermann Hesse described three stages in the pursuit of success. The first, the success of adolescence and early adulthood, comprises a successful separation from parents and survival in the wilderness. The second stage is the pursuit of financial and personal accomplishments. The final stage of success lies in the simplicity of sitting on a river bank and happily listening to the music of the water.

Reaching for the Brass Ring

The metaphor "reaching for the brass ring" comes from old-fashioned carousels. If you "grabbed the brass ring," you'd get to ride again for free. But to grab the ring, which was fastened just out of a tall child's easy reach on the outside edge of the merry-go-round, you'd have to stretch from your bobbing wooden horse, possibly even standing on the outside stirrup and tilting your whole body outward while hanging on to the reins. It wasn't easy to get a free ride.

Mastering problems in achieving may also call for some stretching, at the psychological level. The stretch involves discarding old assumptions that no longer work, whether they're minor stumbling blocks or major barriers to success.

Some individuals can change the pattern of their lives by learning to emphasize positive thinking, by setting realistic, obtainable goals, and by developing positive images about money and success. This approach may be sufficient for those who need only a revised, more positive model to organize new assumptions and change and to more precisely direct ambition. However, those who have a poor or negative self-image, who have unconscious conflicts, or who disavow or ignore their own most positive characteristics face futility and frustration because they are attempting to overlay these problems with positive, supportive material.

Developing Self-Empathy

Self-empathy—listening from inside our own thoughts, feelings, experiences, and perceptions—can be developed for greater self-awareness and understanding.

The real impediment to success may not exist in the language of consciousness. Nonetheless, contradictory messages in the subconscious will make themselves heard daily in self-defeating behavior. The internal struggle trying to find resolution becomes observable at the level of action; the psyche arbitrates the opposing forces into the sort of clumsy compromises that allow survival, but not full success.

We can become conscious of the patterns in our lives by observing, acknowledging, and fully recognizing them in our own behavior. For some individuals with success phobia, these steps alone may be sufficient. But when deeper, more complex issues hide the cause of these patterns from consciousness, psychotherapy, or psychoanalysis, may be indicated. If nearly everything that runs your life is not only out of your own control but even out of reach of consciousness, any change in life patterns will be far easier if you don't try to do it alone.

Once you recognize your own impediments to achieving your potential, do not sweep them under the carpet with a critical, judgmental dismissal: that you're lazy, indolent, stubborn, inept, or any other negative label. Such conclusions are dangerous because they preclude examination of the underlying issues; they place a period to a sentence that's only just beginning. Improvement is more than just exercising your will or persuading yourself. It is a matter of understanding. Full understanding may involve delving into several layers of yourself, some of which may be outside of consciousness. It includes understanding your feelings, your motivations, and your fantasies.

Most importantly, critical or negative judgments of yourself are an abandonment of an internal, empathic listening position. They are a way to distance you from yourself, to put you in the position of a critical observer.

Are You Afraid of Success?

The following questions are designed to reveal some of the impediments in the behaviors, attitudes, and life patterns of people with a success phobia. It's a summary of the questionnaire that follows Chapter 3.

Go over the questions again at least three months after answering the questions in Chapter 3. Write down all your answers, and then look them over to assess your own attitudes about success. Finally, compare your new answers with the old ones to discover whether any of your attitudes or perspectives have changed since you began reading this book.

1. Do you consistently avoid the final step to completing a goal so that you never quite meet the goal?

2. Is there a difference between your abilities and your actual, completed accomplishments?

3. Is there a repetitive pattern that signals some emotional problem in your life, such as consistently having problems with bosses, customers, or colleagues; consistently feeling abused, unrecognized, or passed over; consistently choosing the wrong partner, investment, or timing; consistently *choking* or succumbing to indecision at crucial moments?

4. Do you feel you can truly express yourself in only a few narrow areas, such as maintaining your home, playing in some amateur sport, pursuing a hobby, or amateur art, but never in doing your work?

5. Do you sometimes feel that you are an impostor, as if you've bluffed your way in, and that your weakness and inadequacy would be obvious to everybody if your true abilities and feelings were disclosed?

6. Do you need continual feedback, applause, or admiration to sustain your effort or motivation?

7. Does staying in the background seem safer because you're afraid you'll be revealed as incompetent in the limelight? Does staying safe require that you lower your ambition?

8. Are you afraid that if you succeed at something you'll feel alone, abandoned, isolated, or disconnected from other people?

9. Do you attribute your accomplishments to luck or circumstance rather than sustained effort and skill?

10. Have you responded to success with depression or psychosomatic illness, rather than joy or celebration?

11. Do you constantly accentuate the negative by focusing on what else you could have done rather than finding fulfillment and enjoyment in your real accomplishments?

12. Are you afraid to get too close to anybody, fearing that you'll be rejected and hurt if you do? Have you engineered a number of rejections to avoid being unexpectedly rejected? Do you find yourself rejecting people before they can reject you?

13. Do you avoid setting goals, or are your goals so vague and ill-defined that you never fully recognize when you've reached them?

14. Are you afraid that you'll be disillusioned or disappointed when goals are reached? Do you avoid this expected disappointment by not reaching the goals?

15. Does it seem that nothing you do is ever quite enough, that you can't enjoy the products of your success because of wanting "more" or fearing that they'll be taken away as soon as you get them?

16. Are you addicted to work? Do you have trouble giving up working even on weekends and vacations? Do you use work as a way to regulate your involvement with friends or family?

17. Do you use your work to provide your identity, self-esteem, or basic sense of worth? Do you think "I'm nothing without my work?"

18. Is the past still alive in the present for you? Are you *stuck with* constricting beliefs, attitudes, or assumptions that limit your belief in yourself, your ability to enjoy ambitious accomplishments, or your ability to emerge into a different lifestyle? Do you constantly hear the echo of your parents criticizing you or forbidding you to do things?

Are You Who You Think You Are? And Who Would You Rather Be?

Many people develop inhibitions about success because they carry over from childhood ideas about themselves and about what they ought to be. Ideas that are no longer accurate (if they ever were) and are emphatically not adaptive. They may hold ideals for themselves that no human being could possibly meet; and then feel negative about themselves because they haven't lived up to these impossible ideals. They may also be seeing a very distorted picture of themselves in their internal mirror.

Your Body Self

In human development, the container of our sense of self is our own body. I have studied the body image drawings of over 300 in-patient adolescents and adults in a treatment setting. Of these individuals, whose emotional problems ranged from depression to eating disorders, one finding was consistent: their initial body image drawings were inaccurate and distorted. This is also the most consistent and profound problem of the individuals I see in my eating disorders treatment program.

Here are some exercises to illuminate your basic assumptions about your body self and your body image:

1. Draw with crayon (so you can't erase) the picture you have in your mind of how your body looks, without looking in the mirror. Draw your whole body. If you find it absolutely impossible to draw yourself nude, you can draw yourself wearing your favorite bathing suit or leotard.

2. Turn the paper over and draw a line down the middle, labeling the left half with a plus sign and the right half with a minus sign. List under the plus sign all the things that you like about

your body, how you look, how you feel physically, and so on. Under the minus sign, list all the things you don't like.

3. Set this paper aside for a few days.

4. During these few days, repeat the drawing part again at these times:

    •   When you feel the happiest, the very best.

    •   When you feel the worst, angry, sad, depressed, and so on.

5. Now look at your entire body in a full-length mirror. Draw and write what you see. If you wore clothing in the first sketch, wear the same clothing in this sketch.

6. Have someone take a Polaroid photo of your entire body (even better would be a videotape) wearing either nothing or the same clothing you wore in your drawings.

7. Finally, compare, as objectively as possible, all of your drawings and the photograph. Ask yourself the following questions:

    •   Is my body image (the picture I have of myself, in my mind) accurate and distinct?

    •   Does my body image actually fit with my body? Is it the same?

    •   Does my body image, and how I regard my body, fluctuate over time or across different moods? (It shouldn't fluctuate, because your body doesn't change when your feelings change—although women may experience some minor puffiness and a small weight gain just before menstruation, along with some possible emotional changes—your drawing shouldn't look as though you'd suddenly gained twenty pounds!)

    •   Am I omitting or denying any aspects of my body? (For instance, is your body image roughly equal to your own real age? Is it sex-specific, can you clearly see whether it's male or female?)

Your Psychological Self

Some of my patients have found it valuable to start a journal, a spiral notebook that they keep in an accessible place so they can write in it when they have feelings or urges they don't quite understand. Writing what you think and feel can be like holding a mirror up to your internal experience.

Try the first part of this next exercise when you're alone to determine whether you're blaming yourself for not matching your ideal self and to discover parts of yourself that you can value and use. Enlist some close friends for the second part to discover whether your ideas about yourself actually match the way you seem to others.

1. To begin this exercise, make a list of your ideals: who you are, the standards you want to live up to, your principles, and your goals. Your ideals are the internal directives that guide you.

2. On another page, list your personal characteristics, both *good* and *bad* (for example: sense of humor, intelligent, good-looking, vain, assertive, timid). List all the goals you have achieved.

3. Now compare the lists on the two sheets of paper. How well do they match?

4. Review your ideal characteristics to determine how attainable they are, how realistic they are for your current life.

    Could any human be as perfect as your ideal self? Have you set yourself an impossible goal? Are some of the "good" characteristics of your ideal self more important to you than others? And are you actively pursuing or just passively hoping to meet your ideals and goals?

Is your ideal self stepping all over your real self when you try to achieve your aims? Does your ideal self include characteristics that actively oppose your conscious attempts to succeed? For instance, if you're striving for a vice presidency in an aggressive corporation and you've listed "nurturant," "kind," and "caring" prominently among your ideals, you're likely to have trouble. Or, if you're teaching kindergarten and your ideal is "aggressive," "tough," and "wealthy," you might consider quitting your job and heading for the business world.

Which characteristics do your real self and your ideal self have in common? These are probably your areas of greatest strength, the areas you can draw on to set reachable goals and accomplish them. How much do your parents' aspirations still enter the picture, what they wanted you to do, to be, to make? Altering your ideal to match your own real strengths is a difficult change, but in the long run it may be easier than straining to meet some impossible goal you've been conditioned to strive for since childhood.

Now, compare your real self with the ideals you consider most important. How well do these match? Even in adulthood, people are able to change some of their characteristics by changing their behavior. For example, if you consider assertiveness important but aren't assertive yourself, an assertiveness training course may teach you the skills you need. But after that, it's up to you to practice them.

Instead of blaming yourself for your imperfections, can you consider taking a more positive view of yourself, acknowledging, using, and above all enjoying your own strengths?

5. Ask three of your most intimate and trusted friends to write down (anonymously, if they prefer) how they see you—what characteristics they attribute to you. If they are more comfortable doing this anonymously, give each a sheet of paper and an identical pen, or ask them to use a typewriter while you are

out of the room. Or you can give each an identical pen, sheet of paper, and self-addressed envelope to take home, and ask them to mail the responses to you.

I occasionally do this without anonymity in a psychotherapy group. Each member in turn takes the "hot seat" while every other member gives specific feedback, such as a physical description, personality description, initial and current impression, description of what is most admired, present concerns for the individual, and so on. Although this exercise may sound scary, intrusive, or confrontational, it is one of the most useful, compassionate, and cohesive of group experiences.

6. Compare your friends' lists against the list of characteristics you prepared in step 1 of this exercise.

    Do you see yourself as others see you? Do the responses show a pattern? Have your friends listed some strengths that you never suspected you had? If so, it's time to consider updating your self-image to include these positive attributes and to consider incorporating them into your goals for yourself.

    Do your friends list some of the "ideal" characteristics that you omitted from your "real-self" list? If so, you've got proof that you've met some of your goals; it's time to acknowledge your success.

    On the other hand, do some of your "virtues" seem to others, to be flaws? For instance, if you described yourself as "precise," do they describe you as "petty" or "nitpicking"? If you described yourself as "warm-hearted," do they describe you as "smothering" or domineering? If so, you may be clinging to some outworn *rules* for yourself. For example: *you must do everything perfectly*, or *you must control all your relationships to maintain others' affection*. Don't forget, the people filling out these sheets are your friends, and friends (unlike relatives) choose their associates. They wouldn't have filled out the sheets if they weren't basically fond of you and didn't basically accept you for yourself.

7. Keep your journal handy. Write in it each day, however briefly, something of your own experiences or feelings, not from an objective or descriptive viewpoint, but from your own emotions and perceptions.

8. Each time you have some distinct or profound mood, write of your experience in your journal. It's as important to figure out why you feel happy, as why you feel unhappy, because you create both moods yourself. You have probably had the experience of coming to see something more clearly as you talked about it. The same can happen as you write about your feelings, especially if you feel sad, empty, or down and don't know why. Just beginning to write about your experience can sometimes give it form and focus.

At times, the bravest and most painful thing you can do is stay with your feeling rather than deny it or anesthetize yourself to it by eating, drinking, watching television, running off to an exercise class or a party. Staying inside your experience and writing about it is an active way of *doing something* about it. At times, you may not even have words for what you're feeling (some feelings simply don't have names), so drawing a picture may be enlightening.

The Real World: Models of Achievement

In the working world (and the academic world that precedes it), there are several social models for achieving goals. The most common, the one found in most business enterprises, is the competition model. This model is highly useful in some respects, but it causes a great many people (of both sexes, but especially women) some degree of discomfort, unhappiness, or dissonance between the self they'd like to be, and the self they feel they have to be, to succeed. Another model is the relational model. It mirrors a family that functions well together, but it can also be effectively employed in the outside world.

The Competition Model— and How to Master It

There is nothing inherently wrong with competition; it is often healthy, and it is a part of normal development. Competition does not have to be destructive or *masculine*. For women especially, using competition and power in their own interests does not have to equate with destructiveness and selfishness. These characteristics obviously don't reconcile with the *feminine* identity nearly all women in our culture learn from birth. The use of power does not have to lead to abandonment or isolation.

Competition can be adaptive in certain contexts, particularly in the corporate and business world. In the context of a team and teamwork, whether sports or corporate, competition can be a cohesive process that unites team members and enables them to perform well.

Unhealthy competition, on the other hand, may have its roots in envy, jealousy, or poor self-esteem. It can arise from a drive to compete just for the sake of competing, and lead one to lose sight of the goal or the purpose of the competition.

External Constraints on Competition

For women especially, any competition can be difficult. People important in a woman's life—family, husband, lover, friends, colleagues—may feel uncomfortable as she emerges into being fully expansive, assertive, and competitive. As mentioned earlier, anthropologist Margaret Mead observed that a woman's femininity is often called into question by her success. A woman may fear deviating from a social norm or suffering social ostracism and the loss of love, if she breaks out of the traditionally feminine, nurturing, passive role.

In a few instances, men may also experience external constraints on competition. Some fathers insist on competing with and *beating* their son at every pastime or skill the son attempts. In other instances, a fiercely competitive and vengeful sibling (usually a brother) may exact revenge for any victories or even for any assertiveness shown by the *rival* brother. These family patterns can persist even into adulthood, requiring a definitive emotional separation before the man from such a family can compete effectively. Additionally, in some workplaces, there may be people holding power who compete (or refuse to allow competition) for unhealthy reasons; an example is the boss who treats employees' every attempt at self-assertion as an inexcusable challenge to his or her power. Here, the only competition likely to appear will be based not on work skill, diligence, or even cleverness of tactics, but on skill in mollifying the boss.

Internal Constraints on Competition

Men commonly complain "I am too competitive" or "I can't stop working and relax." Women more commonly state "I can't compete; something is blocking me." This difference is because, starting in infancy, boys and girls are treated differently in regard to competitiveness.

The most common problem for women who have difficulty being competitive lies in the difference between what they consciously want and what their internal models are, their ideal selves. A woman's most basic sense of self is formed in identification with the person most like her, the one most loved and most esteemed and admired: her mother, the self-sacrificing caretaker, attentive to the needs of others above her own. With this identity, a woman may feel profoundly "bad" and selfish if she acts on her own needs and seeks power on her own behalf. Some women even have difficulty separating from ungratifying or self-destructive relationships because they can't tolerate being an *agent of abandonment* and continue to feel totally responsible for the other person's feelings.

Furthermore, many women deeply and unconsciously continue to identify with characteristics they've grown to consciously despise—passivity, for instance, and self-effacement. Growing up and creating a new self-image may seem like an act of aggression toward their mother, and separating from their family may seem like robbing their mother of that essential part of self-worth defined by taking care of dependent children.

Recommendations for Dealing with the Competitive Model

1. To be comfortable with competition and success, you'll need to view competition as healthy, adaptive, and often necessary. Consider that your feelings of restraint were adaptive in some earlier context (for example, in your original family), but ask yourself: How does this restraint affect your life in the present? You must understand where your restraint comes from in order to separate the past from the present.

2. Understand your ideal self. Are your goals and ambitions in accord with how you see yourself? You can be consistently successful at living up to your unconscious goals (being loving, kind, and generous to others, to the exclusion of yourself and your own growth) while failing completely at the goals you consciously desire (your own growth and success).

3. Develop a set of internal standards to live up to, chosen not by what you've been taught is good but by what you consider *good*

enough. A woman recently told me in therapy that she fears not living up to expectations. I asked her whose expectations, and the answer, of course, was "other people's." When your self-esteem depends on a constant flow of affirmative responses from other people, instead of being internally generated, you're extremely vulnerable to the opinions of others. You can be caught between your compulsion to please others and your own need for growth. Self-esteem is created by living up to your own internal standards and by experiencing mastery in this and other enterprises.

The Relational Model

An alternative to the competitive model is the relational model, which applies equally to families, educational institutions, and corporations. In this model, the sort of *cut-throat competition* that is stereotypically glorified in male development is viewed as undermining connectedness to others, affiliation with others, and shared, mutual growth. In one study of perceived dangerous situations in various stories, men saw danger in close personal affiliation; they envisioned entrapment, betrayal, and being caught in a smothering relationship [Reference 15-1]. Compared to the dire dangers of intimacy, they saw no danger at all in competition and achievement. Women, on the other hand, saw danger in competition and achievement, fearing isolation and solitude. They saw enhancement rather than danger in intimacy.

Yet the relational model has proven equally effective in helping both sexes obtain mutual goals. A relational model provides opportunities for collaborative, rather than competitive learning and achievement. It provides an atmosphere that validates relationship needs and connectedness rather than individual, isolated competition. It emphasizes mutual growth as opposed to the sort of competition that aims to achieve power or victory over another person.

The relational model exemplifies a different understanding of achievement and success. Rather than a competitive acquisition of personal power, it values attunement to others and achievement based on connection, affiliation, and cooperation. In many ways, the relational model is more directly goal-oriented than the competitive model, because the benefits of reaching the goal accrue to those who have worked together toward it. With the competitive model, individuals apparently working toward general group goals need not continue once they've reached their own competitive goal, which may be victory over another individual on the team, or over the entire team.

A recent study at Wellesley College demonstrated this principle [Reference 15-2]. A group of students (of both sexes) were given a task in a competitive model, focused on trying to outdo one another. The same students were then given group work requiring cooperation and discussion of their relationships. When the results of their work were measured objectively, they showed that the students were considerably more productive working together than individually. Additional studies of connected-group learning have demonstrated that more is learned and the results of the learning are more creative than when learning is individual and competitive.

These results offer a different view of power, a model for ethical power that both women and men may be able to enjoy. Under the relational model, being powerful enhances rather than diminishes the power of others. Power can be approached more creatively and can be negotiated with others to enrich personal life, work, and business, or professional achievement. Instead of being equated with destructiveness or selfishness, power can be reconciled with a female identity; just as affiliation, empathy, and nurturance can increasingly be incorporated into the male identity.

The relational model can be equally useful for both sexes. Many men suffer, as much as women do, from trying to reconcile the ethical, caring, *nice guy* attitude they express at home with the stereotypical raw competitiveness they must bring to the standard corporate workplace. However, relatively few workplaces currently promote the relational model of power. Despite the fact that more women are entering the higher levels of corporate power, few women or men have thought to even question the competitive model. Even when they do think of it, initiating any change may take a good deal of persistence and a considerable amount of courage, because the affiliative model diminishes the value of the stereotypical masculine characteristics that shaped today's business world in the first place.

Transitions: A Cooling-Off Period

An increasing number of people are making career changes in midlife or are simply taking time off to reevaluate where they're going. For example, Mitch Kapor, the highly successful founder of Lotus Development Corporation, retired from that career while still in his thirties to "pursue personal interests." Many individuals change career directions after achieving success in their original arena.

Bernard, a forty-five-year-old physician, gave up a very successful and profitable medical practice to pursue investments and become an active and dedicated stock market trader. Although he enjoyed medicine, it was something he'd felt he "had" to do; his father and grandfather were both physicians, and it was a foregone conclusion that Bernard would follow the family tradition. He never questioned this family assumption. Now, successful in his own right, he recognized that his passion lay in other areas and decided to pursue these interests for the last half of his career.

At first glance, leaving a *hot* career may resemble a success phobia, in which individuals who can't enjoy their success suspend their efforts just before or after reaching a long-sought goal. Alternatively, it may appear to be burnout, emotional exhaustion from driven competition or from the depletion of constantly giving to others without getting replenished in turn. Although both success phobia and burnout are real, the midlife transition is something else entirely.

Individuals like Bernard are able to pause and become more objective about themselves because they're successful. They are able to shift their point of reference to an internal one—to consider what they really want, think, and feel—and then to actively determine their own course rather than following some family or social tenet.

This process is analogous to the transition many individuals make in the course of therapy or analysis, changing from an external point of reference (pleasing others and being guided by a perception of what one is supposed to do) to an internal point of reference (listening to and developing more fully one's own thoughts, feelings, directives, and initiative). Most healthy individuals are not constricted in extreme ways and are able to undertake this development on their own.

Many people who make a career switch, or simply take time off, refer to an improvement in their "quality of life." Some step away from the prestige of a professional label (doctor or lawyer) to seek the work of their choice. Even those who decide to continue in their career feel renewed by their ability to make that choice.

Attaining success and meeting external goals allow people to reassess their life. Has their original career actually provided what they had hoped or anticipated? Making a million dollars or getting a long-desired promotion may abruptly force individuals to confront their goal's ability to provide the hoped-for answer. And it raises the question "Now what? What am I going to do with the rest of my life?"

For the last two decades or so, our society has strongly emphasized materialism and individual success. Many people are now recognizing, however, that material success does not bring the happiness they'd imagined.

In addition to the limited ability of material things to provide emotional fulfillment, there's a growing awareness, especially at midlife, of the limits of human achievement. Actual achievement of the *more*, that is *not quite enough*, often destroys the illusion that attaining one goal will make everything all right, particularly when mortality begins to stare one in the face. That is the point at which many people begin to redefine success; they hear their own inner master threatening to hit them with a stick. Within themselves, they discover their own answer to that master.

A Caveat and a Warning

The inherent danger is that accumulating wealth, being a success in your work arena, and acknowledging both is irrefutable confirmation of adulthood. Accepting adulthood may be the most difficult step of all.

Taking charge and taking care of people doesn't necessarily mean that you've accepted being grown up. With the passage into emotional adulthood (I don't know what else to call it), we mourn what was and what might have been. Almost all of us come to the end of our childhood assumptions long after childhood. The assumptions most difficult to relinquish are that someone will take care of us, that someone is really in charge and has the answers, that there are absolute answers to be found. When we pass into emotional adulthood, we move from a passive to an active position, to knowing that each moment we are responsible for what we think, feel, and do.

We are all involved with this process. But we all have our own developmental path and timetable.

16

Why Are Successful People Such Lousy Investors?

Everything I do, you blame on me.

—A perceptive six-year-old

It is only a fool who has never felt like one.

—Noah benShea

Keep your eye on the ball, and your head in the game.

—My Coaches
—My Residency Supervisor
—My Analytic Supervisor
—My Investment Advisor
—My CPA

So you're not neurotic, narcissistic, or a sucker. You're highly successful and make plenty of money. Yet, as an investor, your success is merely a whisper compared with your other endeavors.

Van Tharp says, "Most people, even when given a sound recommendation, will often lose money on it. . . . You could give someone a 'magic formula' that is very profitable, yet a lot of people won't make money given that same system—either they won't follow it, or they'll change it in some way . . . and it results quite often in disaster," [Reference 16-1].

Why Investment Decisions Are Difficult

A tremendous amount of information must be sifted through in order to make investment decisions. Unless you have a system or an established set of operating principles, you are subject to natural biases. One such bias is the tendency to abhor losing so much that you maintain an investment position until the loss gets larger, rather than admitting the loss and stopping it by selling. Additional biases include fear, greed, hope, and losing sight of the big picture. These biases are difficult to avoid.

Personal stress also reduces an investor's effectiveness. Stress does two things. First, it narrows focus and reduces capacity; worry about what might go wrong occupies conscious processing capacity that could be more profitably attuned to analyzing available possibilities. Second, stress creates additional energy, which keeps someone doing what they're doing with greater intensity. Both of these consequences of stress are potentially disastrous to investors [Reference 16-2].

The most common inconsistencies are related to either investing without a game plan or failing to adhere to it. You have to know where you are in order to know where you're going.

Running with the Herd

Wayne is a respected attorney in a fairly large city. He has been successful professionally and financially, and has had an above-average investment record. He did particularly well in stocks from 1985 through mid-1987. Success bred more success; he margined his account to do even better.

In early 1987, Wayne inherited $50,000. He intended to place it in a principal-safe, tax-free investment for security. Instead, he decided to "borrow" this $50,000 for a few months, margin it, and make more money on stocks before he parked it in the planned safe harbor.

During the first half of 1987, Wayne was advised to be out of the market by Labor Day. But that summer, he found "running with the bulls" to be such an exciting experience and he was doing so well that he decided to extend his deadline to December 1987. Then came the October crash, and Wayne lost over $100,000.

He had violated two of his own cardinal principles: First, although he had a clear game plan, he didn't stick with it; his emotions caused him to abandon his principle. Second, he violated his resolution to separate his "untouchable" long-term, secure money from his more risky trading/investing money. He learned well from this experience; the tuition was certainly costly enough.

The leading investment authorities give conflicting advice. The most inconsistent and ultimately disastrous approach is chameleon-like movement from hot tip to hot tip or adherence to the advice of the expert of the week.

Develop your own master plan, based on all the expert information and knowledge you can accumulate. Make it yours; be consistent yet objective; adhere to it rather than responding emotionally to trends or illusions. Mark Hulbert, who monitors investment newsletter performance, states, "Time and again . . . I come across advisors who develop very sensible systems and then second-guess them. More often than not, they regret it," [Reference 16-2]. He adds: "To be successful, the investor must resist the emotional extremes to which the markets inevitably swing."

Common Pitfalls

The following are the most common mistakes that typically affect investors:

- Not having a game plan, or inconsistently adhering to it. This leaves you vulnerable to *hot tips* and emotional decisions and to losing sight of the big picture.

- Acting on someone else's formula, methodology, or system. Develop your own principles; set and prioritize your own goals. Clarify the resources you have available, and identify the potential obstacles. Design your own plan, being sure your system and you are a comfortable fit. Objectively monitor your progress at regular intervals.

- Blaming others or something else for mistakes. Own your decisions fully. Don't shoot the messenger, blame the broker, or fault the floor trader. Admitting your mistakes allows you to recognize that the choices you made are your own and helps you avoid making the same mistakes over and over.

- Disregarding stress [Reference 16-3]. Take a self-inventory at regular intervals and especially at stressful times.

- Acting without being certain that you internally, emotionally, accept the move. If any part of you disagrees with what you are about to do, you will not be able to make a full commitment.

- Setting goals to get rich quickly. Fear and greed, the greatest enemies of any investor, lie within the person. Patience and persistence are an investor's best friends.

- Being unwilling to cut losses short. We naturally abhor losses and want to disregard them, holding onto the hope of reversal. When you cut a loss short by selling, you both acknowledge and concretize the loss—it becomes real. This reality is expensive to ignore.

- Not regarding investing as a business. What you do with your money is at least as important as how you obtain it. Investing is a business requiring the expenditure of time and money and yielding return.

- Not designating separate portions of your portfolio for calculated risk and for secure, no-risk investment. Like our perceptions of middle age and old age, our perception of what is risky changes as we come closer to it.

Profile of a Winning Investor

Van Tharp of Investment Psychology Consulting has done research and clinical studies of the key characteristics of successful investors. A composite profile includes the following elements:

- A well-rounded personal life relatively free of stress (decidedly not a life characterized by the drive to succeed at all costs and by all work and no personal life).

- A positive attitude with specific goals—high, yet attainable expectations.

- A positive, nonconflicted desire to be the best in the field and to make money at it.

- A willingness to take responsibility for the results, including owning one's mistakes.

- A system or set of rules for guidance in making decisions, which ensures against following the crowd.

- Money-management skills combined with strong self-discipline.

- Patience, or a willingness to wait for the right opportunity or to take the steps necessary to create the right opportunity.

David Ryan, a three-time winner of the U.S. Investing Championships in Stocks, gave an interview in which he typified these characteristics of an ideal investor: He eagerly and positively anticipates each day, fully enjoying his work. He rates his life satisfaction as 95 out of a possible 100. He sets distinct behavioral goals and achieves them. He has a model to go by, someone whom he admires, and he can, in difficult situations, ask himself, "What would this person do?" He learns from his mistakes, a very important characteristic. Finally, his responses have become automatic—integrated into his own system—not just a set of techniques to follow; success becomes self-perpetuating in this way.

17

Mastering Problems with Money

I have never seen a problem that money has made worse.

—Patient in psychoanalysis

There are two things to aim for in life:
first to get what you want;
and after that, to enjoy it.
Only the wisest of mankind can achieve the second.

—Logan Pearsall Smith

Money is a distinct entity, a medium of exchange for goods and services. But money has at least two additional significant facets: (1) the attitudes and conflicts that have developed around money and (2) the neurotic or emotional issues that use money as their expression or symbol. Money is an increasingly popular and *socially correct* symptom of various emotional issues.

Mind over Money

Some people have to overcome inner obstacles before they can attain, maintain, and enjoy success with money. For many who are otherwise intelligent, aware, and reasonable, the obstacle is emotional, a *circumscribed neurosis* around money. Even people who have undergone therapy may have trouble with money, because money and its meanings are a blind spot for many therapists.

A first step to dealing rationally with money is to directly approach the problem of addressing a taboo subject. Insecurity and embarrassment make postponement of such discussions seem very alluring, and it's difficult to work on such a conflicted, elusive, emotional issue alone. Approaching a close friend, associate, or spouse may be an important beginning, although the discomfort of approaching others to discuss this most *private* of subjects still has to be overcome. For others, self-scrutiny may be sufficient. With an open, exploring mind, you may be able to consider different ways of looking at this issue (or any other) and perhaps to start trying some different experiences.

Trying to guess what other people earn is a popular middle-class pastime. A more formal sizing-up process has been observed among corporate executives, who move through four stages in their approach to the topic of money: (1) friendly, superficial pleasantries; (2) conversation on such seemingly impersonal subjects as sports and travel; (3) an exchange of information and opinions on business topics; and (4) conversations about job, lifestyle, and money. This unwritten code allows executives to create a composite picture from which they can deduce the other person's income. The whole process is based on the implicit agreement that discussion of personal money matters and income is taboo. Permissible topics of discussion include one's car, travels, house, personal possessions, background, marriage—even sexual exploits—but not the ultimate, intimate taboo of personal income.

An increased awareness of some of the emotional aspects of money can lead to further examination, understanding, and finally rational management of money. During this process, you may become attuned to how you really think and feel about money issues. You may become aware of the many times inner tensions arise around money and of the ways your family, friends, and colleagues avoid frank discussions of money.

Parent-Child Money Talk

When your children speak to you about money, listen for clues about what they know and imagine. Before the age of eight, children do not have the ability to understand abstract concepts, including the complexities of money. Understanding their perspective can help answer their questions in a meaningful way. Establishing an atmosphere of open discussion and freedom to question is also important. Money issues can be handled as frankly and openly as anything else, with the same benefits for the entire family.

Children learn by observing; initially, they enact their version of your behavior. Later they may rebel against your behavior on the way to (still later) finding their own style.

They learn boundaries when their parents emphasize that discussions of finances are to be kept within the family. Money discussions also familiarize them with money management and help them establish and maintain limits, priorities, and goals. They need to integrate money into their lives, just as they would integrate any other aspect of family life.

When it is appropriate, perhaps in early adolescence, you can help them understand that the way your family earns, regards, and uses money, is only one of many possibilities. With that understanding, they can use the family system and beliefs as one point of view and then consider other points of view to establish their own beliefs and style.

Don't complicate matters by using money to shape behavior, coerce, reward, bribe, or to punish your children.

Dealing with Financial Phobias

Perhaps the most common financial symptom is a phobia about investments. Money paralysis often combines not knowing what to do with feeling unable to do anything. This paralysis ranges in severity from total immobilization to confusion, reluctance, indecision, or yielding the decision to someone else. Interestingly, impulsiveness with money is less of a problem than indecision, which is fueled by a fear of doing the wrong thing.

Research psychologist Scully Blotnik spent twenty-seven years studying the career and investment decisions of over 11,000 people. Nearly 70 percent of those he surveyed exhibited some serious fear of investing. He also found that approximately a third of that group had all their money solely in bank accounts, having responded to their confusion by making no investments at all [Reference 17-1].

A milder form of money paralysis is procrastination, which may follow a fretful period of extensive analysis and worry about missed opportunities. Procrastination may have its roots in a search for unattainable perfection. Doing research and gathering information may be very time-consuming and require a great deal of effort, but it helps the phobic investor avoid making any sort of mistake.

A financial phobia may take several other forms. One is to take no action at all; another is when an investor, after taking months or years to make a decision, suddenly springs into action based on a hot tip or places savings in an ill-conceived tax shelter, perhaps bought impulsively. Still another phobic variation is avoiding taking action after an investment, such as buying stock for a Keogh or IRA account, is made. Another form is impulsive overreaction to any sign of bad news, selling everything and cancelling all subscriptions to *The Wall Street Journal* and other investment advisories.

Whatever form a financial phobia takes, at its heart is the fact that no one wants to lose money. Having money does represent security, and investing means putting that money and security at risk. Putting money at risk of loss means risking insecurity.

In approaching any phobias, it is important to know first if the fear springs from lack of knowledge. If so, a remedy would be to gradually accumulate basic knowledge about investing; books, magazines, television shows, and consultations with professionals and experienced investors can build confidence and knowledge. What begins as a mystery may gradually pique the new investor's interest and curiosity. The next step might be either to join an investment club or to experiment with buying stocks *on paper*: choosing a portfolio of stocks or other investments, requesting annual reports, reading the daily stock listings, and calculating hypothetical profits and losses—everything except actually parting with money.

A financial planner may be a good coach and valuable support when real money becomes involved. Not only can a good planner impart valuable professional advice, but he or she can help in stabilizing emotional concerns as well.

So that a financial planner does not become a parent figure or a crutch, it is important for you to make your own decisions. A game plan and a set of principles with realistic expectations are important in avoiding ad hoc investing, emotional reactions, and emergencies. Your financial hopes and fears can reach a peaceful compromise and coexistence.

Money paralysis may also occur when money is obtained from misfortune, such as the death of a parent [Reference 17-2]. Among the assumptions activated when money is obtained in this way, is the notion that using the money will reawaken the trauma and create guilt or shame. If this problem arises, it should be worked through emotionally as well as financially. The best way of dealing with something is to deal with it.

Your Money Myths

As you come to understand and resolve the underlying meanings that money holds for you, you can adopt more objective and functional attitudes and allow yourself to consider new alternatives. Along the route, you may confront your personal myths. A compulsion to live to make money rather than making money to live; a belief that money can solve all problems or purchase anything; the tendency to be driven by ambition rather than driving one's ambition—these are a few of the myths about money that shape personal behavior and lifestyle.

The most important first step to understanding money myths is to clarify attitudes about money and to change them if need be.

Some individuals have difficulty seeing money as money. To discover your own money myths, record your answers to the following questions:

1. Are my financial goals consistent with my self-image?

2. Are my financial goals consistent with the way I want to be?

3. Am I pretending to be content with my financial status only because I'm afraid to try to change it?

4. Can I set specific, attainable financial goals? Or do I constantly feel that I need to achieve more?

5. When I arrive at a goal, do I feel satisfaction and enjoyment or the ever-spiraling sense of wanting or needing more?

6. Am I willing to seek suggestions and advice, even differing opinions, to judge a prospective investment or a business decision?

7. Am I derailing my own success by consistently avoiding a final step? Do I consistently pick the wrong investment?

8. Do I consistently expect other people to make my money decisions for me, even if they're not experts?

9. Do I respond to my financial gains with depression? With a feeling of guilt?

10. Can I admit my mistakes and cut my losses?

11. Do I have trouble putting behind me thoughts of "what might have been" if I'd purchased or sold investments earlier?

12. Do I recognize my limits? Or do I feel that my expertise in one field will automatically transfer to another?

13. Do I go on spending binges that I can't afford? Does shopping give me a sort of high? Do I feel let down as soon as I bring home and unwrap a new purchase?

14. Do I spend money to compete with others, get revenge on others, or show off to others? Do I spend money to try to win other people's love or admiration?

15. Do I treat money as a permissible topic of discussion in my family? Is it the same as any other aspect of living, rather than as taboo? In discussing money with my children, do I keep the conversation appropriate to my child's age and level of understanding?

16. Does money control my social life? Do I avoid going out with friends or dating because it costs too much? Do I go only to places and events that are ostentatiously expensive? Do I hate to spend money, even in small quantities or on necessities?

17. Do I feel that I will ultimately have to pay in some way for doing well financially?

18. Do I have a clear game plan for my finances, with definite goals and methods for attaining them?

19. Are my financial goals separate from my emotional goals, from my concept of happiness?

20. Do I have trouble establishing priorities, a balance of work and love, boundaries between work and private life?

Changing Your Frame of Reference

We all have a frame of reference for our internal and external realities. Taking different points of view in order to visualize different options can sometimes be difficult, especially if we're altering lifelong or multigenerational patterns. We create our reality in context; therefore, how we *view* the world determines our experiences and options.

I recently observed a young boy, about twelve years old, walking alone to a seat at a soccer match. He had a scowl on his face and his cap was pulled down almost to his eyebrows—he gave the distinct impression that he hated the world. Soon he began shouting angrily at the players and referees. He obviously felt that no one could do anything right. Several of the players, a referee, and many of the fans eventually glared at him disgustedly. Finally, a group of about five boys banded together and shouted in unison, "Shut up, kid!" In a relatively short period of time, he saw anger, resentment, and dislike everywhere he looked. Judging by the initial look on his face, this was the world he expected to see, but it was a world he himself created. Self-definition occurs only in terms of who you are; it does not occur by comparison, conformity, or defiance.

Children take on their parents' model of money attitudes, meanings, and values. F. Scott Fitzgerald once observed, "The rich are different from you and me." Ernest Hemingway answered, "Yes, they have more money." But that single difference may mean a lot. Children of various financial classes have different models of money, business, and finance. Children of the well-to-do are more comfortable with thinking about and handling large sums of money than children of the less prosperous. Having plenty of money is the matrix of their day-to-day being and is incorporated into their identity. Children also internalize a parent's financial failure, together with any example of the parent's poor self-esteem or feeling of failure; often these children must themselves overcome poor self-esteem to become successful as adults.

Some individuals may reject their parents' values and rebel against them. But an internal struggle remains, because the values are still present even if they're actively opposed. One cause of work compulsion is the need to relentlessly counteract an identification of inadequacy that arose in the family domain. No matter how hard work addicts work, or how much they achieve, this unconscious link to an earlier identification still creates self-doubt. They may feel they're not really capable or successful, but are actually impostors who've fooled everyone. Negative identifications like these can lead people to underestimate their abilities and self-worth, and may also foster a need for secrecy about money, lest exposure of one's fiscal worth also expose one's inadequate self-worth.

Many individuals can overcome their conflicts about money and success by seeking visible, successful models. Mentors are often more valuable for the interaction, modeling, and encouragement they provide than for any specific hints they can give.

Some individuals find it extremely difficult to change their frame of reference. Raul, the psychologist who was the son and grandson of factory workers, had difficulty envisioning himself free from the restricting poverty of his youth. No one from his family nor any of his contemporaries "from the old neighborhood" had changed their lives much beyond the traditional pattern of working very hard and staying poor.

Raul had to work very hard also—but in a different way—to escape from the prison of his background. Until recently, he had been, like his family, inhibited by internal constraints that wouldn't allow him to have new experiences outside the familiar belief system. He still heard the voices from his childhood, telling him there was nothing for him outside the factory. He had to disagree with the voices and endure the anxiety of exploring new experiences and developing new internal and external domains. He learned to view his own assumptions and beliefs more objectively and freed himself to consider other alternatives.

First he learned he could disagree with the voices from his past; then he learned that he re-created these voices in the present; finally he recognized that he could create whatever directives he wished for himself.

Many individuals prefer to maintain a more certain and secure pathway, the one that they've followed all through their earlier experiences; they would rather remain in a predictable situation than suffer the uncertainty of a journey into new, uncharted territory. Of such individuals, writer John Oliver Hobbes states, "Men heap together the mistakes of their lives, and create a monster they call destiny."

Mastering Obstacles to Sound Money Judgment

Three principles regarding money have been discussed. First, money is money. When we view it from a position of simplicity, we can see how much complexity we attach to money. Second, our attitudes and emotional conflicts from our past may involve money itself. Third, other unrelated emotional conflicts may be expressed through money, with money serving as a vehicle for our existing and repressed conflicts.

The following are some emotional characteristics that may improve your money judgment. You may also use this list to weigh the utility of other basic assumptions that affect money judgment.

1. *Having a "big picture" and bringing it into focus whenever necessary.* The *big picture* is our own ideals and principles and the process of objectively organizing our life, decisions, and plans, according to what we believe to be in our best interests. Having a *big picture* doesn't mean that every decision we make will be correct. But having a game plan and operating principles will bring more success than responding impulsively or in a scattered, unorganized way. For guidance, we can ask "What is in my best interest?" With the ability to see the *big picture*, we can discover all that achieving, having, and enjoying money can do, as well as what it can't do.

2. *Being able to establish priorities.* Friendships, family life, leisure time, health, work, tranquillity, and acquisition of wealth may all require continual prioritizing, planning, pursuit, and enjoyment. Conflicts in achieving any of these aims may result in overcompensation in other areas. Establishing clear priorities may involve mourning what we don't have, or what we have to give up, in order to achieve other things. The more success we have, the more demands we will have on our time, money,

and presence. Increasingly, we will need to know what is really important to us, to redefine and refine our priorities.

3. *Recognizing our own limits.* It's often difficult to recognize the limits of our expertise and to seek the advice of others. But denying our limitations, our mortality, and our lack of omnipotence and omniscience can be costly and painful. Choosing and managing investments is serious, complicated, and time-consuming work. Failing to recognize the limits of our knowledge in any area—or being unable to admit our mistakes—can profoundly hamper our judgment. It is thus important that we teach our children limits and priorities. Giving them everything we didn't have, doesn't teach limits. They must know what can and can't be afforded and what priorities we've established and why.

4. *Being able to admit mistakes in order to cut losses.* Our pride and our rationalizations may prevent us from recognizing and admitting mistakes. For instance, the prospect of selling a plunging stock at a loss may make the loss so concrete and real that we will have trouble selling. As long as the stock isn't sold, we can retain the hope it may rise again. It's as though the loss isn't real until the stock is sold; it's only a loss *on paper*. But the hope of salvaging a loss may ensure further losses.

5. *Having specific, attainable goals.* The setting of specific goals helps us recognize whether we've gotten or not gotten where we want to be. Establishing goals can counteract both *greed* and *fear*, two emotions that can seriously impede sound money decisions. Greed can lead to poor judgment and unnecessary risk-taking; fear can lead to the avoidance of some necessary degree of risk.

6. *Being able to distinguish lack of information and organization from unconscious conflict.* Nonexistent or poor financial advice and planning, may prevent us from getting a realistic grip on our financial status or attaining a manageable lifestyle, according

to some financial advisers. Money problems may also arise from spending expansively *out of habit*, falling prey to easy credit availability, or failing to master money management. It is possible to fall deeply into debt through failure to develop a structure for monitoring spending habits. The best prescription for someone who is mismanaging money, or who has no framework within which to operate, may be a financial counselor. But compulsive spending caused by emotional problems (such as depression, anxiety, or stress) is quite different. Compulsive spenders have to stop the addictive spending before they can proceed, even to the extent of destroying all credit cards, just as alcoholics must stop drinking before they can begin to understand all the underlying reasons for their addiction.

7. *Being able to give up "what might have been."* We may be reluctant to purchase a stock or a piece of real estate if we know that it was priced much lower a year ago than it is now. Self-chastisement for not buying at a past low price may only obscure a clear view of the current value. In the words of a popular song, "He lost tomorrow looking back for yesterday." Feelings of competition may enter into the deal; we may be reluctant to pay today's higher price and let the owner make the profit that could have been ours.

8. *Being able to recognize that success and sound decisions in one arena do not guarantee success in others.* Physicians and other professionals are notorious for feeling that, since they've achieved success in one specialized field, their ability automatically spreads to other endeavors. With little time to research investments, or conduct business activities, many of them eventually learn this lesson the hard way. Examples abound of professionals who spend vast amounts of time learning their professional skills but who unquestioningly throw large sums of money into investments they know little

about, with people about whom they know even less. One physician invested $25,000 in a silver mine following the sales pitch of a neighbor who'd recently gone into the investment field. The doctor reasoned that the investment had to be sound because the man down the street had to face him daily. Both assumptions were wrong. The silver mine had no glitter, and the investment seller divorced his wife and vanished from the neighborhood.

9. *Being willing to seek out suggestions, critiques, and advice.* The decision to seek consultation from people knowledgeable in specific areas is sound logically but often difficult emotionally. Consulting someone who will mirror and agree with your own opinions is far easier than listening objectively to critical or contradictory information, without responding defensively or remaining inflexibly attached to your original position. It is even more difficult to listen from the other person's perspective, appreciating it while maintaining (rather than abandoning) your own perspective, and then using the new information to form a flexible and informed position.

10. *Recognizing that there are few true emergencies.* Most decisions are best made by weighing different factors, gathering data, and perhaps consulting experts. Rarely does any legitimate crisis demand that these steps be skipped. Although a promoter may try to push you into an overnight decision, it's not practical to make money decisions in a fraction of the time that it took to earn the money.

Decisions based on impulse, frustration, or anger should probably be postponed until objectivity is regained. Calling a *time out* is a useful maneuver for people who suddenly acquire a large sum of money—perhaps by inheriting it, winning it in a lottery, or signing a lucrative contract. A moratorium of up to six months allows time to recover from the shock, to develop short-term and long-term plans for the money, to obtain some education about handling it, and to integrate the meaning of having it with one's internal image.

11. *Selecting goals that are consistent with one's self-image.* Often obese people who manage to lose a lot of weight regain it soon afterward. Their problem lies not in changing their weight, but rather in changing their internal self-image and body image. Someone who loses weight but retains an obese body image will soon fill back out to match the mental picture. Some people with success phobias have worked at improving everything in their life except their basic self-image of being incompetent, and this incongruency can be powerful enough to destroy any success they attain.

    Similarly, people who cannot imagine accumulating wealth may have difficulty setting step-by-step goals and changing their life to accommodate the transition to wealth. Thus the first requisite for setting a reasonably attainable goal is to choose one consistent with your self-image. If change is indicated, assess and change your self-image.

    Although a self-image is shaped by emotional and unconscious factors that make change difficult, it can undergo transition. However, because transcending a predictable pattern, relationship, or assumption creates anxiety, many people will choose predictability and certainty even at the risk of perpetuating their unhappiness.

12. *Realizing that contentment is different from reluctance to act.* Few people are actually content with the money they have, yet many feel constrained about actively doing anything to change their financial status. Some, however, are content and happy with their current achievements and their life station. We have to honestly assess whether we're afraid of action and change and are rationalizing our inaction or whether we're actually feeling true contentment with ourselves and our accomplishments.

13. *Being able to see money for what it is and what it isn't.* The following are some of the most common money assumptions:

   • Money offers more than financial security.

   • Money can protect me from feeling lonely.

   • Money protects me from danger/anxiety.

   • Money can keep me from feeling helpless.

   • Money is power; with money I can do whatever I want.

   • Money is freedom.

   • Money is self-worth.

   To the degree that we can allow money to exist independent of our emotional encumbrances, we can see it clearly for what it is and what it isn't. We can then be in charge of money rather than letting it take charge of us. Money can never be totally separate from the rest of life. As with any yardstick that measures accomplishments and relative value, emotion spills over from the value of the accomplishments onto the yardstick itself. But it is possible to get your internal point of reference in clear focus. When you're about to make your next major purchase, ask this question: "If no one else were to see me with it, in it, beside it, or know I had it, would I still purchase it?"

14. *Understanding that internal satisfaction can transcend money.* Money means less when true inner peace exists; it becomes a simple medium of exchange, free from complex meanings and from hopes of enhanced self-worth. Usually the people who are most successful (and who usually make the most money) are those who can find work in an area they enjoy, work that is intrinsically motivating. Doing what we enjoy is more satisfying than the money we make from it (given a reasonable standard of living and material comfort). This distinction is fundamental but often overlooked.

15. *Knowing that money cannot buy what it represents emotionally.* Although people who don't have enough money can easily be unhappy, such unfulfilled needs as self-esteem, happiness, contentment, self-worth, and confidence cannot be fulfilled by money, beyond a certain basic level. Money, or the lack of it, commonly represents all the things one wants more of, everything that's missing, and all the supposed answers to all problems.

16. *Knowing that there's nothing the matter with money.* Be careful not to rationalize nonsuccess and not to idealize poverty, compromise, and nonattainment. Money bestows many choices not otherwise available. Albert Camus stated, "It is a land of spiritual snobbery that makes people think they can be happy without money."

17. *Knowing how to use money for pleasure.* Money can be used constructively to enhance enjoyment and satisfaction in life. These joys should not be sacrificed to money accumulation.

18. *Knowing that money does not measure human worth or success.* Money does not reflect the human value of any person or group of persons. Our society is currently in a phase of promoting materialistic values. But materialistic values have little to do with the more important humanitarian values, which measure individuals not by how much they have, but by the quality of their life and the qualities they bring to the lives of others. Many forms of success have no relationship to financial success. The German poet and philosopher Johann Goethe, when asked for the secret of life, replied, "The secret of life is living."

Disentangling Money from Its Meanings

To have a healthy attitude toward money, then, we must disentangle it from its role as a symbol of emotional issues. Unless money is severed from its emotional meanings, it may impede or restrict us from achieving our personal goals. Alternatively, money viewed as a tool to use in the pursuit of our personal goals loses its potential to block that pursuit.

Happiness and contentment involve coming to terms with, among other things, money. Many people face the unfortunate realization that some additional amount of money or the acquisition of some tangible financial goal may not bring happiness. Money, as a tool, is merely an effective means to the end of satisfaction and the realization of personal goals.

People who underestimate their abilities and self-worth frequently feel secretive, insecure, and ambivalent about money and have misperceptions about the nature and purpose of wealth.

Some individuals are concerned about becoming so money-oriented that they lose their idealism and spontaneity or violate their ethical principles. They may try to solve this problem by disavowing or failing to recognize the need for money management or even denying their need for material comfort. But they can retain their ideals, values, and spontaneity while rationally managing money. In fact, rather than losing something by paying attention to money, they will considerably enhance the very things they are trying to preserve.

These people are like artists who reluctantly come for psychotherapy, knowing that pain and internal conflicts have spawned their creativity and fearing that the resolution of pain and conflict will end creativity. What these artists later come to appreciate is that resolving the pain has freed them to be much more creative than before and much more comfortable with creativity.

What they feared losing can never be lost, but only liberated for even greater potential.

Confronting fear, guilt, worry, obsession, or idealization of money and recognizing its myths and meanings can only leave us free to more fully realize our own potential and determine our own destiny.

Money may be a myth, but it is never a fiction. Sometimes the myth is more important than the fact. The recognition of what money is contains the recognition of what it isn't. And we are reminded regularly, as we distinguish the symbol from the real thing, that the things that do not exist are the ones most difficult to get rid of.

References

Chapter 1

1. Jahoda, M., Notes on Work; In: Lowenstein, R.; Shen, M.; and Solnit, A., (Eds.) *Psychoanalysis: A General Psychology*. N.Y.: Int. Univ. Press, 1966.

2. Glenn, N. and Weaver, C. Enjoyment of work by full-time workers in the United States, 1955 and 1980. *The Public Opinion Quarterly*, Winter, 1982.

3. Valliant, G. *Adaptation to Life*. Boston: Little, Brown and Co., 1979.

Chapter 2

1. Krueger, D.. *Body Self and Psychological Self: Developmental and Clinical Integration in Disorders of the Self*. New York: Brunner/Mazel, 1989.

2. Krueger, D. *Success and the Fear of Success in Women*. New York: The Free Press, 1984.

3. Deutscher, M. Adult work and developmental models. *American Journal of Orthopsychiatry*. 38:882-892, 1968.

Chapter 3

1. Krueger, D. W. *op. cit*.

2. Hall, R., Gardner, E., Perl, M., Stickneys, S. and Pfefferbaum, B. The professional burnout syndrome. *Psychiatric Opinion*. April, 1979. pp. 12-17.

Chapter 4

1. Krueger, D. Success and success inhibition. In: Sternberg, R. and Kolligan, J. *Perceptions of Competence and Incompetence Throughout the Lifespan.* New Haven, Yale University Press, 1988.

2. Hennig, M. Family dynamics and the successful woman executive. In: R. Kundsin (Ed.) *Women and Success.* N.Y.: William Morrow & Co., 1974.

Chapter 5

1. Whiting, B., and Edwards, C.A. cross-cultural analysis of sex differences in the behavior of children aged three through eleven. In S. Chess and A. Thomas (eds.), *Annual Progress in Child Development.* New York: Brunner/Mazel, 1975.

2. Miller, J. *Toward a New Psychology of Women.* Boston: Beacon Press, 1976.

3. Epstein, C. Bringing women in: rewards, punishments, and the structure of achievement. In R. Kundsin (ed.), *Woman and Success: The Anatomy of Achievement.* New York: William Morrow & Co., 1974.

4. Hennig, M. Family dynamics and the successful woman executive. In: R. Kundsin (Ed.) *Woman and Success.* N.Y.: William Morrow & Co., 1974.

5. Blumenstein, P. and Schwartz, P. *American Couples.* New York: William Morrow, 1983.

6. Americans and Their Money: The Fourth National Survey from *Money* Magazine. *Time,* Inc. 1986.

7. Krueger, D. *Success and Fear of Success in Women.* New York: The Free Press, 1984.

8. Gilligan, C. *In A Different Voice.* Cambridge, MA: Harvard University Press, 1982.

9. Horner, M. Femininity and successful achievement - a basic inconsistency. In: Bardwick, J., Douvan, E., Horner, M. Belmont, CA. Brooks-Cole Co., 1970.

10. Rubin, L. *Women of a Certain Age: The Midlife Search for Self.* N.Y.: Harper and Row, 1979.

Chapter 6

1. Luria, Z., Friedman, S., and Rose, M. *Human Sexuality.* New York: Wiley, 1986.

2. Rebelsky, R. and Hanks, C. Father's Verbal Interaction with Infants in the first three months of life. *Child Development.* 42:63-68, 1971.

3. Osherman, S. *Finding Our Fathers: The Unfinished Business of Manhood.* New York, The Free Press, 1986.

4. Hite, S. *The Hite Report on Male Sexuality.* New York: Knopf, 1981.

5. Krueger, D. *Success and The Fear of Success in Women.* New York: The Free Press, 1984.

6. Baker, R. *About Men: Reflections on the Male Experience.* New York: Poseidon, 1987.

Chapter 7

1. Kohut, H. *The Restoration of the Self.* N.Y.; Int. Univ. Press, 1977.

2. Krueger, D. *Success and the Fear of Success in Women.* New York: The Free Press, 1984.

3. Goldberg, J. *Money Madness.* New York: Signet Books, 1978.

Chapter 8

1. Rohrlich, J. The dynamics of work addiction. *Isr. J. Psychiat. Relat. Sci.* 18:147-156, 1982.

2. Kohut, H. *The Restoration of the Self.* N.Y.; Int. Univ. Press, 1977.

3. Leland, C. and Lozoff, M., in: College influences on the role of development of female undergraduates. Educational document ED-026975. Bethesda, Md.: ERIC, 1969.

4. Clance, P. and Imes, S. The impostor phenomenon in high achieving women; dynamics and therapeutic intervention. *Psychotherapy: Theory, Research and Practice.* 15:241-147, 1978.

Chapter 9

1. Kernberg, O. Regression in Organization Leadership. *Psychiatry* 42:24-39, 1979.

2. Kernberg, O. Leadership and Organizational Functioning: Organizational Regression. *International Journal of Group Psychotherapy:* 3-25, 1978.

3. Hymowitz, C. Five Main Reasons Why Managers Fail. *Wall Street Journal* May 2, 1988.

Chapter 10

1. Krueger, D. (Ed.) *The Last Taboo: Money as Symbol and Reality in Psychotherapy and Psychoanalysis.* New York: Brunner/Mazel, 1986.

2. Rubenstein, C. Money and self-esteem. *Psychology Today*, May, 1981.

3. Lapham, L. *Money and Class in American.* New York: Weidenfeld and Nicolson, 1988.

4. Slater, P. *Wealth Addiction.* New York: Dutton, 1980.

5. Pittman, F. Children of the rich. *Family Process*. 24:461-472, 1985.

6. Bronfman, J. The experience of inherited wealth. Ph.D. dissertation, Brandeis University. Microfilms International, 87-5730, 1987.

7. Domini, A. *The Challenges of Wealth*. Homewood, Illinois: Dow-Jones-Irwin, 1988.

8. Harris, M. Rebels who get rich. *Money* magazine, September, 1982.

9. Murphy, T. *Money, Love or Respect*. Forbes Magazine, July 19, 1982.

Chapter 11

1. Krueger, D. On compulsive shopping and spending: A psychodynamic inquiry. *American Journal of Psychotherapy*. October, 1988.

2. Bergler, E. Psychopathology of "Bargain Hunters" in Boneman, E. (Ed.) *The Psychoanalysis of Money*. New York: Urizen Books, 1976.

3. Goldberg, J. *Money Madness*. New York: Signet Books, 1978.

4. Sharon, A. *International Research Quarterly*, Summer, 1982.

Chapter 12

1. Blotnick, S. "It Isn't Greed Alone," *Forbes* magazine, March 23, 1987.

Chapter 13

1. Morganson, G., Are you a born sucker? *Forbes* magazine, June 27, 1988.

2. Schwadel, F. For Love and Not Money: Some investors hold on to stock for its emotional value. *The Wall Street Journal*, May, 1987.

Chapter 14

1. Benares, C. *Zen Without Zen Masters*. Phoenix: Falcon Press, 1985.

2. Blotnick, S., Second careers, *Forbes* magazine, February 9, 1987.

Chapter 15

1. Kaplan, A. and Klein, R. Women's self development in late adolescence. *Work in Progress*. Wellesley, MA.: Stone Center Working Paper Series, 1985.

2. Jordan, J. Empathy and self boundaries. *Ibid*, 1984.

Chapter 16

1. Tharp, V. Interview on *Investor's Hotline*; Joe Bradley, Editor, August, 1988.

2. Hulbert, M. "The perfect as enemy of the good." In: Forbes magazine, September 19, 1988.

3. Stahl, C. The trader's ten commandments. In: Bond, R. (Ed.) *Creative Finance*. August 17, 1988.

Chapter 17

1. Blotnick, S. *Ambitious Men*. New York: Viking, 1987.

2. Domini, A. *The Challenges of Wealth*. Homewood, Illinois. Dow-Jones-Irwin, 1988.

Index

A

Adolescence
    ability to think abstractly, 33
    choose realistic goals, 33
    emotional separation, 34
    highly critical parents, 37
    idealizations, 33
    perfectionism, 37
    perpetual adolescents, 33
    pressing real-life demands, 33
    pseudostupidity, 35
    unrealistic expectations, 36

Ambition and ideals
    escape hatch, 143
    extramarital affairs, 144
    feedback, 133
    narcissistic disorders, 136
    narcissistic pursuit, 139
    people-pleasers, 150
    perpetual quest, 138
    realization of goals, 134
    risky business deals, 144
    sense of self, 133
    sexual conquest, 142
    sexual dysfunction, 146
    shameful flaws, 146
    success hunters, 143

C

Changing careers, 277

Children
    academic underachievement, 30
    behavioral problems, 30
    childhood work, 30
    discover answers, 31
    enthusiasm for school, 31
    excessive praise, 38
    healthy children, 30
    healthy self-directedness, 31
    learning disabilities, 30
    learning with pleasure, 32
    magical belief, 31
    parents' attitudes and
        approaches to work, 31
    parents' satisfaction, 31
    school performance, 30
    school phobia, 30
    self-functioning, 30
    something positive, 31
    student's curiosity, 32

Compulsive achiever
    unrelenting ambition, 160
    work compulsions, 160
    worthlessness, 159

P